HENRY PLANT
- PIONEER EMPIRE BUILDER -

Kelly Reynolds

All rights reserved under International and Pan-American Copyright Conventions. No part of this book may be reproduced in any form or by any means, electronic or mechanical, including photocopying, recording, or by any information storage and retrieval system, without permission in writing from the publisher, except by a reviewer who may quote brief passages in a review.

Copyright © 2003

For information address
  The Florida Historical Society
  435 Brevard Avenue
  Cocoa, Florida 32922
  www.florida-historical-soc.org

Manufactured in the United States of America
  ISBN 1-886104-06-9

Published by
  The Florida Historical Society Press
  435 Brevard Avenue
  Cocoa, FL 32935
  phone (321) 690-0099
  wynne@flahistory.net
  www.floridabooks.net

TO

E.J. LIEBOWITZ
and
C.K. REYNOLDS

AMERICAN ENTREPRENEURS

BENEFACTORS

"No man, having put his hand to the plow, and looking back, is fit for the kingdom of God."

Luke 9:62

CONTENTS

I	Last Call	Page	1
II	Barefoot Boy	Page	17
III	Up from Below	Page	35
IV	Lands of Destiny	Page	53
V	Promise in the Ashes	Page	75
VI	Victory in Sight	Page	97
VII	On the Brink of the Dream	Page	117
VIII	Deadline Railroad	Page	141
IX	Striving to the End	Page	159
X	Beyond the Prize	Page	187
	WORKS CITED	Page	207
	INDEX	Page	215

ILLUSTRATIONS

Chapter I .... Page 5
Henry Plant's private railroad car, with troops at dockside (Spanish-American War) and Florida stagecoach.

Chapter II .... Page 32
The First Congregational of New Haven, with the village greet in Branford and a Vanderbilt Line ocean-going steamboat (The *Northern Star*).

Chapter III .... Page 44
Manhattan waterfront circa 1835, with Cornelius Vanderbilt.

Chapter IV .... Page 73
The Planters Hotel, Augusta, with Ellen Blackstone Plant.

Chapter V .... Page 83
Louisville, Kentucky from the Ohio River, with Alvin Adams.

Chapter VI .... Page 107
Charleston, South Carolina in ruins after the Civil War, with notice for Charleston & Savannah Railroad.

Chapter VII .... Page 136
When paved roads lay far in the future, only the coming of the railroad could bring prosperity to the vast agricultural region between Jacksonville and Fort Myers.

Chapter VIII .... Page 157
Work crew aboard Plant System locomotive, with James Ingraham and Henry Haines.

Chapter IX .... Page 162
The Ponce de Leon Hotel in St. Augustine with Tampa Bay Hotel and Henry Flagler.

Chapter X .... Page 193
A map of the Plant System, with its founder (beside trophy fish) and the Plant System headquarters.

- ACKNOWLEDGEMENTS -

Biographies are notoriously works of collaboration. My commitment began with that notoriously collaborative form of endeavor, a theatre production. Denis Calandra, directing FLORIDA CHAUTAUQUA '92 for the Florida Humanities Council, invited me to participate in the role of Senator Claude Pepper. Since the format of the production involved a series of dynamic, largely spontaneous exchanges between figures of Florida's past, my working introduction to biography, and Florida history, came "live."

Over the next several years, the Speakers Bureau of the Florida Humanities Council enabled me to tour the state in a one-man show as Senator Pepper. Frequently, conservative audiences challenged me to renounce Pepper's liberal policies. At least, couldn't I say a few words about life on the other side of the economic hill?

The temptation to do a Dr. Jekyll-Mr. Hyde show was strong. In searching about for a Pepper counterpart, I fixated on the villains of traditional capitalism in Florida, Henry Flagler and Ed Ball. It was the historian David Nolan who suggested that I look into the life of someone close to home here on the West Coast of Florida, a thoroughly untraditional capitalist, a benevolent counterpart to Flagler and Ball, the neighborly Henry Plant.

Soon thereafter a great American writer, Nick Tosches, suggested that Peter Mathiessen's novel, *Killing Mr. Watson*, might inspire me to start working in earnest. He was right.

Pessimists warned me there wouldn't be a great deal of material to work with. But close to home I discovered an extensive historical archive, the Eaton Room, at the Manatee County Library. Here I had the guidance and encouragement of Miss Pamela Gibson.. Using vintage photographs from the Henry B. Plant Museum in Tampa (Cynthia Gandee, curator) I was soon able to mount a one-man show, appearing in character as Henry Plant.

That was in 1995. I have been touring the state ever since with this show, again sponsored by the Humanities Council. Very rarely have I visited a community, from Charleston to Key West, without being presented some rare tidbit of old-time information. In terms of the small but so-significant details of this book, the number of my collaborators went off the record a long time ago.

Once working on the book, I began keeping a more thorough record. Thanks to his well-known contributions to the history of steamboats, I was fortunate to meet and have the help early on of Ed Mueller of Jacksonville. Ed's warm-hearted generosity continues to the present time.

Through the kind offices of Linda Carter of the CSX, I began a long question and answer period with Robert Hanson, of Loganville, Georgia. Anyone requiring information about the minutiae of southern railroad lore or Confederate history will soon know themselves blessed if lucky enough to have an introduction to Bob Hanson.

Others who provided invaluable information were: Annon Adams (researcher *extraordinaire!*), Poughkeepsie, NY; Tom Vince, Western Reserve Academy, Hudson, OH; Linda Bailey, Cincinnati Museum, Cincinnati, OH; Erick Montgomery, Historic Augusta, Inc., Augusta, GA; Ken Thomas, Georgia Dept. of Natural Resources, Atlanta; Ginger Miya, Coastal Georgia Historical Society, St. Simons Isle; Pen Bogert and Rebecca Rice, Filson Club, Louisville, KY; Nick Kallis, Illinois Railroad Museum, Union, IL; Myra Ames, Groton, CT; Catherine Phinizy, Connecticut College; Florence Ogg, Sussex County Vanderbilt Museum, Centerport, NY; Irene Morales, Museum of the City of New York; Dorothy D'Eletto, Staten Island Institute of Arts and Sciences; Jeff Remling, South Street Seaport Museum, Manhattan; Richard Palen, Woodstock, NY; Dr. Don K. Dalling, Murray, UT; Dr. Miles S. Richards, Columbia, SC; Mike Coker, South Carolina Historical Society, Charleston; Susan Griffin, Charleston Visitors Center; and Captain John LeCato, National Railway Historical Society, Charleston; Francis P. O'Neil, Maryland Historical Society; Patricia Cunningham, Halifax, Nova Scotia; Marvin Moore, Maritime Museum of the Atlantic, Halifax; Gary Shutlak, Public Archives of Nova Scotia, Halifax; Faye Matthews and Harry Wells, O'Brien, FL; Sharon Gardner, Haines City; Dr. Fredric B. Ferrar and Dr. John Pyros, Tarpon Springs; Eddie Herrmann, San Antonio; Joe Spann, Polk County Historical Society; Don Copeland, Clarence Hurt, and Ken Murdock, Central Florida Railroad Museum, Winter Garden; Alex McInnes and Ray Myers, Plant City; Arthur D. Johnson, Lakeland; John Witkowsky, Clearwater; and Seth Bramson, Miami.

I hope all those who labor in the vineyards of historical research will share my good fortune in benefiting from the amazing store of knowledge available through the services of dedicated librarians and archivists. Without them, this would not be a book at all, but a series of slender articles. For helping me over and over, I must acknowledge Pamela Gibson again, as well as Frances Skelton of the New Haven Colony Historical Society; Jane Bouley of the Branford Historical Society; Linda Pulliam, Florida State Library, Tallahassee; Alicia Clark of the Sanford Museum, Sanford, FL; Karen Jacobs, Museum of Seminole County, Sanford; Dr. James Cusick, Special Collections, University of Florida, Gainesville; Lauren Brosnihan, Research Department, University of West Florida, Pensacola; and Paul Camp, Special Collections, University of South Florida, Tampa. Others who con-

Henry Plant - Pioneer Empire Builder

tributed their professional expertise were: Debra Randorf, New York Historical Society; Barbara Clark-Greene, Groton Public Library, CT; Pat Euston, Woodbury Public Library; Woodbury; Lisa Becker, Lewis County Historical Society, Lyons Falls, NY; Connie McPhee, Metropolitan Museum of Art; David M. Stokes, Louisiana State University at Lafayette; Peggy Rix, Cedar Key Historical Museum; Susan Carter, Henry B. Plant Museum; Stan Mulford, Fort Myers Historical Museum; Betty Callahan, Okefeenokee Heritage Center, Waycross, GA, Ann Harrison and Tom Hill, Thomasville History Museum, Thomasville; Lisa Lofton, Thronateeska Heritage Center, Albany; Jewel Anderson, Georgia Historical Society, Savannah; Bobbie Levy, Thunderbolt Library, Savannah; and Alice Walker, Augusta Central Library, Augusta; Nicholas Blaga, Wolfsonian Florida International University; and Joan Morris, the Florida State Archives, Tallahassee.

Historical expertise is available and a matter of passionate concern outside the profession. This book owes its existence to the valuable insights and information provided by: Roberta Cole and Joe and Libby Warner of the Manatee County Historical Society; John Viele of the Key West Maritime Society; Dr. Joe Knetsch, Tallahassee; and Joyce Williams, North Palm Beach.

It's difficult to imagine keeping up the pace required to reach the finish line without the good wishes along the way of my old friends Phil Barney, Dan Harbaugh, Ed Beardsley, Arnold Cover, James Danley, and Ann Wykell. Over an especially rough stretch, I was rescued by the stern advice and courageous example of Laurel Goldman.

Then, too, the Henry Plant show brought me new friends. I received fresh encouragement at timely moments from Larry Meyers and Stacy Doty of Savannah; from Hib Casselberry of the Florida Lighthouse Association; and from Clem Heilen and Chuck Billings of the National Railway Historical Society.

Of course for many years I have enjoyed the support of the Florida Humanities Council where I also have some old friends: Joan Braggington, Ann Henderson, Susan Lockwood, and David Reddy. And to Denis and Jeanne Calandra, and to all members of FLORIDA CHAUTAUQUA '92, thanks again, always!

While the book was in early manuscript, I sought the help of Patricia DeFreitas of Bradenton and Susan Joseph of New York. Both graciously provided essential editorial advice. I am particularly indebted to the professionally scrupulous reading of the entire manuscript, in near final form, by Patricia DeFreitas and Dr. William Maillet. Prior to publication, Dr. Robert Taylor offered suggestions in matters of style and historical accuracy that have been gratefully incorporated. The recommendations, which came in close to the last minute from Dr. Gregg Turner were, plain and simple, heaven sent. Whatever errors remain are mine.

Let me add a word of special appreciation to Bobbie Ann Mason for her kindness.

Finally, for all, I owe loving thanks beyond measure to Reda, my wife.

Kelly Reynolds
Bradenton, Florida
19 February 2004

Corporate Inventory
THE PLANT SYSTEM
(Partial Listing)

RAILROAD HOLDINGS

    Savannah, Florida, and Western Railway (1879)
      [Formerly the Atlantic & Gulf Rail Railroad]
    Affiliates:
    Florida Division
    Live Oak & Rowlands Bluff Railroad (1883)

    Florida Southern Railroad (1889)
    [Formerly the Gainesville, Ocala & Charlotte Harbor Railway]

South Florida Railroad (1883)
    Affiliates:
      St. Cloud & Sugar Belt Railway (1892)

Jacksonville, Tampa &Key West Railway (1899)
    Affiliates:
      St. Johns & Lake Eustis Railway (1889)
      Deland & St Johns River Railroad (1890)
      Sanford & Lake Eustis Railroad (1887)
      Sanford & St. Petersburg Railway (1895)
        [Formerly the Orange Belt Railway]
      Silver Springs, Ocala, & Gulf Railroad (1892)

    Tampa & Thonotosassa Railroad (1893)
    Florida Midland Railroad (1896)
    Barr's Tram Railway (1888 approx.)
    Winston & Bone Valley Railroad (1892)
    Northwest & Florida Railroad (1888)

Georgia Division
  East Florida Railway - Waycross Shortline (1880)
  Charleston and Savannah Railroad (1880)
  Affiliates:
    Green Pond, Waterboro & Branchville Railway (1887)
    Waterboro & Western Railway (1894)
  Brunswick & Western Railroad (1884)

Alabama Division
  Alabama Midland Railway (1887)
  Montgomery Belt Line Railway (1888 approx.)
  Abbeville Southern Railway (1893)
  Southwest Alabama Railway (1898)

STREETLINE CARS

  Jacksonville Street Railway (1879)
  Pine Street Railway - Jacksonville (1882)
  Jacksonville Suburban (1885)

OTHER RAILROAD INTERESTS

Henry B. Plant served on the board of:
  Northeastern Railroad
  Wilmington & Weldon Railroad
  Richmond & Danville Railroad
  Southern Security Company (1871-78)
  Richmond Terminal Company (1888-93)

EXPRESS HOLDINGS

  Southern Express Company (1861)
  Texas Express Company (1866)

MARITIME HOLDINGS

Steamboats and Steamships, predominant assignments:
Coastline /Inland Fleet

People's Line
Operating on Apalachicola, Chattahoochee, Flint, and St Johns Rivers

Side-Wheelers:
H.B. Plant, Chattahoochee, Thronateeska, Flint, Apalachee, Milton H. Smith, Lotus II, William D. Ellis

Operating on St. Johns River
H.B. Plant II, Uncle Sam, Jennie Lane (formerly *Big Sunflower*), *Chattahoochee,*

St. Sebastian

Port Tampa and Manatee River Line
Margaret I, Margaret II, H.B. Plant II, Kissimmee, St. Lucie, Alice Howard, Thomas A. Edison

Suwannee River Line
Caddo Belle

Canada, Atlantic, and Plant System Limited
Halifax, La Grande Duchesse, A.W. Perry, Evangeline, Pretoria

Gulf Fleet
Port Tampa, Key West, and Havana Line
Port Tampa and Mobile Line
West India Fast Mail
Olivette, Mascotte, William G. Hewes, Naugatuck, Juanita, Florida, Tarpon, San Antonio, Whitney, Yarmouth, City of Tampa (formerly *Fredrick DeBary*), *Caloosa*

HOTELS

Tampa Bay Hotel (1891)
The Inn at Tampa Bay (1888)
Seminole Inn (1887)
Tropical House-Kissimmee
Ocala Hotel
Hotel Belleview (1893)
Hotel Punta Gorda (1888)
PICO Hotel (1887)
Fort Myers Hotel

Above, a listing of Henry Plant's investments and corporate activities, that may be partial and must be unadorned. My book is a biography in a somewhat restricted meaning of the word where the subject is a tycoon. It attempts to tell the story of a businessman's life as a man.

Henry Plant's financial success, as I see it, and as my abilities best permit me to explain it, was not the result of a grand scheme but of a grand dream—abetted by implacable patience and determination. Moreover it is clear that without a wizardry for number crunching and corporate organization, without an accurate and capacious memory for details of every sort, his plans would have gone nowhere. Essentially his success as an entrepreneur followed from his success as a human being.

Today we'd say he was a great guy to work for, a great guy to do business with—*a prince.* For a Railroad King, considering others of the species, what greater compliment?

~ I ~

LAST CALL

He was going to live a notably long life for those times, almost to the millennium, to the summer of 1899. Throughout his youth, through the 1820s and 30s, it was a terribly hard life by our terms, and it was the same for nearly everyone. Still, year by year, despite a regular succession of political disappointments and financial catastrophes, Americans were able to dream more realistically, somehow, of a better life. When they did, they dreamed simply, but intensely, of a life occasionally blessed with the safeguards and comforts that we take for granted today.

By the 1840s, in the years of Henry Plant's early manhood, came the glory times of steamboats and railroads, and people were beginning to dream occasionally of more than just a better life. Traveling "in style," they began to dream of living in style, however temporarily. Of course permanent living in style was something in a class by itself. The everyday conveniences and benefits that we take for granted today were available then only to the lucky few, the very lucky few.

By the 1850s, amid the troubles that would lead to the Civil War, Henry Plant was on his way to joining the luckiest of these lucky few. From a modest start, he discovered the secret all his own of making his dreams come true. Starting literally from the mailroom, he would grow rich by helping to make the dreams of others come true.

He began with our everyday dreams. With the simple, necessary little dreams that we all still have of reliably claiming our luggage at the end of a trip, of receiving package deliveries in one piece, on time. Henry Plant became a successful young man by dramatically lessening the possibilities that these everyday, necessary dreams would fail us.

From there he could go on to make the dream of living in style much more available for the lucky few, and possible for everybody, eventually. The actual making of such an ambitious dream, he knew, must begin with the place to build it on, somewhere in the warmest part of the United States. His eighth grade education had served him well; the schoolhouse map provided an introduction to the vast real estate opportunities on the peninsula of Florida.

But Florida? Pirate romances aside, from his boyhood, and for long after—until he settled there, really, and went to work changing it—Florida's reputation was constant. It was a territory where dreams went to die.

Until the age of the automobile, only the wealthiest could afford to leave home for extended stays in more comfortable and exciting places, that is, could take vacations, as distinct from holidays. But not even the super rich, the jetsetters of the early Steam Age, dreamed of going to Florida for a vacation—to Florida as it was then—except in their nightmares.

For Florida, the land that for generations now has meant the good life, the soft life, then meant something worse than the end of the trail. At least, everywhere else in America, the end of the trail meant the start of the frontier, meant opportunity. On the map, there were no trails to Florida. Even long after the Civil War, suppose that Henry Plant could have taken you on a buggy ride along the best road in the state—the ever incomplete Bellamy Road, running west from St Augustine—encouraging you to invest in the real estate opportunities hereabouts. For all your host's wise and genial manner, you might have been hard to persuade, watching the dismal scenery of neglect and ruin go by, on the edge of an all-conquering wilderness.

In 1899, going north, Henry Plant watched the scenery along the old Bellamy Road, Florida's first "turnpike," roll past for the last time, a stately succession of well-tended farms and village streets. He was traveling the main route of his own mighty Plant System railway, 2,235 miles in all, between Tampa and New York. On his first brief visit to Florida in 1854, it would have meant grueling weeks on a military-style expedition if he had taken the same trip, from the Tampa Bay to where the broad, dusty Bellamy Road crossed the tracks up ahead, near Palatka. Since 1886, however, smoothly clattering along on the gleaming rails of the Plant System, past the yellow-painted Plant depots, you made the trip all the way to New York in just over twenty-eight hours. Guaranteed for all passengers on the

Plant system was a safe, comfortable ride from north to south in just twenty-eight hours.[1]

Especially comfortable for Henry Plant, who was riding as he always did—as did all the "big" men of the time, all the nearly 500 "captains of industry"—in his private railroad car, the famous Plant System Car 100.[2] Often in the thousands and thousands of miles he had traveled this way, he must have thought back to the boy whose first experience of extended travel had been atop a furniture-loaded cart, creaking cautiously toward every stone and pothole, great rivers somewhere before him, and the steep and forested Alleghenies in a purple distance, insurmountable, the end of the world.

Now he had been to the far corners of the earth, to Europe, to Asia. And he had come back with the treasures of history's proudest civilizations, with cargoes of carpets and tapestries and statues and clocks and elaborate music-making contraptions. And cargoes not by the cartload—by the boatload!

How could anyone find the place for such spectacular heaps of treasure? Even the wealthiest of the wealthy would have to store most of it away. But Henry Plant, who had ended his first day's work slung in a hammock in the dingy crowded forecastle of an ocean-going steamboat, now owned eleven fabulous dwellings in south central Florida. Here the wealthy and the almost wealthy came to stay, and paid to stay in those eleven grand hotels. One of these he had commissioned to be the grandest hotel in the world, a massive, rambling edifice of ornate brickwork and carved wood, his Tampa Bay Hotel, set amid flowering orchards and surmounted by silver minarets. And this fabulous structure he had dared to build in a wilderness village that was now, thanks to the touch of his hand, a thriving metropolis.

The untamed land that destiny held for him became United States property in 1819, the year of his birth. The scrappy, youthful USA, wheeling and dealing to acquire the Lousiana Purchase and Florida, had pitched into the last decade of what amounted to 300-years worth of world war and diplomatic intrigue between Spain, Britain, and France. Such a tangle of hostilities only gradually unwound; it took two years to officially close the Florida deal. This occurred at Pensacola, the last European foothold in the Southeast.

On his way to the Battle of New Orleans, General Andrew Jackson had easily

---

[1] Grismer, *Tampa*, 172.
[2] Beebe, *Mansions on Rails*, 103-4. Smyth, *Plant*, 103-4.

captured Pensacola in 1812. Now, appointed Florida's first governor by President James Monroe, the impetuous and bloody-minded hero was required to endure weeks of mournful old-world protocol before the Spanish garrison's final withdrawal. At last, amid scenes of the merrymaking and idleness that he would soon attempt to outlaw, Old Hickory raised Old Glory over the courthouse square on July 17, 1821. Florida, sprawling 361 miles east-west, from the Perdido River to the Atlantic Ocean; Florida, rambling 447 miles north-south, from the St Mary's River to Key West—58,600 square miles in all—now belonged to the United States.[3]

—o—

In the year of Henry Plant's birth, Florida's population was best estimated at 12,000—less than half of what it had been when the first Europeans came ashore in 1513. For then the original inhabitants—the Calusa, the Apalachee, and the Timucua—numbered close to 30,000. These tribes quickly became statistics in a horrifying reality. Between 1492 and 1650, European diseases, the slave trade, and wars of conquest resulted in the nearly total extermination of the indigenous peoples of the Americas.[4] On that jubilant day when Old Glory first flew over Florida, only a few Calusa survived, huddled inaccessibly far away, deep in the swamplands of the peninsula.

Even today, census figures are notoriously deceptive. Of the 12,000 estimated in the Florida census of 1821, less than half were whites. The destruction of the aboriginals attracted other Indians to the empty hunting grounds and prairies. Immigrating in the early 1800s from Alabama and Georgia into remote regions of the interior, powerful elements of the Creek nation established hunting villages and tended crops and grazing lands.[5]

By the time Henry Plant was halfway through his schoolhouse education in 1830, the population on the enticing T-shaped peninsula had almost tripled in one decade. Nearly everyone, 34,735 in all, lived on the bar of the T—the panhandle—and there concentrated on the east-west ends, in Pensacola and Jacksonville. The exception would be a thriving little community of scavengers, wreckers, and traders at the end of the island chain on the tip of the peninsula. Half a century later Key West became a jewel in the maritime department of Henry Plant's transportation empire. Tampa, the crown jewel itself, had been first recognized by an

---

[3] Tebeau, *History of Florida*, 110.
[4] Milanish in *New History of Florida*, 1-15. Zinn, *People's History*, 6-17.
[5] Canter Brown, Jr., *Peace River Frontier*, 3.

As he rode to New York for the last time, memories of the chaos at Port Tampa during the Spanish-American war (inset) were still fresh in Henry Plant's mind. Yet solace was at hand. From his private car he could watch the country roads flash by — roads he had once traveled in horse-drawn vehicles.

adventurer named Richard Hackley. In 1822 young Hackley, a Manhattan lawyer, bought a Spanish document granting its owner purported title to the southern part of the Florida peninsula.

The coastal area in the heart of the region would become home to a fishing and farming community established by runaway slaves; then destroyed by Indian raiders; then an outpost of the U.S. Calvary, Fort Brooke, later Tampa. White settlers soon began to drift down. In Colonel Brooke's opinion, "The chief, it may be said, the only object of these settlers is to dispose of whiskey to the troops and the Indians, which they have and continue to do, to the great annoyance of the command and injury to the Seminoles and Indians."[6] Who were these first Floridians of the United States? Those of European descent were rugged souls, highly resourceful and fiercely determined, the last frontiersmen to go south. For these early pioneers to Florida faced risks and difficulties far greater than those encountered by early settlers in Georgia or Alabama. On the Florida border, law and order ended more conclusively than anywhere on the western frontier. Generations of wanted men, of outlaws and desperadoes, had regularly moved in and would continue to do so throughout the first half of the 19th century, forming a unique social stratum still influential into the 20th.[7]

Meanwhile, a steady source of pioneer stock in the early Florida territory had always been fugitive slaves. Many were unlucky enough to join the British army in time to oppose Andrew Jackson at New Orleans on January 8, 1815. The survivors returned to Florida where they became the first agriculturalists to settle the Tampa Bay region. Other blacks, fleeing across the panhandle from bounty hunters, allied themselves with—or were taken into slavery by—the newly-arrived Indian tribes.[8] The tribal Seminole and Mikasukee nations arose. These mighty and elusive peoples—despite forty years [a minimum] of coercion, warfare, broken treaties, and bribery—would remain unvanquished.[9]

Henry Plant was nearing middle age when the thrust to settle Indian-occupied territory would propel Florida decisively into the future. From the start, U.S. policy aimed to crush the supposedly undisciplined Indian warriors on the battlefield and remove the survivors west of the Mississippi. Old Hickory and his Tennessee frontiersmen initiated the hostilities in 1818 with a ferocious campaign along the

---

[6] Brown, 11, 35, 41, 53.
[7] Brown, 35-41.McWhiney, *Cracker Culture*. Glisson, *Yesterday's Florida*, 21-8. Tosches, *Dead Voices* 141.
[8] Brown, 19. Landers in *New History of Florida*, 175-77.
[9] Mahon and Weisman in *New History of Florida*, 183-205

Suwannee River, destroying everything in their path that looked Indian, mainly crops and villages. Finally, frustrated by the elusive quarry, Jackson had a couple of footloose Englishmen strung up. This set off a diplomatic crisis that curtailed the invasion.[10]

Only in the Second Seminole War could the army and local militias bring their wily opponents to pitched battle. And then, until the capture of Osceola by treachery, the "savages" often held their own. It was enough to bring the vicious conflict to a temporary halt when a hardcore contingent of 1,000 Indian survivors agreed to withdraw to a huge reservation in the central interior.[11]

In 1845 Florida became a state, with a white population of nearly 60,000.[12] Soon afterwards Florida's second governor, Tom Brown, put the issue for settlement with rare candor, if a long way from accurately, "the most interesting and valuable part of our state [is] cut off from any benefit to the citizens and sealed to the knowledge of the rest of the world, to be used as a hunting ground for a few roaming savages."[13]

The Third Seminole War began in 1852. When Henry Plant first came to Florida two years later, its miserable conclusion was near, strictly a cash deal. In a removal costing $800 a warrior, $450 a woman, $400 a child, the main body of Florida's Native Americans withdrew to Arkansas. Two hundred recalcitrants, in three scattered bands, remained in the Everglades, clinging to their heritage.[14]

The original Seminole grazing and hunting lands in the central highlands swiftly became cowboy cattle kingdoms, still thriving today. But by the 1840s, in the fertile regions of the northern peninsula—in Leon, Jefferson, Hamilton, Madison, Jackson, Gadsen, Alachua, and Marion Counties—an agricultural system would thrive. Throughout Florida's vast and fertile Black Belt, panoramic fields of the bright-green cotton crop were meticulously tended and harvested by labor gangs of African slaves.[15]

Long hard times awaited the children and grandchildren of all these folk, looking for their chances. But they would still be there, and they would be ready, when near its end the century entered the unexpected youth of its Gilded Age—and Henry Plant arrived to begin the making of a new Florida.

---

[10] Brown, 7, 9. Mahon and Weisman, 191-2. Tebeau, 113-4.
[11] Brown, 41, 48. Mahon and Weisman, 193-99.
[12] Hanna, *Lake Okeechobee*, 53.
[13] Hanna, 58.
[14] Mahon and Weisman, 199-201. Tebeau, 158-68
[15] Rivers, *Slavery in Florida*, 11, 16-33.

—o—

Thirty minutes past the Bellamy Road, the train pulled into Jacksonville's Union Station, the last (or the first) stop in Florida. Once, before the Civil War, he had passed through here with the first Mrs. Plant, on a mission of hope and sorrow. They beheld a frontier community, surrounded by water and desolation, and pushed on. But now Jacksonville was prosperously sprawling, one of the busiest railway junctions in the country, all owing to the activities over the past quarter century of Plant and his friend, colleague, and rival, Henry Flagler. The "union" at Union Station meant, above all, the convergence of the Plant System's north-south line with Flagler's Florida East Coast Railway.

Not many businessmen could boast having survived such a friend, much less such a rival, as Henry Morrison Flagler. John D. Rockefeller had found him a quickly calculating, bright-eyed young man, undeterred by hard times on the Ohio frontier, and brought him into the oil business.

These days, Flagler's mighty railroad had come to a halt far short of achieving the grand dream of running track out over the ocean to Key West, an engineering feat that would make it the Eighth Wonder of the World. One day Plant hoped that his friend would wake up and dream this dream to reality. After all, who was it brought Henry Flagler into the Florida railroad business? It never displeased Henry Plant to say that he had. Soon Henry Flagler would lead the honorary pall-bearers at his funeral.[16]

Leaving the station, coasting through the outskirts of the city, the clickety-clack, clickety-clack of the rails had been almost surreptitious. Suddenly, though, they were crossing into Georgia over the St Mary's River, and the gentle sound of rolling metal jumped dramatically, a steady, drumming clatter on the Waycross Shortline Bridge. Even in his most troubled and gloomy rest, and no matter the many, many times he had made this crossing, Henry Plant must have smiled, if just customarily, to hear the racket because the Shortline bridge had made for his first big winning in the railroad business. When he'd put over this bridge, it might rightly be stated that he'd put over a fast one, now mightn't it? Up 'till then, the folks here in North Florida used to say that no one would ever bring another of those things—a railroad—into Florida. But he'd proved them wrong, overnight—overnight!—and, for the most part, they'd been thanking him ever since.

The steamboat men had been the worst, with their lawyers and money runners in Tallahassee. And he was a steamboat man himself, and lived right back there in

---

[16] *Branford Budget*, June 30, 1899.

Jacksonville harbor, and up ahead in Savannah, on one after the other of the most gorgeous steamboats ever put in the water, the *H.B. Plant* and the *Margaret*.

The *Margaret*, and Margaret. His second wife, Margaret Loughman Plant, his close companion for 26 years now, was back at the hotel in Tampa. If Margaret was resting, hers was a troubled rest, too. Ever since he went in with the War Department on that Cuba business, Margaret had her look for him–her look of not looking at him.

And his son, Morton, at the new hotel on the Gulf, probably not resting too well either. Busy all the time, but busy in one place. The brand-new hotel in Clearwater still wasn't brand-new enough, still wasn't up-to-date enough, not for Morton.

A former deckhand on a Long Island Sound paddle wheeler, Henry Plant, would live to see his steamships carry passengers and cargo to ports between Halifax and Havana.

Though for little Henry's sake all this fussing would be all for the best, now wouldn't it? Four years old now, the child who would carry on his name, his grandson, Henry Bradley Plant II. At least one thing you could count on, Morton had a good heart. Morton's grandmother, his own blessed mother, had seen to that.

Let the hotel be the best home in the world for the little boy, and the father in it.

And other things, too, were making him feel poorly these last years. Everybody knew that his biggest venture in one place, the Tampa Bay Hotel, had never, well, had never quite caught on the way it should. Some suspicions, even in his own mind, that maybe he'd given the hotel's fancy architect too much leeway. Then, what about the personally commissioned steamship meant to make his cruise line the pride of the maritime world, *La Grand Duchesse*? Who but himself had been the fancy pants on that one? The engineers had warned him, more than once, that he was asking too much. But liners were crossing the Atlantic now in thirteen days. What else to do? He had to catch up, get ahead! So through all the troubles at the shipyards, he stuck to the super-charged boilers, his own idea! Well, maybe this sleek new world of steamships had been a little too swift for him. The *Duchesse* had been one disappointment after the other. What were they saying about her now? "A sea-going lemon." The blueprint boys had been right, so far.

So far! Lots of folks had been right so far. The precious soul his grandmother had been—so sure he'd grow up to be a preacher—putting all the money aside she could, to put him through Yale College. How she and mother took on, that he day he came back from the Long Wharf, signed aboard the *New York*. Just eighteen— wasn't too long after, though, he had more money than his grandmother saved that day he came back. And now, well, he could buy a pretty good part of the Yale campus.

In every sense, transportation brought Henry Plant to Florida. Early on, life gave him the classic choice of staying at home or going to sea. At sea in the 1830's as a "captain's boy" on a Long Island Sound packet steamer, he was quick to appreciate what there could be in it for a man ready to put all his energy into finding ways to move people and their goods ever more rapidly, safely, and reliably. His awareness of transportation as a life-changing event had come even earlier.

He was a six-year-old when his father died. When his mother remarried two years later, the family relocated to Martinsburg in upstate New York, a distance of some 300 miles. At least such a trip was feasible in 1825. At least, setting out, a family knew that it could be done, that the odds of arriving intact were in their favor.

The Plants were one of the old New England families, arriving from England in 1636. Then, an inland journey of 300 miles would have been unthinkable. Settlements in the interior were still likely to be no more than hard-won, heavily fortified, isolated clearings. The warlike Mohawks occupied and held the western forests with uncanny vigilance. For generations, any significant travel or transfer of goods in the American colonies meant going by ship, along the coast.

Even between adjacent settlements there would be no roads for a long while.[17] The early "roads" through the wilderness were Indian paths, between fourteen and eighteen inches wide. Indians walk through a forest single file, placing one foot exactly in front of the other., and this practice determined the width of the paths. These centuries-old paths had been worn according to customs that knew no hurry, no effort. Indian trails found the indirect ways of least resistance around steep grades and arduous descents. Rocks and fallen trees were never cleared.

The first alternately muddy and dusty roads in the Colonies—for families walking abreast to church, for wagonloads of market-day commodities—were extensions of township streets that developed with the arrival of new settlers and the spread of farm lands. The "highways" between settlements generally followed the Indian paths. A mile of such a road built to the standard width of a rod (16-1/2') required the clearing of an acre of forest, felling trees, uprooting stumps, breaking and hauling stone. Then, the unremitting effort required to maintain the roadway year-round in a community where everyone's survival was already a matter of working one day after the other to exhaustion. When six-year-old Henry Plant traveled across the Alleghenies, between New Haven and upstate New York, the teamsters and coachmen had aboard the tools to clear and repair the road ahead.

Yet 1825 was a momentous year for travel in America. In the middle of New York harbor aboard a freshly christened canal boat, Governor DeWitt Clinton held aloft a gushing keg and emptied five gallons of Lake Erie water into the Atlantic Ocean. Bands struck up, cannons boomed. The opening of the 364-mile-long Erie Canal, eight years in the digging, made New York the nation's commercial center overnight, surpassing Philadelphia–"A mile an a-half and hour, a cent and a-half a mile!" Roadway transportation from the rich farmlands of the Mid-West simply could not compete. In the first full year of operation, 18,000 boats passed through the locks at Schenectady, paying $765,000 in tolls.[18]

The great mercantile cities of the colonial era felt the pinch right away. Pennsylvania built 1,000 miles of canals by the end of the decade. Businessmen beyond the reach of canals held desperate confabulations. They would need to act quickly, and empty their deepest pockets. In 1825 the world knew that in Great Britain a steam-powered railroad had gone into operation, hauling passengers and freight 15 miles through the industrial midlands. When Henry Plant was three years old,

---

[17] Larkin, *Everyday Life*, 211-13. Parks, *Roads*, 5-21.
[18] Butterfield, *American Past*, 76-7.

there had not been ten miles of railroad track in the United States. By the 1830s, America's first locomotives were running trans-mountain routes out of Baltimore and Charleston.[19] The hectic days of the languid canals were over almost as soon as they began. Across a rapidly expanding network of iron rails, in chuffing clouds of steam and in long plumes of spark-showering black smoke, Henry Plant's future now awaited him.

But in Florida? To begin with, Florida was a long way from taking shape. The territory proclaimed itself by the formal distinction of East Florida and West Florida, essentially, a peninsular and a panhandle Florida. Proponents of this division would maintain considerable influence over the state's future, even after one Florida entered the union.

The geography of East Florida created the dilemma. On a map the situation might look promising, at first. The harbor-rich coastlines and navigable streams suggest ideal opportunities for shipping, but, as nature provides, these opportunities are strictly longitudinal. To join the territories of East Florida and West Florida, and to consolidate the peninsula south of St. Augustine, that would be a matter of waiting for Henry Plant. Meanwhile, Gulf-Atlantic transportation was required to go the long way around via Key West.

Of course, the hazards and sheer cost inefficiency of rounding the Florida Straits had set men dreaming, since the Spanish Conquest, of a cross-Florida Canal. And the dream of this engineering impossibility would long appear a more feasible solution than a cross-Florida road.[20]

During Henry Plant's lifetime, no sort of paved roads connected the towns and cities of the South—though some places might boast brick—or cobble-paved streets. Not until 1894 was the first concrete-paved road laid, experimentally, in Ohio. In Florida the earth itself compounded the difficulties of road building. All over the world a good rainfall will turn a dirt road into wheel-sinking mire—and good rainfalls in Florida are traditionally abundant. Worse, whereas dry weather produces dusty dirt roads over most of the world, dry weather in Florida can turn even her best hard-packed sandy roads into another aspect of the wheel—sinking phenomenon—wheels sinking into powdery grit. In the South, when a good road—which is to say, a popular and propably essential one—had been made impassable due to the waer of heavy traffic, the expression was that the road had been "plowed up."

In 1824 Congress appropriated the inglorious sum of $20,000 for a desperately

---

[19] J Derr, *Paradise*, 333-5.
[20] Tebeau, 140-41.

needed road across the panhandle, 624 miles between St. Augustine and Pensacola. Eventually a plantation owner named John Bellamy undertook the job. Following a trail blazed by Spanish missionaries, Bellamy finished 240 miles of the project using his own slaves and equipment.

As long as it lasted, though, only teams of the most determined oxen could pull loads any distance over the soft, sandy soil of Bellamy's road. Ruts deepened, and stumps left low-cut down the middle tore the bottoms out of wagons. No bridges were ever built. Streams and inlets of any depth required passage in one primitive ferry after the other, poled by ferrymen trudging fore to aft. And, instead of causeways to span the boggy patches there would be spoke-snapping, axle-busting, passenger-tossing, spine-fracturing "corduroy"—logs laid cross-wise. When Henry Plant traveled stretches of the "finished" Bellamy Road in the early 1880s, the experience must have literally jolted his ambitious plans for a new Florida over and over.

What did it take to build a better road? Hard workers and smart, experienced management, out on the job every day. None of his top men were college men. Oh, some few might qualify. For one, that young colonel from Harvard, down with his New York brigade a year ago, destination Cuba, destination glory. The wild old neighborhood around the Tampa Bay Hotel never would know a wilder bunch, but—for all that—gentlemen. Didn't they have some swell times? Grand long sit-downs after dinner, good brandy, smoke cigars, play cards all night. Then every morning, exercise their horsemanship, go tearing down the sandy roads, out to the woods. Henry Plant could tell a hot pistol when he saw one. That young Theodore Roosevelt was a go-getter. Needed putting in his place, true. "Mr. Plant, if you can't get us to Cuba on time, I will order the government to seize your System." "Colonel Roosevelt, seize it and be damned." But think how he grabbed the headlines when he did get to Cuba.

Yes, telling a hot pistol from a toy gun, telling a go-getter from a big talker, you better keep that secret to yourself, building a railroad business, a steamboat business, a hotel business. He hadn't wasted a second, had he, and not spared a dime to put Colonel Henry Haines and young James Ingraham on his side. When it was the big job had to be done, let some folks lift their hands, shake their heads. "Does that fool Plant think he can build a railroad halfway 'cross the state in three months?" But his go-getters, they already had the job half licked. All the pistols he cared to pack, Haines and Ingraham.

How smart was he then, trying to run that whole Cuba business himself? Where were his go-getters last year? Well, couple of years ago, all the big jobs were done, that was supposed to be the idea. Promised Margaret another Paris trip, another China trip. But when the *Maine* blew, the war was on, and Tampa was the big-time port for Cuba. He had made her so, from his dream, from way back. And when the dream became a nightmare, who else could make it work? Who else could take shipment for so many tons and tons of men and horses, weapons and goods? Everything into Port Tampa by his trains. Then—some delay here, of course—by his ships, mostly, loading at his docks, out on the water, to Cuba. They had that mess down there over in ten days. Who else, his age, could take on so much?

Sad thing about it was, according to some, the mess was in Tampa. The men arriving too soon, shipping out too late, drunk and disorderly on the streets. His rail yards backed up outside of town, one long bottleneck of spoiling meat and vegetables. Overnight, his magnificent facilities at Port Tampa became a bewildering chaos of mixed-up uniforms and a pandemonium of underfed horses and mules. According to some, that's what brought him low. Too old to take on so much, alone.

The train slowed, switching tracks, sliding into the familiar yards at Savannah. To the west was all of Georgia, where it all started, really, his years with the Confederates, the long years of widowhood and grief. How often had he seen his own boy then, when he was busy building all this? Well, didn't he visit the home in Connecticut every chance he got? Once, maybe twice a year, all through Morton's childhood. Hardly enough for little Henry, of course. The way it turned out, Morton couldn't help but be a better father. Later on he would understand why, for almost that reason alone, everything must go to the boy. As for how Margaret might take it, anyone could tell by looking at Margaret that she gave herself credit for knowing Henry Plant's reasons better than he did.

"All aboard! Brunswick, Beaufort, Charleston! Last Call! All aboard!" Immediately, up and down the long platform, the emphatic closing of heavy doors. All the doors except the door of Plant System Special Car 100, which would not open until New York City. Next, after the ritual calling among the brakemen and crew, that expectant moment of silence along the platform so peaceful it had you fooled every time ... that it might last forever. Then, from far up ahead, an angel's ding-ding-ding and a monster's wuff-wuff-wuff. Seconds later, the successive rackety groan of stiffened couplings came traveling down the cars. The train was moving out in a series of soft jolts—jolts that were extra soft when the engine pulled Special Car 100.

Soon the white-jacketed steward entered. With just a nod, finding Mr. Plant dozing at his favorite window, he parted curtains of swaged brocade, turned down and smoothed the bed. All night, crystal and silver appointments on a little screwed-down Regency desk would be jiggling, just audibly, merrily. Mile by rushing mile, they were leaving the South. The empire of trains and steamships and grand hotels that fanned out from Tampa Bay, now dwindling behind him, preparing to vanish, like the magician's trick it had always seemed. And why not, hadn't he created all this from nothing?

Yet, for his long lifetime of astonishing feats, Henry Plant would scoff at the suggestion that he had been a magician. The Plant System wasn't up his sleeve, certainly not. He kept everything inside his head, inside his heart. And there it would stay safely tucked away. He mustn't let go until his New Haven lawyers could execute the cunning contrivance of unalterable stipulations and doled-out entitlements that, yes, he had been dreaming of for quite some time now.

Years to come, another Henry Plant would put forth his hand. The little boy growing up in the big hotel would be a man. This glorious empire, based on convenience and comfort for all mankind, would spring forth once more. To last another lifetime, and another, and another, Henry Plant was going to see to that. He had only to stay alive long enough to make sure this last work done, according to his will.

~ II ~
BAREFOOT BOY

Incomparably, there never has been a more popular place to spend an American childhood than Mark Twain's hometown on the muddy banks of the Mississippi. On the rocky headlands of the Atlantic Coast, Henry Plant's home town seems to have been pretty much Hannibal, Missouri's counterpart. When the United States was growing up, Branford, Connecticut, like Hannibal, offered the two advantages a growing boy needed most: education and adventure.

In the white-maned years of his Hartford residency, Mark Twain may have rambled along the Branford River outside New Haven—to his regard no more than a large creek. But with a sense of well-earned assurance, the swiftly flowing waters meet the ocean at an inlet of massive craggy boulders, forming a slender beach of almost white sand and a classically snug harbor.[1]

Originally founded in 1646 by families from the county of Middlesex, on the rural outskirts of London, Branford would remain a typical village, even a Hallmark-worthy village to this day. Henry Plant's first American ancestor, his great-grandfather John Plant, reached the vicinity by 1637.[2] He was just in time to join the war that destroyed the remains of the original inhabitants, survivors of a devastating measles epidemic brought by the white man twenty years before—the amalgamated tribes of the Pequots and Mohegans.[3]

---

[1] Federal Writers Project, *Connecticut*, 340-41.
[2] Smyth, *Plant*, 37.
[3] Osterweis, *New Haven*, 10.

Kelly Reynolds

Even in the early part of this century, youngsters in New England grew up hearing stories of the Indian Wars told over and over around the fireplace. Later in life, the merciless prosecution and pitiful outcome of the Seminole Wars would come as no surprise to Henry Plant. More assertively even than the Seminoles under Osceola, the Pequots under chief Sessacus sought to re-establish their territorial rights, steadily being "treatied" away in Rhode Island and along the Connecticut River. In their shrewd bargaining, the colonists had allied themselves with the Pequot's traditional enemies, the Narragansetts. After a number of provocations, armed conflict began in 1836. John Plant must have taken part in one of the bloodiest battles of the war, when the Pequots were defeated on Sachem's Head, a rocky promontory on the Atlantic, just east of Branford. A Narragansett chief, celebrating the victory, placed the severed head of a Pequot brave in the fork of a tree.[4] It remained there for a long time to come. For generations, doubtless, every child in the village could have eagerly led us to the place.

And John Plant was likely present at the final battle of the war. A combined colonial and native force smashed the last Pequot fort, slaughtering 500 warriors. Sessacus and a few braves escaped to the west, where the Mohawks put them to torture and death. Pequot women and children taken captive at the battle went either directly into slavery with the Narragansetts or were sold by the colonists in the West Indies.[5]

That was in 1637. In 1674, during King Philip's War, the colonists destroyed the Narragansetts. Until economically resurgent in our time via casino gambling, the days of Indian power in New England were over. Meanwhile, the village of Branford had been incorporated, a satellite township of then New Haven Colony.[6] And, thanks to a thriving trade in wax-producing bay berries and a fine harbor full of coast-wise sailing vessels, through the first half of the eighteenth century Branford seemed ever about to surpass New Haven itself.[7] In this promising locality John Plant was rewarded with two acres of farmland for his military services, and established the family home.[8]

The main features of the household and the colonial village remained intact throughout Henry Plant's childhood. Southern New Englanders eschewed log cabins; instead, by overwhelming choice, their homes were framed, floored struc-

---

[4] Writers Project, 339.
[5] Osterweis, 10.
[6] Osterweis, 12.
[7] Simonds, *First Church of Branford*, 62-3.
[8] Smyth, *Plant*, 37-8.

tures, snugly clad in clapboard. Wealthy families might add a projecting second story; later, with greater wealth, would come the architecture of gables and widow's walks. Many houses had steeply sloping shingle roofs that almost touched the ground in the backyards. There, all would be tidily, lovingly maintained, a kind of mercantile system in crowded miniature—orchards and gardens, compost heaps and seed beds, stables and cow barns, hen coops and rabbit hutches, outhouses and wash houses, wood sheds and tool sheds.

Like the households, a New England village aimed at self-sufficiency, self-containment.[9] The family farms that replaced the surrounding woodlands were the "developments" of the 1800s. At the time Henry Plant's childhood Branford had attained a population of around 2,000. Local agricultural prosperity had reached its peak, and, in addition to a venerable iron works, several small industries had sprung up, including six distilleries, three fulling mills, a carding mill, and—surely best of all—several shipyards which held on through the 1860s. Little remained, however, of Branford's early promise from back in the days of its rivalry with New Haven. Only six ships, capable of coast-wise trade, rode in her harbor. One such ship, a schooner of greater than forty tons, would have been enough to capture the daily fascination of a growing boy.

Yet it would have been within and around the triangular Branford village green that young Henry Plant found the center of his weekday life, outside his home. More than a park in New England for almost three centuries, until the coming of the automobile and radio, nothing could diminish the importance of the village green. By the definition of village, no one lived far away. The familiar American front-porch and front-yard lifestyle would be an innovation of the far future. Originally, you came out your front door and went to the "common"—to the pasture-like green—and on serious business, as a rule.

Few recreational opportunities were permitted by the regulations of the original New England townships. So much as an inclination for a good time, for leisure even, would have been frowned on and worse. True, every town had its tavern near the common. But above all, the village green was the heart and soul of every inhabitant's commercial, political, and religious life—where the religious aspects of life stood predominant and unquestioned.[10]

---

[9] Simonds, 128.
[10] Writers Project, 340. Osterweis, 32-4.

However diabolic their business schemes and ethics, strong religious convictions characterize the private-life practices, pronouncements and lavish bequests of a number of the most successful financiers of the robber baron Era: Rockefeller, the pious Baptist; Carnegie and Flagler, staunch Presbyterians; Morgan, an ardent Episcopalian. While in so many ways atypical of his financial peers, all his life Henry Plant was to remain a firm and active Congregationalist.

The two principal characteristics of Congregationalism, enunciated 1582, have always been a stern avoidance of "show" and a zealous concern for independence. All the early Protestant sects had the first characteristic in common, "protesting" the pomp and ritual that had often assumed grotesque overemphasis in the Roman Catholic and Anglican faiths. But it would become a characteristic of many Protestants to stress a certain kind of vigilant uniformity that, as in Massachusetts Bay Colony, produced a grotesque overemphasis of its own.

So marked, however, was the Congregational opposition to vigilant uniformity that the entire collective unit of the early church was known as "The Independents." The prime organizational theme stressed fellowship among houses of worship. Doctrinal unity would be maintained not by a detailed creed or hierarchical supervision but by something more like mutual trust among members of the same loving family.[11]

Of course members of loving families can squabble a good bit. But that would come later for the Congregationalists who came to America. Initially they enjoyed the benefits of a desperately enforced cohesion. In John Plant's time, settlers who came to New Haven Colony entered a monolithic, extremist theocracy, run by Puritan fathers for whom life in Massachusetts Bay had been too soft. Little towns like Stamford, Guilford, and Branford were intended to remain satellites of theocratic New Haven.

But the authoritarian excesses of the New Haven founders proved self-defeating. The Congregationalists in their unsupervised way won out, and in 1708 succeeded in establishing a theocracy of their own. Much less monolithic and extremist, it would be the established state religion of Connecticut for the next 110 years. Mostly this was a time of ferocious squabbling. The "Great Awakening" of 1730 bitterly divided the church into radical and conservative parties, the "New Lights" and the "Old Lights."[12] Doubtless the Old Lights held power at the Branford Church, for the radicals did hardly anything on behalf of the American side during the Revolution. We can be sure that Henry Plant, in his life-long quiet

---

[11] Atkins and Fagley, *American Congregationalism*.
[12] Osterweis, 85-6. Simonds, 85-9.

way, took pride in his family's enthusiastic and evidently heroic record of patriotic activities.

Yet while on the winning side in the most important event in American history, the conservatives were the underdogs and eventually the grimly die-hard losers in the power struggle that shook the Congregational church long after its disestablishment in Connecticut in 1818, the year before Henry Plant's birth. From the time he could walk, when he went with his family across the village green to church, the First Church and Society of Branford, Henry Plant was taking his place in a membership of proud, resourceful, and embattled forbearers, independent to the last. The presence of his grandmother would have intensified his awareness of this tradition.

Proud, resourceful, embattled, independent to the last, the church as meetinghouse on the village green was also the vital center of political participation in the destinies of both Branford and New Haven. Owing to its fiercely assertive sense of itself, New Haven had almost disastrously resisted incorporation in 1662 when the state of Connecticut was formed. Branford would do the same even closer to the last minute, as it would always resist incorporation into "greater" New Haven.[13] And these same qualities, of initiative and stubbornness that dominated the historical environment of his youth, would characterize Henry Plant's later life and the fate of his financial empire.

About the time Henry Plant's parents were courting, issues of initiative and stubbornness brought years of desperate crisis and profound change to Branford, to New Haven, to Connecticut, and to faraway Florida. In the course of the ten years (1804-14) that England fought Napoleon, 42,000 seamen went permanently AWOL from the subhuman conditions of the British Navy. To make up for these losses, Union Jack recruiters invited themselves aboard foreign ships at sea. By 1807 American sailors were being regularly snatched up. Finally the number of American citizens serving involuntarily approached 10,000. Then, in retaliation for resistance to a particularly overzealous recruiting effort, the British blew up a U.S. Navy ship.

Though no pacifist, President Thomas Jefferson wished to avoid war. But after what did amount to a vicious war of political resistance on the eastern seaboard, he put into effect the hugely unpopular Embargo Act of 1808. U.S. ships would simply stay at home for the duration. American seaports were sealed. In the great

---

[13] Osterweis, 10-12.

harbors of Charleston, New York, Philadelphia, Baltimore, and Boston, merchantmen flying the U.S. flag rotted at the docks.[14] The same occurred in such lesser but significant harbors as New Haven.

Meanwhile the British and French scoffed at the embargo, running goods freely through border ports in Canada and Florida. Thanks to the "open" possibilities in the Florida ports of Pensacola and Apalachicola, Southern planters hardly noticed. Along the Atlantic seaboard, such a snug little harbor as Branford may have thrived on small-time smuggling.

With peace, the great seaports quickly regained their glory. But, while not crippled to the extent proclaimed during the "Dambargo," New Haven would never fully recover, not as a seaport.[15] Indeed, it was all going to turn out much for the best, thanks to what had already become famously known as the locality's "Inventive Spirit."

Throughout his life Henry Plant would move among daily reminders of his birthplace; reminders, too, of the gratifications that ingenuity and hard work could produce. The 19th and early 20th Centuries would rejoice in the abundance of New Haven quality goods pouring steadily, profusely forth to the markets of the world—clocks and locks, boots and shoes, springs, small arms, carriages.[16]

Even during the Panic of 1819, the rapid growth of commercial and industrial activity sustained New Haven's carrying trade. And soon the latest technological breakthrough was promising boom times for the port cities on Long Island Sound. Best of all, when the Lake Erie-New York Harbor connection became a sure thing, the great 1820s canal craze struck Connecticut.[17]

Today we camp out for space launches. The people of the 19th Century took picnics at construction sites. All during the time Henry Plant was a boy, a tremendous canal-digging project was underway between New Haven and Farmington.[18] From far off, you knew. Every hot summer day, all day long, steel clanged on stone. Clouds of dust rose above the trees. Tatterdemalion troops of Irish "navies" came marching by, straight off the ships, hefting picks and shovels.[19] Oxen dragged timber-loaded sledges. Wagon teams of mules brought the great levers

---

[14] Smith, *John Marshall*, 380-85.
[15] Hegel, "Jefferson's Embargo." Osterweis, 193, 201-2.
[16] Osterweis, 226, 237.
[17] Kirkland, *Transportation*, Vol. I, 71-2. Osterweis, 169.
[18] Osterweis, 283-4.
[19] Simonds, 124-31.

Henry Plant - Pioneer Empire Builder

and gearworks that would swing the locks. And all the time, families in their buggies, bringing picnic baskets, maneuvered through the turmoil, looking for the best place to spend the day. Later, in the same spirit, to witness a new world in the making, they would come to watch the work on Henry Plant's railroads.

The 1836 completion of the canal multiplied the quantities of agricultural goods requiring transshipment up and down the coast. By this time the character of the New Haven waterfront had altered dramatically. The age of sail was passing. Steamships now dominated coastwise transportation. Was the future transportation king aware of any of this? Clearly, he would be. At eighteen, owing to the exciting possibilities of the steamboats in New Haven harbor, he faced a crisis of life-making or life-breaking proportions.

When we judge the qualities of Henry Plant's personality based on the friendships and business associations of a lifetime, loyalty stands at the top of the list—above all, loyalty to his family. Now, all at once, in his last year at school, he was required to choose between his own adventurous plans and the stay-at-home destiny cherished by his beloved grandmother all the years of his growing up.

Well after Henry Plant's time, an eighth-grade education stood for a high school diploma in America. And far more so than in our times, the quality of pre-college education was uniform. Uniformly poor, that is. A literate citizenry need only be functionally literate in a society where, by iron necessity, upwards of 70 percent of the people would be on the land. In colonial times, many schoolmasters were hardly more than functionally literate. With crops in the fields, endless chores in the barnyard, and cattle forever straying away, it meant a considerable sacrifice to allow a good young hand time off to sit half the day in a cozy little shelter, huddled over a chalkboard.

Fortunately, by the time of Henry Plant's birth, the ideals of Franklin and Jefferson had been in energetic application for two generations. A somewhat itinerant body of well-qualified and highly motivated pedagogues was the first, best practical result of the drive for a democratically superior national schoolhouse.

Certainly the chances were slim that one of these rare outstanding teachers would appear in such an obscure village as Branford, and stay. Henry Plant was to be blessed with rare good fortune most of his life. In 1812 a committed young man named Timothy F. Gillett stepped off the stage from New Haven, prepared to serve the rest of his long life in the dual capacity of minister and schoolmaster. He had a keen awareness of the limitations of what had been passing for an education at the time.

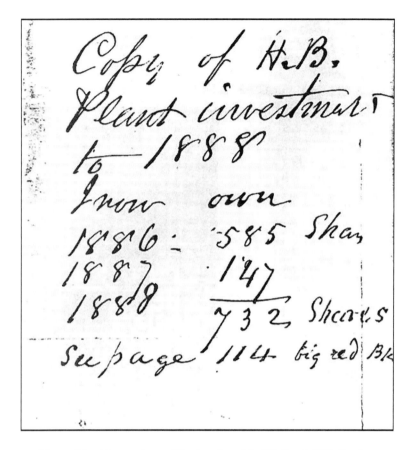

Henry Plant learned a swift, clear hand in "Father" Gillet's classrom. He dashed this notation on the back of a brochure for the American Museum of Natural History, NYC.

For eight years Reverend Gillett held classes in his home. Known to all as "Father Gillett," he soon began to promote the idea of not just a schoolhouse for Branford, but an academy. The difference far surpassed our present distinction between public and private facilities. First, the original schoolhouse in America was universally a one-room schoolhouse—in every sense, a beginning. In his retirement discourse (1858), Father Gillett provides a thumbnail history, "It will be remembered that our fathers carried with them the school as well as the church. The principle was, a common school education for every child. Probably three or four months in the year was deemed sufficient to acquire the necessary education. As the settlements spread, schools were multiplied. Reading, writing and arithmetic were taught. That was all that the law required, to entitle school societies to a share of the public money. There were no select, or grammar schools, until your present pastor commenced one."

Then with particular reference to what this improvement would mean in Henry Plant's lifetime, "[We] now have eight districts, and ordinarily one, sometimes two, select schools. The requisite qualifications of teachers have been increased, and the branches in which pupils are taught are quite sufficiently multiplied for utility. But I feel constrained to say this great subject is still undervalued. Branford has raised but few publicly educated men."[20]

The Branford Academy commenced in 1820 and doubtless must have been thriving handsomely six years later when Henry Plant was ready for school. But at just this time, in October of 1825, an outbreak of typhus occurred. With terrible suddenness, the dreaded disease struck the Plant household. Behind closed shutters, Anderson Plant, the father, lay wrapped in wet sheets. Soon his six year-old son and an infant daughter, Eliza Ann, joined him. Only the little boy survived. The mother, Betsey Bradley Plant, and her stepmother, Sarah Plant, were not touched.[21]

Most of us no longer fear that epidemic-borne death will catch up with us any place on earth, least of all in small-town America. We no longer live in the expectation that we will be called on to comfort and care for family members dying at home, in horrific and protracted agony. Yet sweeping epidemics and household deathwatches were the common lot of mankind throughout all but our very recent, tiny share of human history.

For the commonly typhus-stricken communities of the 1800s, medical science could offer no resources whatsoever against the onslaught of the infection. After two weeks, survivors would be those with sufficient undestroyed tissue to start over. The salmonella virus ravages every system in the body. In all cases, high fever and diarrhea demand a constant supply of fluids and a protein-rich diet. Symptoms of highly toxic cases, such as the four in the Plant household in 1825, will be hemorrhaging of the intestines, acute dehydration, and delirium. Before the miracles of modern medicine, the care and survival of typhus patients required miracles of human dedication and endurance.[22]

---

[20] Gillett, *Congregational Church of Branford*.
[21] Smyth, 41-2.
[22] Karlen, *Men and Microbes*, 114-15.

New Haven established a County Medical Society after smallpox and yellow fever epidemics in 1794. For plague-stricken Branford in 1826, however, no significant outside help was available. Medically, none existed. There were no remedies. Quarantine was the only known defense against the hosts of "putrid and contagious diseases" of the time.[23] This would be so throughout Henry Plant's lifetime. He was going to witness countless deaths by epidemic, especially during his years in Florida.

Betsey and Sarah Plant, isolated in a village of the dying, in a house of the dying, did all the desperate nursing, all the futile "doctoring" themselves. The two women kept up with the work that had been the family work, with the endless survival chores at the washboard, the chopping block, and in the garden. With only snatches of sleep, they did all the cooking, washing, cleaning, and fetching on their own.

The very young and the very old are first to go in an epidemic. When the acutely dehydrating and hemorrhagic fever struck, two-year-old Eliza Ann Plant must have been wrenched away after few days of intolerable pain. In the same terrible suffering, Henry should have been the next to go. Instead, the little boy clung to life even through the death agonies of his father and aunt.

It was a very close call. Later in life, he would remember little of it. He had been comatose when his father died. His only memory of Anderson Plant would be one of those typical fragments of early loss–a big arm reaching down, and the work-stiff hand that a child holds onto one bright morning, outside the front gate, on the way to some eagerly anticipated village event.

Henry probably started school that spring or even the next year. At the Branford Academy he would have benefited immediately not only from Timothy Gillett's enlightened teaching methods but also from a structural facility far in advance of contemporary village standards. The two-story building, with steeple and bell, was roomy, airy, and bright. In bad weather it was kept snug and warm, thanks to the expert attention of the learned gentleman who opened the door every morning—schoolmasters of the time did custodial duty. Through his forty-six years at the academy he founded, Father Gillett maintained the building, provided the firewood, and never charged his pupils more than the nominal fee of two dollars a term.[24]

---

[23] Osterweis, 184.
[24] Simonds, 137.

—o—

Near the end of his life, the pupil destined to become one of the great American railroad kings would acknowledge Father Timothy Gillett's profound influence and bemusedly claim to have been among his most indifferent scholars. True, Henry Plant was never, according to the exalted criterion of the time, a "publicly educated man". Yet, as with so many other men of the era—men as far apart as Abraham Lincoln and Henry Flagler— Plant's early preparation enabled him to develop all the skills required for social and financial success. As for personal influence, the connection between teacher and pupil must have been of the profoundest sort. The elegiac description of Father Gillett provided by a colleague, Rev. W.T. Eustis of New Haven's Chapel Street Church, is eerily close to a likeness of the adult Henry Plant, "His face was the index of his character; placid, yet resolute; kind, but restrained; a gentle eye and firm lip; thoughtful and self-controlled, denoting a man of courtesy, who never suffered himself to be shaken by passion."[25]

Other profound influences were closer to home. During the epidemic of 1826, the village turned more intently than ever to the resources of faith. Branford folk were on their knees hour after hour, day and night, praying. Every moment that could be spared, families went to their churches by the common, Episcopalian and Congregational. This would have been the time when Sarah Plant committed herself to accumulate the savings intended to provide for her grandson's education for the ministry at Yale College.[26]

On this score, over the considerable time he was going to spend with his grandmother, the boy must have lived with an increasingly ambivalent sense of his destiny. He knew that he was to prepare himself—that he was being prepared—for Yale Divinity School. At first, this future may have been keenly appealing. He had the ideal example of a clergyman's life constantly before him in Father Gillett. Particularly the first years after Anderson Plant's death there could scarcely have been a better father figure in the village than the schoolmaster and minister—popular, warmhearted, vigorous, articulate, reliable, and decisive. Henry Plant would be known by these same characteristics all his life.

Soon, though, in 1828, there would be a father again. His mother probably became acquainted with Philomen Hoadley through church activities, and Henry Plant would always remember his stepfather as "a religious man." Mr. Hoadley, a

---

[25] Simonds, 146.
[26] Smyth, 41-2.

widower, was the father of two boys. Henry, the eldest, was four at the time, and James, two. After the marriage the family moved to the Hoadley home at Martinsburg, in upstate New York.[27] This was an arduous journey of some 300 miles. The only easy stretches would have been by canal and riverboat. Mostly they made plodding progress in one stagecoach after the other. But moving along outdoors, eight-year-old youngsters are rarely conscious of discomfort. And here was a stupendous new world of forest and mountain going by, of prosperous farms and villages, settled in what had been the fearful *terra incognito* of John Plant's Indian fighting days, the dark domain of the Mohawks. To the end of his life Henry Plant would be in love with the physical and mental adventure of scenery and conveyance, riding along, whether by canoe or buggy, steamboat or "palace car," watching the sights go by, and making his plans.

Over the next ten years he would often have the experience of traveling the route between Lake Erie and the Atlantic Coast. His mother and stepfather remained in Martinsburg where two more children were born, George in 1831, and Horace in 1833. Clearly their household became a busy one. Nothing interfered with young Henry's education, however. He attended the newly rebuilt school in nearby Lowville, an academy of traditional excellence.[28] But, more and more often, the boy made extended visits to Grandmother Sarah. For him, the Plant family home in Branford would always be the family home.

His ties with the church in Branford, too, would always be strong.[29] Even past the time when he knew that a clergyman's life was not for him, probably in his mid-teens, he kept the decision strictly to himself for a long while. In Branford, Henry Plant attended services dutifully with his grandmother. Summoned by a drum to the unadorned white meeting room, they listened to Father Gillett's earnest sermons, preached from a plain barrel-shaped pulpit. This congregation had always kept to the old ways. Back during the young man's childhood, when the notion was put forth to install a stove, the members met in the bitter cold of a winter morning and voted down the proposal by a large majority. The big treat of Henry Plant's Sundays was the picnic lunch that Grandmother Sarah prepared, and that they enjoyed in the meetinghouse after services.

---

[27] Carr, "Old Branford," 18. Smyth, 40-42.
[28] Keen, "Loweville Academy."
[29] Carr, 37-44, Smyth, 40.

Outside the ordeal of the typhus epidemic and the burden of his grandmother's expectations—which must have been shared by his mother and stepfather—Henry Plant seems to have been the typical village youngster of his era. Even had the miracles of modern medicine been available, growing up then was never less than hard. In most places and for most of our history, the survival of a human family has required grinding daily work, unremittingly repeated, generation after generation. As still happens in many parts of the world, many children were simply put out to jobs, to bring their scant wages home. When the Industrial Revolution triumphed, Henry Plant, by then a millionaire with a Fifth Avenue address, would see too much of this in America.

For his village childhood, though, in an established, moderately well-to-do family, survival was simply put—chores, chores, and more chores. It must have seemed that he was forever fetching, forever toting. One day, away off yet in the future, a hand-pump for the kitchen sink would be an undreamt-of modern convenience. Most people born in 1819 would never see indoor plumbing or kerosene, much less electricity.

There was heavy work, too, that could be dangerous. After 1900, a Plant System employee had this to pass along, "An incident of Mr. Plant's boyhood [shows] how we were almost deprived of his useful and noble life. When a boy of eight or ten, he was riding a plow horse at work in the field. The horse ran away, carrying plow, boy, and all with him. Barefooted and bareheaded, the brave lad clung on until entirely exhausted, when he fell and was severely injured. He was found by friends who carried him to their house. After several hours hard work by the doctor and others, he revived sufficiently to be taken to his home. The fight for life was severe and protracted."[30]

Still, these youngsters of almost two centuries ago led lives filled with every bit of the joy and excitement that our children know today, though few of them ever had the opportunity to enter a store and buy a toy. For that matter there were no stores at all in villages such as Martinsburg and Branford; peddlers brought around household wares and sundries, and would still be doing so into the 1900s. Eventually a boy would own a pocketknife; a girl would have her needle and thread. But toys were made. The children of each village and neighborhood had their own versions of the familiar games like jump rope, ring toss, crack-the-whip, prisoners base, mumblety-peg, and marbles.[31]

---

[30] Smyth, 40-41.
[31] Schwartz, *Long Ago*.

Then, what we know so well from Mark Twain, there was swimming and fishing. Henry Plant would spend much of his adult life on the water and he would always be an avid fisherman. In his teens, visiting his grandmother on Long Island Sound, every fishing trip he took must have carried him just that much further from Yale College. When he came trudging down the dusty lane at sunset, swinging his catch, Grandmother Plant was there. His happiness filled her, too. No wonder—the scholar she dreamed of was dreaming of a life at sea!

In 1838 his mother and stepfather returned from Martinsburg and settled in New Haven.[32] With the move came a scholastic bonus, attendance at New Haven's famed new Lovall Academy and exposure to the Lacasterian system of "magic" arithmetic where Lovall students learned such feats as mentally multiplying 21-digit figures.[33] Later life would prove he must have been an apt pupil. As Mr. H.B. Plant of the Plant System, he would keep the books of his many large and complex business organizations inside his head.

With young Henry at the Lovall Academy, Grandmother Plant's hopes for him must have soared. By her schedule, her grandson was due at Yale College the next year, and then the ministry. Of course the young man was familiar with the campus. He must have passed nearby many times a week, on his way to the ships. If the little harbor at Branford had set him dreaming of the sea, the waterfront at New Haven would set his heart on it.

Even though a little sister to the great Atlantic ports, New Haven kept up a busy trade to the West Indies. Moreover, her cool breezes and cultural benefits had brought New Haven a brisk tourist trade from the region beyond the nation's capitol, from that *terra incognita* across the Potomac. For only under urgent circumstances did New Englanders travel to the South, which, under the slave system, resembled a vast agrarian wasteland, given over to the cotton producing "industry." In the summer months, on his way to the dockside excitement at the Long Wharf, the young man with the sea in his blood may have heard Southern accents for the first time, at the Pavilion Hotel, a favorite spot for the frolicsome Charleston crowd.[34]

Whatever their enthusiasm for local color, however, New Haven's early vacationers rarely chose to promenade along the famed picturesque prospect of the

---

[32] Smyth, 42.
[33] "John Lovall."
[34] Osterweis, 238, 251.

Long Wharf. The custom of curing Patagonian sealskins right off the ships made the harbor even more famed for its summer-long stench of putrefaction. But the seafaring men who lounged about the grog shops, waiting for their next berth, never noticed. Here, too, coveys of retired sailors sat perched all day in the sunshine, smoking their pipes and swapping yarns. A few afternoons on the Long Wharf, and a young man with any sort of hunger for adventure would have his appetite pretty keenly whetted.[35]

—o—

Shortly after Robert Fulton ran the first successful steamboat in 1807, he started a shipping company with Robert Livingston. Since Fulton had chosen the Hudson River for his run, the state of New York rewarded the company with exclusive "steamboat navigation rights" in New York waters. On March 3, 1815, the Fulton-Livingston Company inaugurated a regular New Haven service, carrying 30 passengers up Long Island Sound in the record time of eleven hours. Very soon the trip was booked solid weeks in advance.

Ready to climb aboard a good thing when they saw it, a group of New Haven investors built their own steamboat, the *United States*, in 1821. But the New York monopoly required that passengers transfer to Fulton ships at the New York line. Swiftly, legislators in Hartford declared a state monopoly on Connecticut waters. Political and legal battles ensued that might be going on to this day. Fortunately, the U.S. Supreme Court soon rendered a judgment disallowing interstate transportation monopolies. By 1828 the Connecticut side dominated the New York run, offering a weekly service to Philadelphia as well. The equitable $2.50 fare included a good meal. But in the most thrilling news story of late summer 1830, the *United States* blew up in New York harbor with considerable loss of life. Though the disaster left a temporary power vacuum on Long Island Sound, nothing set back the popularity of this new craze, the steamboat craze.[36]

—o—

What was a steamboat, really, originally? Here are the specifications and brief history of a vessel we shall meet again, "The steamboat *NewYork*, built by Lawrence & Sneden, 250 feet length, 23 feet beam, 11 feet depth of hold. James P. Allaire built the engines, having 52 inches in cylinder diameter by 10 feet stroke, and single boilers located in the hold. The paddle wheels were 24.6 feet diameter,

---

[35] Writers Project, 223.
[36] Osterweis, 238.

Henry Plant's early path in life might have led from the village green in Branford (insert) to Yale Divinity School and a pulpit at one of New England's foremost Congregational churches. But the call of the sea was stronger. Nonetheless, Henry Plant remained steadfast in the faith of his upbringing. The First Congregational Church of New Haven embodies the solidity and ardor of his religious tradition.

buckets 12 feet length and 39 inches dip. The *New York* began regular trips April 4, 1836, and continued twenty years on this run, thereafter going to the Hudson as a towboat."[37]

A top British reporter observed the *New York* and wrote:

> The great difference in appearance between these [American] packets and ours is that there is so much of them out of the water, the main-deck being enclosed on all sides, and filled with casks and goods, like any second or third floor in a stack of warehouses, and the promenade or hurricane deck being a-top of that again. A part of the machinery is always above deck; where the connecting rod, in a strong and lofty frame, is seen working away like an iron top-sawyer.
>
> There is seldom any mast or tackle, nothing aloft but two black chimneys. The man at the helm is shut up in a little house in the fore part of the boat (the wheel being connected with the rudder by iron chains), working the whole length of the deck; and the passengers, unless the weather be very fine indeed, usually congregate below. You wonder for a long time how she goes on, for there seems nobody in charge of her; and when another of these dull machines comes splashing by, you feel indignant with it, as a sullen, cumberous, ungraceful, unshiplike leviathan; quite forgetting that the vessel you are aboard is a direct counterpart.
>
> There is a clerk's office on the lower deck, where you pay your fare; a ladies cabin; baggage and storage rooms; engineer's room; and in short a variety of complexities that render the gentleman's cabin a matter of some difficulty. It often occupies the whole length of the boat (as it did in this case) and has three or four tiers of bunks on each side. When I first descended into the cabin of the *New York* it looked, to my unaccustomed eyes, as long as the Burlington Arcade.
>
> Charles Dickens[38]

The waters of Long Island Sound were alive with such ships by the middle of the 1830s. Then the "steamboat wars" began.

"Commodore" Cornelius Vanderbilt, founder of the dynasty and by popular acclaim America's original robber baron, initiated a New York-Hartford steamboat service on the Connecticut River in 1833. But a neighborhood concern, the New Haven Steamboat Company, which had financed the railroad connection at Hartford, refused to honor tickets of transfer from the Vanderbilt line. Unwisely—

---

[37] Dayton, *Steamboat Days*, 109.
[38] Charles Dickens in Dayton, 110-11.

for soon the Commodore's steel-shod foot was well inside the door of local transportation affairs. His steamboats, led by the big *Kosciusko*, began running cut-rate trips on the New Haven-New York route. From then on, every time the Hartford railroad men came around a little bit, the passengers paid the price. With every concession, their rates went from cut-rate to cut-throat. Then, to keep up the pressure on his steamboat rivals in the harbor, the Commodore would insist that the railroad raise its fares accordingly. In the case of non-cooperation, he could cut back, or eliminate, his schedule on the Connecticut River.

With variations, this vicious game of kicking each other under the table went on between New York and Hartford for five long years. New Haven passengers felt they were being shanghaied, keelhauled, and put out to dry with the sealskins. Eventually they incorporated a steamship company of their own.[39] That was in 1838, the year the Commodore prepared for war in earnest. It was also Henry Plant's first year on Long Island Sound. In the magnitude of what was to follow, the young man could have stayed ashore, even at Yale Divinity School, and learned a lot about running a transportation business.

---

[39] Osterweis, 240-41.

~ III ~

UP FROM BELOW

First, after graduating in the class of 1837 at Lovall Academy, eighteen-year-old Henry Plant announced that he would not be attending Yale College that fall, long after the plan had become the central family expectation.[1] His mother and stepfather were probably not surprised. In the household, there must have been some indications of adolescent wavering. Moreover, Betsey P. Hoadley and her son would be on the closest terms all their lives. When Henry Plant had a personal problem, he shared it with his mother, if he was going to share it with anyone.

Certainly the best way to break the news to his grandmother would have been with his parents at his side, backing him. That way Betsey could take Sarah Plant aside with words to the effect, "This notion will pass. The boy's just not sure what to do with his life. You'll see, he'll come around."

With Yale to the side, he was ready to find his way in the world. Characteristically Henry Plant went one step at a time. Later he would say that at first he tried his hand at any number of different things. In 1837 there were nine livery stables in New Haven, always looking for help. There was one nearby, on Crown Street, and he had a way with horses. Among the shipping merchants along the waterfront, a pleasant young man quick with figures would always be an asset, and likewise at the dry goods stores on Chapel Street and the grocery stores on State

---

[1] Smyth, *Plant*, 42.

Street.[2] It was just right for him, while the shock of his decision died down, to assert his independence with these modest opportunities.

He knew better in any case than to try going to sea right off. His days at the Long Wharf had given him a sense of reality that other young men would only learn from reading Richard Dana's gritty expose of seafaring "romance," *Two Years before the Mast*. Besides, his Plant family had all been farmers, his Hoadley family, townspeople. A proper ship's berth would not have been conveniently waiting for him. Besides, once aboard ship, he was going to be unusually choosy about where he slept. Any berth at all would never do.

—o—

In the fall of 1837 and the winter of 1838, store clerks in New Haven were receiving a daily earful of news from the harbor, told around the stove.[3] The steamboat war might be about over, and it looked like the local boys might win it. They had just closed one smart deal, an exclusive contract to carry mail on Long Island Sound. Instead of operating an uncertain two-or-three-day-a-week schedule, the home team would be out there every day. And did you hear? At the last minute, moneybags crowd from New York, who'd been so eager, just hemmed and hawed. Come right down to it, they didn't have the starch! The war with Vanderbilt was as good as won. All over Connecticut, cracker barrel philosophers pictured the Commodore in his counting house, rubbing his big hands in sorrow.

He was rubbing his big hands in glee. He knew his competitors would soon be squealing in agony all the way to Washington, there to beg on their knees before stony-faced bureaucrats. On a three-day-a-week schedule, the steamboats carried cargo and passengers to capacity. Now, required to run every day of the week delivering mail, they were running half empty. "Please, please give the contract to Vanderbilt with our blessings. A few more months like this and we'll be bankrupt."

Undismayed by the fiery demise of the *United States*, in 1835 the New Haven Steamboat Company had launched a trio of state-of-the-art vessels, the *New York*, the *Hudson* and the *Splendid*. But when—watching from the window of his counting house—the Commodore beheld these costly investments, he saw three thoroughbred steeds of Neptune, prancing in his feckless neighbor's meadow. Thoroughbreds of championship potential too, capable of making the trip up the Sound "in eight hours, against the tide and without sails." Taking everything into

---

[2] "Town and City Directory, 1830," *Connecticut Herald*, January 5, 1830.
[3] Covington, *Plant's Palace*. 43. Osterweis, *New Haven*, 241-2.

account, the *New Haven Register* could add without undue pride, "There is probably no line in the Union superior to this in speed and accommodations."

A bankruptcy auction was already in the offing, however, when Henry Plant joined the New Haven Steamboat Company in 1837. Soon, alongside the once upstart *Kosciusko*, the *New York*, the *Hudson*, and the *Splendid* would bear the Vanderbilt arms on Long Island Sound.

All Henry Plant's sea-faring ambitions at this time were confined to the waters of Long Island Sound. It would be many years before he went *out* to sea. For that matter, once he officially became a sailor, he would concern himself less and less with a sailor's customary duties, with aspects of the ship's nautical operation. Indeed, assigned to duties as a deckhand, he turned his considerable power of resolution against the deck itself. And exactly his shipboard residence, his berth, had a great deal to do with what followed. Indeed, finding his first ship, and then locating a suitable place to live aboard it, would rank among the most critical undertakings of his young life.

The ship that finally met with the approval of the apostate divinity student was the grand packet steamer—soon to be the pride of the Vanderbilt Line—the *New York*. Had he ever been inside a ship before? Once he was taken to his berth, to his theoretically permanent shipboard home, where exactly was he? He was in that area within the ship's bow too awkwardly wedge-shaped for cargo, the forecastle. From an authority on life aboard 19th century ships, Joseph Conrad, we catch a glimpse of what greeted Henry Plant when venturing into his ocean-going abode, "The forecastle, with only one lamp burning low, was going to sleep now in a dim emptiness traversed by loud breathings, by sudden short sighs. The double row of berths yawned black, like graves tenanted by uneasy corpses. Here and there a curtain of gaudy chintz, half-drawn, marked the resting place of a sybarite. A leg hung over the edge very white and lifeless. An arm stuck straight out with the palm turned up, and thick fingers half closed. Two light snores, that did not synchronize, quarreled in funny dialogue."[4]

Making a move to better quarters, to private quarters, seems to have become Henry Plant's top priority from the first night he spent at sea. What could have been less likely? Perhaps the ship's officers were well "berthed." The overnight passengers went steerage. Men and women occupied separate dormitories that amounted to little better than elongated versions of the forecastle. For the comfort

---

[4] Conrad, *Nigger of the Narcissus*, 22.

"NEW YORK."

On this Vanderbuilt steamboat, Henry Plant's first shipboard accommodations were the opposite of luxurious.

and privacy he had in mind, the young deckhand would need to be more than ordinarily lucky and opportunistic. He would have to summon forth his own possibilities. Simply enough, he was required to create his own category of seamanship. In turn, meeting this demand would lead to a whole new category of career, to the start of his fortune, and ultimately to Florida.

His immediate success did begin with luck and opportunism. On a New Haven—New York steamer, there was the luck of his situation—the right place at the right time. Then he had the gumption, the "business sense," to recognize history in the making where it can be hardest to see–right under one's nose.

It was going take some time, however, for the key factors of luck and opportunity to combine in the interest of upgrading his accommodations. For the next year would be a short one on the Vanderbilt line. When the New Haven & Hartford Railroad refused another suggestion to raise their rates to Vanderbilt standards, the Commodore not only pulled his regular service off the Connecticut River for 1838, he also replaced his steamboats at the Long Wharf with a single battered ferry. When tickets were available, Connecticut passengers no longer enjoyed even the comforts of going steerage.

Still, a famous "pioneering attitude of mind" had made New Haven wealthy. Surrender was a long way off. New Haveners grimly set about bankrolling another locally-owned steamship company, the Citizens Line. In 1840 they were making ready to challenge the Vanderbilt juggernaut with three state-of-the-art vessels, the *American Eagle,* the *Telegraph* and the *Belle.*[5]

---

[5] Osterweis, 242.

Plant was to remain a faithful Vanderbilt employee all his remaining days on the Sound. When, in early 1839, the Commodore briefly suspended his anti-Connecticut actions, the *New York* was in dry dock. The company transferred Henry Plant successively to the *Splendid,* the *Bunker Hill* and the *New Haven,* all lesser vessels than the *New York*—doubtless with forecastles that much smaller, too. In later years he would look back wryly on these discomforts, "[We] took our meals in the kitchen, standing up. Taking it all and all it was a rather rough life on a fellow that had just left a good home, and when some of my fellow townspeople would come aboard and catch me with swab or broom in hand, I didn't feel altogether happy, but had too much pluck to quit."[6]

In the spring of 1839 he went back on board the *New York,* refitted with twin copper boilers amidships, a daring, spectacular breakthrough in steamship technology. Now his destiny directly awaited him. He would always pay tribute to the encounter in all its significance.

"About then a considerable lot of package freight, express matter, began to be sent back and forth. This was stowed just anywhere on board and not properly cared for. One day the captain had the idea that a big double stateroom could be used in which to store it, and I was given the duty of looking after it, and a berth was put up there for me to sleep in. As I look back on my early career, the day I was transferred from the dingy forecastle to the express room was by far the happiest, and it was there that I took my first lessons in the express business."[7]

The express business has always been one of civilization's essential components. Yet since ancient times to the 1840s, very little had changed, aside from its vehicles. So, the day marked an epoch when the master of the *New York,* Captain S. Bartlett Stone, conceived his idea of a shipboard express department, which was, simply, *to organize* one. Most likely, in the way of most great ideas, he developed the conception in its fullness by putting two and two together. Later, Captain Stone would speak of a special fatherly relationship with the young Henry Plant. And what would have attracted his favorable attention to any member of the crew, if not outstanding work? Was the new deckhand making it a custom to go out of his way on behalf of the "express matter," otherwise "not properly cared for?"

---

[6] Smyth, 43.
[7] Smyth, 44.

In any case, this much is clear from Henry Plant's own statement, the future potential of the "express business" dawned on him from the moment he beheld all the priority cargo on the steamboat, for one day's voyage, put together in one place. It was all his responsibility, too. Twenty years old when the express business was just beginning—and destiny had made him an expressman. Advancing the efficiency and reliability of package and postal deliveries would be his main concern for the next forty years, until something bigger came along. In the 1880s he would go from the business of expressing material to the business of expressing people, and providing for their special handling.

The immediate, the local development responsible for the volume of priority cargo heaped aboard the *New York* had its origin in New Haven's famed Inventive Spirit, now producing a flood of highly desirable manufactured goods. A gentleman farmer in Maryland might procrastinate for years before ordering a shotgun from the Remington Arms Company. When at last he did so, the item became "express matter." As we all know, the customer expected delivery *now*. Many such orders arriving in New Haven daily kept the packages piling up on the steamboats docked at the Long Wharf.

At this time, however, in the mid-1800s, our version of "now" was in its infancy. After the Remington Company made a routine delivery to the harbor, both the Vanderbilt and the Citizens Line would have been waiting to carry the package to New York. In the best circumstances, elapsed time from the factory gate might be less than ten hours. But in New York there would have been no reliable, efficient—much less rapid—means of delivery between the New Haven steamboat and any connection to Baltimore. Then, what connection from Baltimore to the countryside? Here, with a simple matter of local delivery, might occur the worst breakdown of all. Likely the gentleman came to the docks himself–another day lost to hunting right there.

The problems of multiple-connection long-distance delivery mounted as commerce grew, as the country grew. Fortunately, New Haven had no monopoly on the Inventive spirit. Captain Stone's expedient had been a solution in miniature. An overall solution was going to require the merger and re-organization of countless local delivery services. This complex, massive consolidation over the next quarter of a century would ultimately produce the means, financial and technical, that Henry Plant would use to solve the problems of Florida's isolation, and to create her golden future.

——o——

The opportunity that Plant was going to capitalize and re-capitalize on had its start from the time he was first relishing his liberation from the forecastle. Up in Vermont, a so far luckless businessman, Alvin Adams, had been watching the proliferation of traditional little delivery outfits. The country was splitting its seams with prosperity. New Haven may have led the way, but by 1838 the Inventive Spirit was spreading all over the Northeast. From everywhere to everywhere, a glut of merchandise and business correspondence waiting for delivery—while the U.S. Post Office dawdled in protracted infancy.

A horse and wagon, desk and chair, was about all it took. With $100 to his name, Alvin Adams went to Boston and found a partner. Pooling their life savings, $200, they established a route to Worcester, just in time for the Panic of 1839. And throughout the following year the business was less than brisk. For Adams's partner, the Depression meant depression. He lost his "pluck" and sold out. But, strapped to meet the cost of doing business, $10 a month, the determined Adams struggled on. Fourteen years later, with Henry Plant its supervisor for the Southern District, the Adams Express Company would dominate the delivery of freight, valuables, and "rush" communication throughout the eastern U.S.

In 1842, though, Adams was still struggling. Then along came a partner of his own canny persuasion, a former shopkeeper on the Boston waterfront, one William Dinsmore. Daringly, the two began renting space on railroad trains and steamboats.[8] Soon an air of profound consideration possessed the demeanor of the Vanderbilt Line's young freight manager. The following notice appeared:

> Adams & Co.'s New York and Philadelphia express cars leave this depot daily (Sundays excepted) at 4 o'clock P.M.
>
> N.B. The subscribers would respectfully give notice that they have completed an exclusive contract with the Union Transportation Company, to run two crates daily between New York and Philadelphia for the transportation of merchandise. Packages will be received and forwarded to Norwich, New London, Hartford, and New Haven, Ct. Notes, bills, and acceptances will be collected on the above named cities.
>
> Small parcels will be received until 1/4 to 4 o'clock P.M. and will be delivered in New York the next morning.
>
> N.B. The subscribers are alone responsible for the loss or injury of any articles or property of any description entrusted to their car; nor is any risk assumed by the owners of the New York and Norwich steamboats, or the Norwich and Worcester and Boston and Worcester railroad companies.

---

[8] Harlow, *Old Way Bills*, 25-29.

Kelly Reynolds

ALVIN ADAMS
W.B. DINSMORE[9]

—o—

When—in the near future—the chance was going to come for him to start out with the progressive Adams Company, Henry Plant would be exceptionally well prepared for promotion. His "first lessons" aboard the *New York* had already set him on the way to the executive level. Once there, a trainee in the area of corporate negotiations, he rose with astonishing ease. Sent out to open and to take charge of a new territory, a couple of old hands went with him, his tutors. Before long, the old hands were learning a few things for themselves. Finally, just a few years later at the bargaining table, the Adams Company would take a high-stakes lesson from the former captain's boy.

Yet, no wonder. Consider the thoroughness of lesson learned on his way to the executive training program at the Adams Company. As the newly appointed freight supervisor on Commodore Vanderbilt's steamboat company, young Henry Plant had been treated to a doctorate in the top-level negotiating skills of the day. Skills that were sly, skills that were, more often than not, brutal. For instance– at one point during the Panic of 1839, when bread lines were a common sight in every large city, the Commodore lowered his New Haven-New York fare to 25 cents. A popular move, to be sure, but in the long run hardly a benevolent gesture. For the House of Vanderbilt had the resources to continue floating serenely along, while, up and down Long Island Sound, local banks and small businesses went under. In New Haven only pride kept the feebly resurgent Citizens Line hanging on until times were better. But, with the Commodore holding the high hand, even better times meant worse to come.[10]

By the spring of 1841, with both rival lines operating busy schedules, service out of New Haven Harbor had reached the saturation point. Inexplicably Vanderbilt added another ship, a decrepit grand dame from the Connecticut River, the *Cleopatra*. Docked inconspicuously, most often the aging beauty simply kept to her berth. Months went by. Then, on the morning of July 7, the New Haven Line's popular favorite, the *Telegraph*, cast off on schedule from the Long Wharf. The course to open water took her past the Vanderbilt docks. Suddenly wide-awake,

---

[9] Harlow, 29.
[10] Osterweis, 242.

though far behind any conceivable schedule, the *Cleopatra,* bound for the scrap heap anyway, charged forth to claim her shipping lane. In the collision, at least no lives were lost. But the *Telegraph* was damaged beyond repair. By the time the authorities could separate the factions and muster a quorum, another busy summer had come around. It was common knowledge that with only the *Belle* left to keep the Citizens Line going, another collision might occur at any moment.

A court of inquiry quickly determined that the Vanderbilt's *Kosciusko* had smashed into the *Belle* "deliberately." New Haveners were still relishing their moral satisfaction when the news came from Hartford that the railroad would henceforth begin offering concessionary fares to Vanderbilt passengers. A storm of protest arose over this obvious "collusion" between Hartford and New York. All that autumn, angry public rallies convened as far away as Meriden and Branford. None of this fazed the Commodore, however. On the front page of the *New Haven Register* for November 5, 1842, was the story, "The Citizens Line has sold the *Belle* to the Connecticut River Steamboat Company. The citizens have now no defense against Vanderbilt."

After Henry Plant became one of America's foremost "Railroad Kings," the feeling around New Haven would be that he turned his back on the town that gave him his start. Likely he never saw it that way at all, ever. In terms of the ascent he was following, New Haven came naturally, the next step after Branford. Arriving in Manhattan Harbor aboard the *New York*, any ambitious young man sees his destiny vividly written before him. And while leaving New Haven behind might be more dramatically felt, for Henry Plant "leaving behind" never meant turning his back, certainly not on the places that he called home. His Hoadley relatives remained in New Haven, and he would always be on close terms with them. His mother was often in New Haven when he came to visit. His son grew up there. Indeed, one of the great, final regrets of Henry Plant's life was going be that he did not live in New Haven long enough.

Many ambitious young men have come into New York Harbor, the breeze in their face, and beheld the place their destiny has kept in splendor for them, for the taking. The young deckhand would eventually create his own splendid places. But in a way that even Florida was not to be, this place would be home for him. Not so much the place of his abode as the place of his establishment.

Whenever the young seaman Henry Plant came ashore at the south end of Manhattan Island he entered a scene of high-energy commerical activity. New York by 1835 had come to dominate Atlantic Coast shipping. And the dominant figure in all this was the man Henry Plant worked for, Cornelius Vanderbilt, "the Commodore."

Henry Plant would live to see the beginnings of the New York skyline. At his death in 1899 the tallest buildings stood ten stories high. But when he sailed into New York harbor on a day in 1837 he beheld a city that was level with his gaze– a hive of commerce, and especially of industrial activity. For the great port cities of the Northeast were also great manufacturing centers. On Manhattan Island, especially along the waterfront, fortress-like smithies and factories stretched up the East River. Their brick chimneys belched towering columns of black smoke, gathering above in a thick canopy, a noxious, down-sifting layer of ash and murk. And, where the young seaman would come ashore, beyond the fortress-front of factories, was Lower Manhattan, a kind of hurricane-tossed but frozen gray sea, a dreadful wilderness of wooden tenements and shanties.[11]

But most of all, amid terrible squalor and social disorder, he beheld the glorious results of the central enterprise of his future, transportation. In New York City, the year Lake Erie waters began flowing into the harbor, 500 new shops opened. So did twelve new banks and thirteen marine insurance companies. In 1800 the banking capital of the city had been $3,400,000; in 1825, $25,100,000. And the moment young Henry Plant stepped off the gangplank, he stood in the midst of this source of enrichment. "Bales of cotton, wool, and merchandise: barrels of potash, rice, flour, and salt provisions; hogsheads of sugar, chests of tea, puncheons of rum, pipes of wine. Boxes, cases, packs and packages, of all sizes and combinations, were strewed upon the wharves and landing places, or upon the decks of the shipping. All was noise and bustle. The carters were driving in every direction, and on board the vessels, were moving their ponderous burdens from place to place."[12]

Moreover, a pervasive, all-surrounding sense of nautical abundance and possibility was always going to be the primary aspect of the city that he came to know, Walt Whitman's "mast-hemmed Manhattan." Henry Plant loved it, it was in his blood. His son, as soon as he was able, would give his life over to his own ardent re-creation of the age of sail. But the father's first sea-faring love was the throb of great engines at work, moving the ship entirely at the will of man. With his first voyage, in the choice of the ship he made, Henry Plant gave his life over to the principal theme of his time, the all-embracing ideal of the age of steam and the Industrial Revolution—progress.

When he was born, shipping one ton of wheat between Schenectady and New York cost $120. In 1830s, thanks to the Erie Canal, the rate was dropping below $20. By then the whole nature of daily living, and thereby of human consciousness, was being transformed. When the boy Henry Plant lived in a small town near Schenectady, the clothing that his family and neighbors wore was homespun. By dint of one of the most labor-intensive and tediously repetitive activities in human history, each household in the rural regions of New York produced well over ten yards of its own sturdy cloth annually. But, instantaneously, after the opening of the Erie Canal, a distribution network of itinerant peddlers sprang into being.

---

[11] Homberger, *Historical Atlas*, 80-1, 84, 111. Stott, *Workers*, 54.
[12] Ellis, *Epic of NYC*, 228. Homberger, 57.

They brought commercially produced garments within the means of small-town, rural incomes. By 1855, annual production of homespun cloth in New York State had dropped to under 1/2 yard per household, on its way to zero.[13]

Moreover, by reaching out to hitherto inaccessible markets, the new transportation systems could bring the agriculturalist something unheard-of in farm country—disposable income. Between 1820 and 1860, agricultural products passing through New York Harbor accounted for one-third of all USA exports. In those years, an ambitious young man could stroll along the docks at East River and estimate the source and flow of the treasure. Fully sixty percent of the nation's imports came in at New York harbor. The most extravagant items and lavish supplies were consigned for transshipment down the coast to Baltimore, Wilmington, Charleston, and Savannah. Owing to the seed-picking engine recently devised by New Haven's most inventive son, Eli Whitney, cotton was king. Far the largest and most profitable aspect of New York's commerce derived from the southern states, from the slave-run cotton industry.[14]

During Henry Plant's deckhand days, one luxury transshipment in particular must have received his close personal attention. Thanks again to the Inventive Spirit, New Haven had become the Detroit of the horse-and-buggy era. At the heart of the city's prosperity was the manufacture of fine carriages. Revenue for a typical year, 1836, amounted to $12,000,000.[15]

Southerners vacationing in New Haven were exposed to continual temptation. The leading carriage workshops had their showrooms near the popular Pavilion Hotel. Handled with the utmost care, a regular succession of custom-made phaetons and barouches came aboard the Vanderbilt line, destined for the South via New York. To an ambitious young man's eyes and to his touch, as sleekly potent, elegant, and delicate-seeming as thoroughbreds themselves the embodiment of all that man could put in the world of luxury, precision, and power. "A visitor to the Charleston or New Orleans race track, in this period, could see long lines of New Haven-made carriages, their panels bearing the heraldic devices of proud owners, moving toward the grandstand."[16]

---

[13] Stott, 9.
[14] Stott, 9-10.
[15] Osterweis, 251-52
[16] Lord, "Diary."

In his years of success in Florida, Henry Plant would take great joy in traveling the back roads, driven in a gleaming custom shay, known all over. When he stopped in a village, round-eyed young folks would gather around as closely as they could. Then, one or two would run off with the news. Quickly the men too gathered close, according to their status, introducing themselves, hope leaping in their hearts. Soon, with all the pluck, spunk, sport, and charm they could muster, asking how far the railroad might reach this year? What about the steamboat service? Any chance, soon? Any chance at all? They knew, everyone knew—up on the high-upholstered seat, the calm friendly man in the wide hat and broadcloth suit had "the magic touch." He could raise his hand and produce a shower of gold.

These men with the golden touch appeared in America, in New York, for the first time in the 1830s. But, except for the robust and crude-mannered Commodore himself, they were not often seen in the East River neighborhood of the Vanderbilt docks at Peck's Slip.[17] Here Henry Plant, a greenhorn deckhand, prepared to come ashore. With the decks at last empty of passengers, he looked for a companion to follow down the gangplank. By now the dense congregation of horse-drawn cabs on Front Street had vanished. Heavy freight wagons came rumbling up. All around him, stevedores were hoisting off the cargo. He made his way—a familiar way, after the Long Wharf—through stacked-up mountains of crated merchandise, produce, and household goods. Amid the chaotic immensity of Manhattan's waterfront, a New Haven greenhorn could move about with a confident stride.

And so too, with mounting confidence, the youngster would enter the orderly layout of foundries and warehouses. But at the edge of a brickyard he stood motionless. Before him, the crooked commercial streets of Lower Manhattan, that he had only glimpsed from the deck, out in the clean harbor air. And close by, down these streets, what he could sense—a dismal human wilderness of tenements, far more inhospitable than any arctic.

The contemporary American writer who studied this region most closely was Stephen Crane. He depicts the scene that would have greeted a young seaman just beyond the waterfront, "the dusty foul air, thick with curses, shot through with the sharp smacking of leather on horse flesh, and the cries of the beaten horses [and] at every corner, 'a hideous tangle' of rattling, cumbersome drays. Drunken teamsters, contesting for advantage, might leap down from their top-heavy loads and fight in the street. Pedestrians were always fair game. In pairs, policemen com-

---

[17] *NYC Directory*, Doggett, 325.

monly climbed up on the wagons to beat particularly vicious or uncooperative drivers."[18]

His shipmate took young Henry Plant by the arm, led him through this chaos to a sedate residential district on the West Side. A Connecticut family, the Judsons, had established a hotel where New Englanders of modest means could feel at home.[19]

For in the 1830s this neighborhood still belonged to its settlers, the last full generation of Manhattan's "native working classes," or essentially Henry Plant's generation, and class. Already the floodgates of immigration were creaking open. A decade later they would burst open. During the 1880s, when Henry Plant desperately needed workers for his railroads in Florida and Georgia, less than twenty percent of America's labor force was native-born.[20]

Of course in the 1840s an ambitious young man would soon discover Broadway, then the upper-class district of grand homes and elegant shops. Here, a sweeter air, almost fresh. Thanks to the tall town houses of marble and granite, one could barely hear the hubbub of the commercial traffic just blocks away to the east. Broadway was shorter then, running from the Financial District to 14th Street. The thoroughfare, though still unpaved, and despite the occasional wandering pig, was immaculately tended.[21] Here he recognized multitudes of New Haven-made coaches and phaetons, as good as the best the Southern planters could afford.

And here too, by their dazzling and heraldic equipage, he would recognize the golden men with the magic touch, and their families, the Vanderbilts and Astors and Vanrenselers. These were not men of the "native working class," surely. These first golden men started out with the advantage of an old family in a new republic. Largely, they made their own rules between themselves; then busily, and with a certain disdain, went about piling up everybody else's money.

An ambitious young man with a duffel bag on his shoulder could only observe the grand goings-on from a distance. Soon enough, though, he would be strolling among the elite himself, in the best finery a freight supervisor could afford. By then he was beginning to learn that, for a fact, some new rules might apply. Hadn't he seen the Commodore make up a few? Well, he was moving up pretty fast him-

---

[18] Crane, "Maggie" in *Collected Stories*, 50-54.
[19] Smyth, 51.
[20] Stott, 29.
[21] Lyman, *New York*, 110, 148.

self. He was going to find his own berth in this neighborhood one day. He had his eyes open for the means to achieve it.

—o—

But first he would fall in love. He had known Ellen Elizabeth Blackstone through family friendship, going years back.[22] Her brothers were ambitious young men too, and the younger, Lorenzo, would be a life-long friend. But this was not a family of "the native working class." Ellen's father was State Senator James Blackstone. The Blackstones traced their New England ancestry back even further than the Plants, to the Pilgrim days.[23]

When Henry and Ellen were courting, the liveliest topic of discussion at New Haven dinner tables centered around the increasingly outrageous events of the steamboat war. The year of their betrothal, 1842, was the year of the Commodore's total victory. Before their wedding in September of 1843, Henry was beginning to concede that a seafaring life might not be the best life for a married man. By then, politics dominated dinner table discussions. The enterprising folk of Connecticut bitterly opposed the upstart Andrew Jackson and backed the Whig Party of Daniel Webster.[24]

On the supremely divisive issues of slavery and the protective tariff, Webster stood rock-solid for compromise, compromise, compromise, and more compromise. But in the upcoming presidential elections the Whigs suffered a defeat that would seal their doom within the decade. Appealing to the abolitionist cause, a repentant slaveholder from Alabama, James Birney, split Whig support in two. New Haven's "protective" champion, Henry Clay of Kentucky, lost his best chance at the presidency. An Andrew Jackson protégé was sent to the White House in 1844, the feisty James K. Polk, who would soon launch the Mexican War.[25] The next year Ellen Plant gave birth to a healthy baby boy. That settled it for the sea-faring life. The influential Blackstone family could help him in a new endeavor. Henry Plant was by then well along in forming the idea of a new career for himself. The ambitious young man had learned considerable about making improvements in the delivery business at sea. As of 1845 he was going to start thinking about what improvements might be needed on land.

---

[22] Smyth, 45-6.
[23] Harrison, "James Blackstone."
[24] Osterweis, 294-6.
[25] Hofstader, *American Political Tradition*, 148-9.

The New Haven listing of business establishments for that year notes significant change at 14 Court Street. One of the city's oldest firms, Washington Webb & Company, had become Webb & Plant.[26] Clearly, anyone minding the store at 14 Court Street would be in an ideal position to learn the landlubber's side of the import-export business. Mr. Washington Webb had a lifetime's experience in one of New Haven's principal and traditional markets, the West Indies trade.[27] (Since colonial times Connecticut had enjoyed close ties with the Caribbean; frustration under the British mercantile system had fostered her revolutionary ardor.) The new partner was now able to study in detail the operation of the ages-old trading system that exchanges commodities of little value at their source, but "priceless" at distant markets. A good part of his study, too, would have been devoted to keeping the books. It was doubtless from old Mr. Washington Webb that Henry Plant acquired the rudiments of what became his uncanny mastery of financial records.

At the time of so much sudden success, however, he and Ellen experienced the deepest sorrow a young couple can know. Their infant son, George Henry Plant, died suddenly at eighteen months. His father would always remember "a promising child." Members of the Plant and Blackstone families gathered at the churchyard in Branford for funeral services led by Father Gillett. The bereaved parents remained childless until the arrival of Henry Plant's only surviving issue, Morton Freeman Plant, in 1851.[28]

Long before then, the routine at the store had become as confining as a clergyman's life would have been. He longed for the sea, for new places, fresh challenges. Certainly the times were in tune with his ambitions, as they would be all his life. Local express businesses were continuing to proliferate throughout New England. Soon the perfect opportunity presented itself in thriving New Haven. An eager rival to Alvin Adams's expanding Boston-based business was looking for a manager. Beecher & Co announced the opening of an express delivery office at the Long Wharf, using the Vanderbilt Line to New York. In this line of endeavor, very few young men anywhere could offer Henry Plant's combination of credentials, connections, and experience.

---

[26] *New Haven Directory, 1845*, 120.
[27] Smyth, 45.
[28] Smyth, 45.

The position was by no means purely a desk job. He was the whole office, usually the messenger, too. Perhaps with the excitement of starting up, and with so many small businesses all around him likewise struggling, it may have taken awhile to recognize a shoestring operation. When he did, his future was taking care of itself. The New Haven and Hartford Railroad acquired Beecher, and put Plant in charge of business at New York harbor.

By this time the Adams Express Company was a giant in New England, with a New York headquarters. It absorbed the former Beecher interests in 1850. Assembling a workforce of uncompromising reliability and integrity had been the key to the Adams success story. The young manager from the Long Wharf, now on the Manhattan docks, had made a reputation. His expansive employers promptly decided he belonged in the main office.[29]

It could not have happened at a worse time. Ellen Plant was pregnant and in poor health.[30]

Surely, his marriage had implied a commitment to New Haven. But he wouldn't be that far from home. He would be starting out at a substantial raise. Best of all, this line of work could lead to a modest fortune, soon. In New York he was going to be in the company of such men as William Dinsmore and E.A. Johnson—men not much older than himself but already grand masters of the express business.

Aside from all this, the opportunity was literally golden. The Adams Company had just landed a government contract to transport specie between the New York Custom House and the Philadelphia Mint. Likely as an inducement to leave New Haven, E.A. Johnson offered the assignment to the new man. Henry became the special courier to the Mint five days a week, a duty requiring extraordinary responsibility, stamina, vigilance and daring. Riding the trains in those days was not for the faint hearted. A pioneer figure in American railroading, James Baldwin, describes the experience in the Philadelphia area, circa 1835, "The locomotives burn pine wood, & the sparks, from the velocity of the cars, fall upon, round, & into the cars so as to endanger the cloths. Great patches are already burned in the lining & curtains of the cars. A bag of biscuits on the top of one car took fire, & the man thru it off to prevent the car from taking fire."[31]

But all in a day's work. From the Battery, with valises of gold coins strapped under his arms, and escorted by armed guards, a dapper Henry Plant would dis-

---

[29] Smyth, 46.
[30] Smyth, 46.
[31] Kirkland, *Transportation*, Vol. I, 308.

creetly enter a baggage car, but a special baggage car, virtually a fortress on iron wheels. In Philadelphia, guards escorted him to the Mint.[32]

Afterwards he checked in at the new five-story Adams office building, being hailed in the *Illustrated American News* as "one of the lesser lions of the city, which should be seen by every visitor. It presents almost as magnificent an interior as any found in the United States."[33]

While this may have been an exciting routine, fairly soon it was just a routine. Still and all, for a family man, wasn't this an improvement over life on a steamboat run? Twenty-five years later in Florida, building his own company, Henry Plant would move swiftly to reward energetic, talented young men for their job-proven abilities. He would remember that eager young men are eager to move up, or on. He kept his eye on such young men, the way he knew that his New York mentors had kept an eye on him. After Plant had served six months as the company's highest ranked messenger, E.A. Johnson and William Dinsmore promoted him to an office near their own.

At this time, a father again, Henry Plant must have been aware that he was stepping into the first glow of a dazzling future. Behind his splendid new desk in his office at Adams Express headquarters, 16 Wall Street, he was seated not far from where he had come ashore ten years before.

Back then, even after living in New Haven a few years, he was still a village lad. He might have joined the college men. Instead, he had joined shopkeepers. Sometimes he had run a store by himself, a businessman at seventeen. But all along he had been looking to join the sailors. Soon, his first voyage out, eight hours down Long Island Sound and he was, at last, a seaman. Then, his legs on the solid earth again, amid all the dynamism and disorder of the Manhattan waterfront, the great city went rushing past him, faster than the dark river at ebb tide—knowing himself a village lad still.

Now, whenever he stepped outside the Adams building, the river was a gleaming river, dark no more, and he was a part of it. His wife and son had joined him at the Judson Hotel, on the West Side. Time had been, when strolling that way down Broadway—hanging back from the crowd somehow, his heart still back home—he would find himself gazing on a fabulous world, unapproachably far away. These days, he regularly took his way home along the broad thoroughfare, along mannerly, luxurious, residential old Broadway. Though much preoccupied with business matters, from time to time he would look about and note its genteel charm with assurance. In New York from then on, and in all the places that counted, he would never hang back, never look back.

---

[32] Smyth, 106.
[33] *Illustrated American News* in Harlow, 69.

~ IV ~

LANDS OF DESTINY

In the winter of 1853, a Northern man with an invalid wife brought her down to Jacksonville to benefit her health. The present metropolis of Florida was then a settlement of five or six houses, one of which was called a hotel, but the hotel was so badly kept that the gentleman was cautioned against going into it. He had letters of introduction to a Florida settler, whose home was five or six miles out of Jacksonville. The settler sent his boat after the Northerner and took him to his house. The boat was an immense 'dug-out' canoe, made from a single mammoth log.

In the course of the winter the lady's health improved to such an extent that her husband decided upon taking her to St Augustine for a pleasure trip. There was in the household a beautiful Indian girl, the daughter of one of the Seminole chiefs and she volunteered to accompany [them]. The only road between Jacksonville and St. Augustine was so grown up with trees and bushes that it was barely passable. The gentleman and his wife and the Indian girl set out in a buggy, their host going before them on horse back to select the road and blaze the trees.

The journey was made in safety; but the return trip took a little longer than was intended, and just as the deep shades of a Florida night were about to fall [the party] found the blazed trees, but were unable to follow them. The gentleman, however, managed for some time to pick his way by finding the indistinct wheel tracks in the sand and the broken twigs; but as the dryness increased this became impracticable, and there was every prospect that the invalid lady and her husband and the Indian girl would be compelled to spend the night under the pine trees. But their host set out on horseback to hunt them up, and his shouts soon gave them welcome assurance of succor. The lady's health was so much improved that during the remainder of her life every winter was passed in Florida. Her husband is now spending his thirty-ninth winter in the state.

The gentleman who found Jacksonville a settlement of a few shanties, who came so near the opportunity of passing a romantic but uncomfortable night in the woods with his wife and the Seminole girl, told me the story of his adventure a few days ago, while I sat in his gorgeous private car, so far down in the State of Florida that, in 1853, few white men had reached it. The Florida climate never did a better winter's work than when it restored the health of the gentleman's wife, and thus interested him in the new country, for the gentleman was Mr. H.B. Plant, who no longer does his Florida traveling in a dugout, but sends his own cars over his own tracks to the furthermost corners of the state.

[From a *New York Times* of the 1890s][1]

From "Henry Plant's Busy, Busy Career Is Ended," *Jacksonville Times-Union*, June 24, 1899.

The coming of Mr. Plant to the Southern States really marked the opening of Florida to the people of the country as a winter resort.

When Florida, the land of his destiny, first appeared to Henry Plant, it did so gradually, indistinctly, unobtrusively. The grand steamer *Marion*, departing New York on March 25, 1853, had made an appointed connection at Charleston with an only slightly less grand steamer for Savannah, the *Calhoun*. But there was little scheduled shipping from Savannah to Jacksonville in the Florida territory. When a captain of the distinctly modest steamer *Waleka* mustered a cargo down the Georgia coast via Brunswick, passengers came aboard.[2] The same low-lying marshy shore would have been slipping by to starboard since Baltimore. The land that finally hove into view at the mouth of the St. Johns River by then had become repetitively, softly familiar; certainly no surprise. In the years ahead, the territory

---

[1] *New York Times* in Smyth, *Plant*, 47-50.
[2] Mueller, *Steamships*, 3.

was going to remain familiar for him, a beloved vacation spot. Then, in loneliness, Florida would become an afterthought, at times the kind of afterthought perhaps better forgotten about altogether.

In the winter of 1853 Henry and Ellen Plant had come as far South as they could, for about the only reason that Northerners would make the journey, a cure for painful, dangerous illnesses. As far back as her pregnancy with Morton, Ellen's health had been a cause for concern. Now she had been "taken with a congestion of the lungs."[3] By the turn of the century in the USA, tuberculosis was claiming 7,000 lives annually. It had been a kind of "steady state" epidemic all through human history, but with the pollution and urban overcrowding of the Industrial Age, the "wasting sickness" had become a scourge. By the 1900s so many were dying in the tenements of London, Berlin, Paris, and New York that the end of Western civilization appeared at hand.[4]

Many years would go by before methods of therapy, totally ineffectual in most cases, were at least organized.

Returning "comparatively well," Ellen must have gone straight to New Haven where Morton, now three, was living with his grandparents, Philomen and Betsey Hoadley. Morton would be spending the better part of his childhood with the Hoadleys, and doubtless with his maternal grandparents too, the Blackstones in Branford. He was destined to grow up this way, as did so many children of the time when extended families were a requirement of family survival. The combination of severe illness and severe business pressure effectively took his parents out of young Morton Plant's life.

Indeed, in coming years, business pressure removed Henry Plant even from what would always be the grandest devotion of his life, his care for Ellen. The express business was booming as never before, and no one rode the boom any higher than his boss, Alvin Adams. In a lesson that would not be lost on his youngest executive, the cunning Adams had been building a substantial cash reserve. Between 1853 and 1854 he absorbed four major rivals and reorganized his firm. Adams himself would be president, the redoubtable William Dinsmore, vice-president. On July 1, 1854, Adams and Company became the Adams Express Company, a thousand-share joint-stock venture capitalized at the then staggering sum of $1,200,000. Many of the most experienced men in the express business

---

[3] Smyth, *Plant,* 46.
[4] Ryan, *Forgotten Plague,* 5-7, 23-5.

were serving on the board of directors, some from the just-absorbed companies–Edward S. Sanford, Clapp Spooner, Joe Hoey, S.M. Shoemaker, A.B. Kinsley, and Johnston Livingston.[5]

All these prominent businessmen became Henry Plant's close associates in coming years. Soon a highly cultivated young man from Woodbury, Connecticut, joined the board, Henry Shelton Sanford.[6] With him Plant would eventually form perhaps his most important, life-long friendship.

The reorganization gave the Adams Company the opportunity to dominate the express business throughout the Southeast. When Ellen Plant's husband took her to Florida for the winter of 1854, she must have been aware of his keen interest in the accommodations and transportation facilities centered between Charleston and Savannah—especially the accommodations. Their life together was about to alter radically. Ellen Blackstone Plant would sacrifice the remaining years of her motherhood for the sake of her own health and her husband's career.

The key to the control of the most vital geographical corner of the Southeast was Augusta, Georgia. Immediately after the 1854 reorganization, the Adams Express Company sent Henry Plant there in temporary partnership with Clapp Spooner.[7]

Until his move to Florida fifteen years later, Augusta would be Henry Plant's principal home base.

Eli Whitney had made Augusta an important city, a kind of up-river extension of Savannah. Originally a conquistador campsite and a 1740s frontier outpost, Augusta had become a cultural and commercial center by the 1830s thanks to an annual procession of wagonloads of cotton from all over northeast Georgia, arriving to be "ginned," warehoused, and transshipped. But there was more to Augusta than cotton when Henry and Ellen Plant arrived. Prosperity and population were growing only modestly, 1839-45. Then the seven-mile long Augusta Canal came in from the west. Immediately, within the city limits and in surrounding Richmond County, some 56 mills and factories sprang up, producing flour, textiles, dye, paint, agricultural implements, boiler plate, machine parts. Between 1846 and 1851 the population increased by 4,600, including 1,500 slaves. Most newcomers, however, were foreign immigrants—a rarity for the South.[8] Though by the Civil War total southern manufacturing capacity would be less than 25 percent

---

[5] Harlow, *Old Way Bills*, 288.
[6] Harlow, 122.
[7] Harlow, 67
[8] Corey, *Confederate City*, 7-8.

of New York State's, Georgia—leading the region by far with better than 450 miles of railroad track—had become known as "The New England of the South."⁹

Still, after so long in fastidious New Haven and bustling, upscale Manhattan, the Plants may not have been immediately at home in their new home. A British observer with a particularly keen eye for lapses in tidiness and sophistication visited the South in 1856. In his *American Journal*, William Makepeace Thackery describes Augusta as "a queer little rustic city, a happy dirty tranquility generally present."¹⁰

The canal had been dug over the strong protests of the gentry who correctly foresaw its potential for aesthetic disruption. And factories might prove "breeding grounds for abolitionists."¹¹ But all Augustans came to favor one form of disruption, of progress, that arrived coincidentally with the Adams Express Company, railroad tracks quartering the city north and south, east and west. For without trains through Augusta, the city was doomed. In a very real sense the future "Railroad King of the South," a die-hard Connecticut Yankee, grew up with the railroads of Augusta. Here, Henry Plant would learn a history and witness developments exemplary of the way Southern communities might turn the uncertain future of a new technology to their benefit.

Fittingly, at the onset of an age of ruthless and often clumsy economic competition, the theme would be a struggle for survival, with a dazed Augusta triumphant over a vanquished foe, expiring somewhat unwittingly at her feet. The story began when the river city's favored relationship with Savannah threatened the shipping magnates and merchant bankers of distant Charleston. Up to the early 1820s the cotton farmers of upstate South Carolina had been hauling their wagons the long, slow turnpike way over the Blue Ridge Mountains to Charleston's great port on the Atlantic. Then Savannah offered a much better deal, down river via Augusta.

In January 1828, the Charleston city fathers secured a charter for the South Carolina Canal and Railroad Company and began laying tracks westwards, a move every bit as audacious as it would have been for an American city in 1927 to begin building a spaceport for interplanetary travel. And at a time when "railroads" meant horse-drawn tramlines, the South Carolina Canal and Railroad Company dispatched an epoch-making order to the West Point Foundry in Cold

---

⁹ Boney in *History of Georgia*, 170. Stover, *American Railroads*, 27.
¹⁰ W.M. Thackerey in Corey, 8.
¹¹ Corey, 8.

Springs, New York–construct and deliver America's first working steam locomotive.

The vertical boiler engine, christened the *Best Friend of Charleston* and resembling a bright red and green and gold toy, made the first passenger run on the continent along six miles of track, Christmas Day, 1830. "We flew away on the wings of the wind at 20 miles an hour." Rejoicing, the merchant bankers financed the laying of track across the state. For a western terminal, they chose an upstart town, Hamburg, South Carolina, directly across the river from Augusta. At some distant but foreseeable time, when the railroad was complete, every bit of the produce of South Carolina's cotton plantations and farmlands would again leave for northern markets at the port of Charleston.

The history of the railroad was exemplary, too, right up to an incident of human error of the sort that would be repeated with many variations on rail-lines and river-ways throughout the early age of steam. Leisurely hauling freight on a June day of 1832, the *Best Friend* was brought to a pause while her crew dismounted. For eighteen months their naps had been interrupted by periodic whistles of steam escaping from the safety release. This time the fireman took the precaution of tying down the emergency valve. The tremendous explosion that occurred shortly thereafter scattered the *Best Friend* across the countryside. Public enthusiasm for railroads was much dampened all over that part of the South. But the city fathers of Charleston were resolute. They ordered a new locomotive, and in October of 1833 completed what was then the longest railroad line in the world, 136 miles to the terminal at Hamburg, across the Savannah River from Augusta.[12]

What would happen if the profit-hungry South Carolina Canal and Railroad Company decided to cross the Savannah River just above or just below Augusta? The produce of northeastern Georgia, its many tons of cotton, would be siphoned off directly to Charleston. Augusta would wither, replaced by already flourishing little Hamburg. To the city fathers of Augusta, this development was something worse than a stick in their collective eye. It was a knife at their collective throat. But it was the city fathers of Athens, some 100 miles to the west, who took the initiative. Construction of a line commenced eastward—and this did fairly quickly arouse the participation of investors in Augusta.

Meanwhile, additional railroads, notably the Western & Atlantic, began construction in the eastern part of the state. Soon the rivalry between Charleston and Savannah was turning hotter—and more productive—than ever.[13] In 1833,

---

[12] Jensen, *Railroads in America*, 26-7. Phillips, *Cotton Belt*, 132-56.
[13] Boney, 159. Phillips, 17-8. Waring, *Savannah*, 50-51.

months after the completion of the Charleston-Hamburg line, a daring group of Savannah investors incorporated the Central Rail Road and Canal Company of Georgia. They were led by their ambitious mayor, William Washington Gordon, who had sold them on a dream very much like the one Henry Plant was going to buy for himself when, after the Civil War, the original dream lay in ruins, a nearly 200-mile-long westward route to Macon. Raising the capital for such a complex and monumental construction project in a particularly prosperous corner of the antebellum South, however, was to prove the easy part. Assembling a labor force to do the murderously hard roustabout work, and do it right, that was something else entirely. Half a century later the great railroad builders of Florida, coping with fever-ridden swamps and hurricanes, would learn much the same lesson for themselves.

Just as well Henry Plant, then a sturdy seagoing lad of fourteen, and already a practiced observer of commercial activity, had not come to the South in those days. In his part of the US, labor gangs of experienced Irish navies had just finished digging the Farmington Canal. Why not bring them to northeastern Georgia? They built railways as well as canals, and could finish the project in a jiffy, despite the hardships. But the mere suggestion would have caused uproar—Bring down "free labor?" Never! Indeed, throughout the future Confederacy, the passage of time would scarcely dint this pervasive antagonism toward non-slave labor. At the outset of the Civil

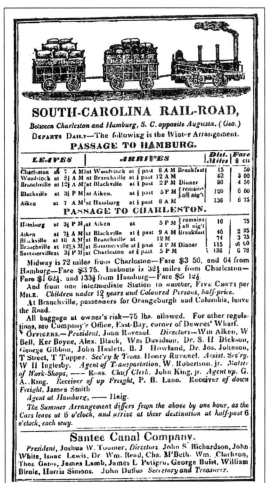

At the outset of his business career in the South, Florida's future railroad king had the change to ride behind some of America's first steam-driven locomotives.

War, 4,200,000 first-generation immigrants were living in the USA. Barely 600,000 of them lived south of the Ohio River.[14]

Well, what about native-born free labor? This railroad work meant good pay. Everywhere able-bodied men sat about, with time on their hands. What was it that accounted for their reluctance? A leading Southern thinker of the time, Thomas Cobb, explains, "Since the mass of laborers are not recognized as citizens in the South, everyone who is a citizen feels he belongs to an elevated class. It matters not that he is no slaveholder; he is not of the inferior race; he is a freeborn citizen; he engages in no menial occupation."[15]

Meanwhile, the ambitious plans for making Georgia the leading railroad state of the Deep South pressed on. As with most such projects, bringing William Washington Gordon's dream to reality required perseverance and compromise. The original scheme had called for using hired labor, possibly Irish "imports," from start to finish. The nation-wide depression caused by the Panic of 1837, however, lingered on. The payroll was cut and cut again. Soon management called on the less costly expedient of slave labor; the line to Macon was finally completed in 1843.[16] To the north, as worked on by the available labor force, the steam-powered Athens-Augusta line began service in 1837—the Athens-Union City branch was not powered by steam until 1841. Soon the young executive from Adams Express, Henry Plant, was crisscrossing Georgia on over 1,400 miles of 5-foot-gauge track.[17] Gordon's line, now the Central Rail Road and Banking Company of Georgia, was "the longest continuous railroad under one management in the world," operating 246 cars and 24 locomotives. Moreover, on 35 acres by the river, Savannah boasted the largest railroad repair and depot facility in the South. During the Civil War a line operating between Savannah and Bainbridge, the Atlantic & Gulf, ran a route south, across the border to Live Oak, Florida—creating thereby the opening gambit in the destiny of the Plant System.

Augusta had entirely succumbed to railroad fever the year before Henry and Ellen arrived. The fever had even conquered the tradition of state-line-inviolability that was making the southern railroad "network" a state-by-state system. With the long-awaited bridge across the river at last in its proper place, the rolling stock

---

[14] Shore, *Southern Capitalists*, 50. Newby, *The South*, 108.
[15] Newby, 156.
[16] Boney, 159.
[17] Boney, 161. Mitchell, *Right Way*, 19.

of the South Carolina Railroad Company began rolling to a satisfying daily stop at a depot on the corner of Reynolds and Washington Streets.

Then, on the opposite side of Augusta, other railheads were being made ready. It would be a good while, however, before the tracks joined at a "union" depot. Everywhere in the US at this time the enormously awkward, expensive handling and short distance transportation of freight through city streets, between railheads, meant prosperity for legions of porters, draymen, and tavern keepers. Just after the welcome for the SCRR&C, the Georgia Railroad, under the leadership of the famed Pennsylvania engineer, John Edgar Thompson, completed a connection from Athens. Its depot opened in the western corner of town. And soon, from the south, the Central of Georgia began running mostly empty freights into its yards in the Waynesboro district. Their lightsome metallic clickity-clicking conveyed a merry tune. At the end of the long late-summer days, long trains of cars would inch away, squeaking and clanking, laden with cotton for the docks at Savannah. The wheels of each car bore down with a firm thump at the joints in the rails, and this set the bric-a-brac dancing in the best homes. But in the best homes they slept all the more deeply afterwards, dreaming of coins in weighty sacks.

So much progress was adding up to civic salvation, to Augusta's victory over the upstart little Hamburg across the river. How had it all come about? Clearly, in the southern sky over racetrack meetings, hunting camps, and cotillions, a new constellation had arisen, an Augusta-Savannah-Charleston triangle. The age of steam had converged on the region.[18] Cotton shipments that once went down the Mississippi to New Orleans were being siphoned eastward by the Western & Atlantic connection to Memphis. Close to home, Augusta's traders had only to bid high and higher for the commodities of the Georgia countryside. The South Carolina Railroad and the Central of Georgia would do the rest. Soon warehouses on the west bank of the river bulged. By 1857 freights picked up speed across the bridge and passed through Hamburg without a whistle. The upstart little town was emptying out, folding up.

—o—

In his lifetime now, Henry Plant had witnessed all the ways by which the new means of transportation—canals, steamboats, and railroads—could alter the land and human lives. In New Haven and New York, and now in Augusta, he had seen these marvels close up, had experienced their power. Certainly there was nothing

---

[18] Boney, 156-7. Corey, 6-8. Gordon, *Passage*, 138. Hanson, *Georgia Railroad*, 4-7. Phillips, 156-63, 221-31. Stover, 27

like the railroad for producing a suddenness and efficacy of transformation.[19] The year the Plants arrived, 1854, the Central of Georgia completed the Savannah connection. Augusta became a major railroad terminus and an authentic metropolis, the second largest in Georgia, surpassing Savannah. In the decade before the Civil War $1,000,000 would be invested in Richmond County industries, the greatest local investment in the South. By 1860 only 102 cities in the U.S. had populations over 10,000. Augusta made the list with 12,493.[20]

Probably no one in Georgia, no one in the South, was better positioned to note these developments than Henry Plant. To begin with, his background gave him an immediate appreciation of the causes and effects of daily history that his new Southern neighbors scarcely noticed. Hamburg might have vanished from the map thanks to their wishes, so far as wealthy Augustans were concerned. And this feat of inattention was not entirely a factor of denial. After all, Plant had been sent to the South, as if to a foreign land, in the calling of an American businessman precisely because there were so few Southerners ready to act in such a capacity.

Of course it was the "peculiar institution" that made the South a foreign land and Southerners inexperienced in business. By 1850, chattel slavery was disappearing everywhere in the civilized world. But in the South its perpetuation instituted a siege mentality.[21] A movement was underway in the late 1850s to found a central university for what would soon become the Confederate States, "Southerners must be educated as Southerners, as slaveholders. [They must] be taught to support and defend the institution of slavery, and all the rights of the South at all times and in all places."[22]

Consider that in the 1850s the Adams Express Company was expanding to California with the Gold Rush. It was never the policy to send managers from the New York office to manage affairs in the West.[23]

From the time Henry Plant left his stepfather's New Haven household in 1834, his only official home address—where he rarely stayed any length of time—would be the Plant mansion at 584 Fifth Avenue. During his 23 years of doing business in Georgia, between 1854-63 and 1865-79, he stayed in one hotel after another. During all his years in Florida he would live in self-appointed accommodations—that is, aboard his own steamboats and trains, and in his own hotels.

---

[19] Corey, 8.
[20] Wiley in *Confederate City*, viii.
[21] Newby, 163-5.
[22] Newby, 163.
[23] Harlow, 140-52.

Was Henry Plant ever at home in the South? Or why was he so little at home, really? The Adams Express office he opened was in the heart of the Broad Street district, a commercial and residential district. Most of his neighboring businessmen lived on the second or third story of their buildings, handsome brick structures with balconies, chimneys, and dormer windows.[24] The Yankee couple certainly had the means; it must have been tempting. But when Henry and Ellen Plant took up a residency on Broad Street, they moved into the Eagle and Phoenix Hotel[25]

They were automatically a people apart. At this time one out of three Southerners owned slaves. And slaveholders were ten times more prosperous than non-slaveholders; they owned 93 percent of the South's immense agricultural wealth.[26] Wherever Henry Plant traveled in the cotton states during the growing season, the broad, fertile land seemed covered with slaves.

Likewise for the urban profusion of unskilled and semi-skilled jobs—slaves were everywhere in the towns and cities of the South. In an age altogether without "conveniences," when every menial task was done by hand and started from scratch, Southern labor was slave labor. No wonder Henry and Ellen Plant, for all their substantial income, never invested in southern real estate. No wonder, despite their commitment to a long stay, they never seriously considered owning a home in Augusta. For owning a home would have required owning a slave, or slaves. There was no other way. It was unthinkable in the South of those days to work land or staff a household with any form of "hired help."

Unavoidably, for northerners of principle, residence in the South—staying in the South—presented a series of moral, intellectual, and emotional challenges. Plant's Victorian biographer, G. Hutchinson Smyth, offers a perfect example.

> When the express office was opened [in Augusta], help was needed, a sort of man-of-all-work for the many requirements of the office. Dennis Dorsey, a colored man, was hired from his owner to act as porter, and in whatever capacity he might be required. One summer when Mr. Plant was about to go north, Dennis came to him and said that his master was about to sell him, and that he wanted Mr. Plant to buy him. "What does your master want for you?" asked Mr. Plant. "Fifteen hundred dollars," Dennis replied, "but I am not worth that much. You can buy me when you come back, as there is little danger of my being sold at that price." But Dennis was sold in Mr. Plant's absence. When Mr. Plant returned [to Mobile],

---

[24] Corey, 8-10.
[25] Martin, "Henry Bradley Plant," 270.
[26] Kolchin, *American Slavery*, 180.

Dennis besought him to buy him from the trader who then owned him. Mr. Plant bought him for eighteen hundred dollars and brought him back to Augusta. In a short time after this Mr. Plant was stricken down with gastric fever, and Dennis proved a good and faithful nurse to him. Mrs. Plant was in her grave, and Mr. Plant lived alone at the hotel, so Dennis was gratified by the opportunity to return the kindness rendered him by his generous purchaser.[27]

From this, one of the rare occasions when the slave trade was bent on behalf of a humanitarian purpose, we can surmise that Henry and Ellen Plant took something amounting to a vow of silence when they moved to Augusta. Just on such a basis, Southern hospitality could prove a trying experience.

And vice versa. The North had long been trying Southern hospitality on the issue of tariffs. At stake had been, for example, all those New Haven manufactured goods stowed aboard the Commodore's steamboats by young Henry Plant. The protective tariffs, designed to coddle infant USA industries, kept out the cheaper European goods coveted in the agrarian South. But the votes were in the North. In early 1830s, the often incandescent pro-slavery firebrand, John C. Calhoun of South Carolina, bemoaned the victimization of the South by "a system of hostile legislation . . . an oppressive and unequal imposition of taxes . . . unequal and profuse appropriations . . . rendering the entire labor and capital of the weaker interest subordinate to the stronger."[28]

Immigration had made all the difference. The populations had been evenly distributed on both sides of the Mason-Dixon in 1790. Then the floodgates began creaking open. The census of 1850 foretold the overwhelming Republican majority that would nominate and elect Lincoln ten years later: the North— 13,527,000; the South—9,612,000.[29]

Beyond economics, beyond politics, the moral issue. By 1854 Northerners were more and more unwelcome, per se. The abolitionist movement was at its height, and freeing the slaves was only the obvious goal. Abolitionists recognized that putting an end to slavery meant putting an end to the plantation culture that supported it—or, rather, that slavery supported. Such anti-slavery leaders as Horace Greeley and Wendell Phillips were passionate, thoroughly professional agitators.

---

[27] Smyth, 58-9.
[28] Hofstader, *American Political Tradition*, 78.
[29] Hofstader, 77.

To suppress their views, and possibly their agents, Southerners created what amounted to a police state.

Still, it would be unlikely that the Plants were ever suspects during the early days of their residency in Augusta. Abolitionism was still an extremist cause. Not so much slavery as that necessary national contingency of slavery—its impact on free labor—had become the central issue of American political debate. In the fall of 1854 the man that Wendell Phillips distained as "the slave-hound from Illinois,"[30] Abraham Lincoln, came out against slavery for the first time in his career.[31] But he did so purely in defense of free labor. The issue here was that by its extension to the western territories slavery might be institutionalized nationwide. From 1856 the platform of Lincoln's Republican Party would capitalize on this fear, "Slavery not to be confined to the Negro race, but to be made the universal condition of the laboring class of society."[32]

Henry Plant, given the chance of making his own way in life, had made the decision to belong to that "laboring class of society." To a perceptive Southerner, behind the young businessman's potential contribution loomed an ominous warning. For in addition to Connecticut Yankee "know-how," Henry Plant fully embodied Lincoln's free-labor ideals. By earnest hard work, thrift, and sober living, he had risen. The former grocery store clerk and deckhand was now, if not quite a captain of industry, a first mate. Without the skills and personal force of such men, the South was headed for the dustbin of history. What could an ambitious young man have hoped for, born without privilege in a small village outside Augusta? That he might rise to become a slaveholder.

Instead, from a small village outside New Haven, the ambitious young man now 35 had come to Augusta with the responsibility of establishing a communication network that would modernize the entire region. Stockholder gratification aside, his mission was profound—set the people of the South if not on the road to tomorrow, at least on the road to today. For the Information Age began with the express outfits. And on the way to the future in the 1850s, the Adams Express Company was around the curve, out in front.

Henry Plant arrived in Augusta the battle-scarred veteran of an underground war. He had joined the express business just in time to participate in the last

---

[30] Hofstader, 110.
[31] Hofstader, 114-5.
[32] Hofstader, 119.

pitched battles against the U.S. Post Office. The prize was no less than the ultimate prize of the Information Age, the transfer of communication.

Originally, the typical express company was an in-town parcel delivery service. Then, as roads connected, parcels were delivered over longer and longer distances, and exchanged between express companies. It was the genius of Alvin Adams to consolidate the companies and extend their routes, and to make efficient use of steamboats and railroads. These improvements occurred when industrial growth began to generate a tremendous volume of communication, and when the U.S. Post Office was not fully up and running. Congress accordingly protected its fledgling public delivery service in much the traditional way of protecting fledgling private industries with a monopoly. Under severe penalties of law, all stamped correspondence, all letters, must be carried by the U.S. Mail. An exchange of memos.

From an Adams affiliate in Philadelphia, "Receive nothing mailable. You will have no small number of Post Office spies at your heels. They will watch you very close. See that they have only troubles for their pains."

From the New York Postmaster to a Massachusetts Postmaster, "The young man who has the care of the Adams & Co.'s express from New York to Boston is making great inroads on the income of this office."

Again, "A merchant told me that he wrote and sent to Boston from six to ten letters daily, and that he did not think one in fifty of them were conveyed by mail. His custom was to do up all he had to send on any particular day in one packet and send it by the express carriers at the charge of twenty-five cents. Answers were received the same way."[33]

Since colonial times, official postal services, overpriced and bogged down in absurd regulations, had been a target of scorn and ridicule. Now, as the government began searching and arresting expressmen, the express companies devised swifter and stealthier routes—thereby cutting their rates. Throughout the Northeast, as quickly as the popular private-sector messengers could be tossed in jail, concerned citizens, their partisans, bailed them out.

None of this happened in the South, however, where there were no major express routes until Henry Plant arrived in 1854. And though locally the federal government's postal service was always far less efficient than in the North, South-

---

[33] Harlow, 1-7, 36-42.

ern scorn and ridicule had been traditionally mitigated by the bountiful sweets of the patronage system. Besides, commercial activities were still puttering along on the smooth and gentle basis which best reflected the leisure principles of a plantation society.[34] In such an atmosphere the go-getter, tight-fisted spirit that Alvin Adams exemplified might be easily resented. By the nature of Plant's selection as the Southern representative of the Adams Express Company, we gain our first glimpse of his legendary genius for doing business, his poise and equanimity, and his status as an all-around "good fellow."

Surely, too, we glimpse the amazing complexity of Henry Plant's abilities in a way that his colleagues and superiors were perhaps—as later events were to prove a little slow to recognize Henry Plant's abilities. For as well as an inexhaustible supply of diplomatic patience, the job of creating a regional corporate empire in the antebellum South required an aggressive dealmaker. Success could only be achieved by that rarest kind of American businessman, capable of dominating a negotiation without ever seeming to. It tells us a lot that the veteran executive Clapp Spooner, the Adams Company director who had come south as Plant's mentor, instead became his assistant, almost immediately.

Arriving by steamship in Charleston—with the ailing Ellen Plant in the care of a nurse—the two men called first at the offices of the South Carolina Canal and Railroad Company, probably by invitation. In any case, they quickly secured the line to Augusta, locking up their most essential interstate route. Next, over the gently rolling coastal plain to Georgia. They could proceed on either a four-day trek by packhourse and wagon—and this would still be the popular choice for a generation to come—or a take the four-hour "flight" aboard the the facilities of the South Carolina Railroad and Canal Company. Of course the tenderfoot Yankees chose the four-hour journey, "flying along" on the line where once the daring little *Best Friend* had flown. Appropriately Henry Plant, the man who would build the region's premier railroad system, took his first extended train ride on this pioneer line.

The routes within Georgia were the Adams Company's long-range and most important goals. Spooner and Plant would begin with the Central of Georgia's Augusta-Savannah route. The key to all the early Georgia railroad connections, Savannah was a place where Henry Plant was always going to enjoy great good fortune. Probably soon after watching his protégé's initial success there, Spooner

---

[34] Boney, 168-73.

decided to return to New York.[35] The board would know their man in the South was doing just fine on his own.

On his own, Plant first pounced on Atlanta, then Montgomery. His enthusiasm was infectious. Why, the South was past ready for the express business. It was just a question of benevolently introducing new ways of doing things. As early as 1829 there had been a textile factory in Athens, Georgia. By 1856 the Industrial Revolution was coming to the Georgia countryside, visibly.[36] Progressive plantation owners, on their trips to New England, had toured the mills that astronomically multiplied the profits of the cotton trade. They had called on machinery manufacturers in Chicago and abroad, eager for new orders. Engineers had come. Georgia's sources of waterpower were wondrously abundant; textile mills could be set up in many, many strategic centers, next to the cotton fields. The first such major center had been Augusta. On his travels though Georgia, in Columbus and Thomasville, New Manchester and Macon, Henry Plant was witness to the steady growth of a Southern textile industry. On the eve of the Civil War, Georgia's textile mills employed better than 3,000 workers, nearly half of them women. Almost 12,000 Georgians were doing industrial work. Indeed, the potential need for express services had been tremendous. Once the exponentially accruing benefits of up-to-date transport communication were made even perceptibly manifest, only someone of Plant's boundless energy could keep up with the demand.

Consequently, within months of the moving to the South, Henry Plant turned himself into a fully qualified chief executive officer. Survival demanded it. Suddenly he was in the midst of a hugely thriving enterprise run at street level by largely and often totally inexperienced operators. For a long time he alone would be responsible for the swarms of decisions necessary to keep its complex daily activities cohesive and profitable. And the more he expanded the Adams territory, the greater his executive responsibilities. Plainly, an intuitive gift made him a superb judge of character. It soon became necessary to delegate authority, to put together a staff of able regional administrators, and to appoint scores of competent, reliable managers on the local level.

—o—

By the time Henry Plant was sent south, the Adams Company had become a sprawling giant. In size, complexity and power to dominate, it ranks among the

---

[35] Harlow, 66-7.
[36] Boney, 170-2. Graham, "Economics" in Gispen, 103-10. Nordan, "New Manchester," *Georgia Journal*.

foremost early American "octopus" organizations, on a par with anything the Vanderbilts created. In fact, when Alvin Adams toured the California gold fields in 1853—the express companies had put the rush in the Gold Rush—he had been hailed as "a Vanderbilt."[37]

By 1858 Plant was in New Orleans where several years before the Adams Express Company had attempted to launch its southern operation. A yellow fever epidemic had accounted for his predecessor. Acting decisively, the new man established a route eastward along the Gulf Coast.[38] When he visited its terminus in Mobile, Henry Plant could easily have sailed across the bay to Florida, thirteen years in the Union. If he had gone on cruising down the coast to Florida's fifth-largest city, Cedar Key, he would have discovered a promising base for express operations. In 1858 the citizens there were celebrating the realization of a seemingly impossible dream, the completion of a cross-state railroad from an Atlantic port in the northeast.

Sailing a little further into the tropics, he would have come to a sleepy little fishing village tucked back in a sprawling bay. The site had all the possibilities to become one the world's great harbors, his seaman's eye would have told him; as indeed it did tell him, twenty-five years later, when Tampa, Florida, was an even sleepier place.

For most of the year 1858, though, the residents of the little fishing village slept very poorly. Because in Tampa, too, they had dreamed the Florida railroad dream. But their part in it had turned out to be just that, a dream. For a while folks down there were staying up all night, burning public figures in effigy. But soon the sleepy little place went back to sleep again, for twenty-five years. Then Henry Plant would bring the dream back to life, and make it real, bigger than ever.

But 1858 was much too busy a year for him to think of sailing down a tropical coast. From Mobile he hurried back west, to the West, before those distant spaces were taken over for all time. A dangerous-sounding gentleman, one Mr. Starr S. Jones, had announced the formation of the impressive-sounding New Orleans and Texas Express Company. It turned out that Mr. Jones's outfit consisted of himself in a tiny office and an eleven-year-old boy on the streets of Galveston with a

---

[37] Harlow, 158.
[38] Harlow, 67.

handcart. Overnight, Henry Plant "benevolently erased this small business," and extended the Adams territory as far as El Paso.[39]

The next spring Morton, now eight, joined his parents in Augusta. The family's time together was drawing short. In May they visited Atlanta, stopping at the fashionable Trout House. But almost immediately, and inexplicably for the child, the parents decamped for Louisiana and the Mardi Gras season, leaving him behind. Morton's young life would be a succession of sudden and unexpected goodbyes.[40]

Perhaps some trouble with the Texas expansion explains the odd itinerary of Henry and Ellen Plant in the spring of 1859. It was more urgent than ever to maintain a strong base of operations in New Orleans, the greatest port on the Gulf of Mexico, the gateway to the Caribbean, the Mississippi River, and to land routes east, west and north. Plant began promoting a shrewd and assertive ex-soldier from Tennessee, A.B. Small, to positions of responsibility in the southwestern district, including Texas. Small anchored himself securely in New Orleans.

Wherever he traveled, Henry Plant's status as an Adams man gave him prestige and an introduction to community notables. In Memphis, for instance, Jefferson Davis. Or certainly about this time he established a contact that would open the door for him, when the time came, to the future president of the Confederacy. At the time Henry Plant arrived in the South, Davis was U.S. Senator from Mississippi. His parents had been born in a log cabin. A West Point graduate, he had served with distinction in the Mexican War, and he had been Secretary of War in the Pierce administration. His passion for logistics was well known, for transportation in all forms. When Henry Plant began setting up express offices in the Delta, Senator Davis was at the head of a group of investors planning to launch a railroad from Memphis to the Pacific.[41] Nothing could have been more vital to the interests of the Adams Express Company. Nor, in ever-busy Memphis, could there have been a busier source of message activity along the new Adams telegraph lines than from Jefferson Davis and his friends.

During the whole antebellum era, from colonial times, it would be hard to find a professional person who covered more ground in the South than Henry Plant did over the years 1854-61. How did he do it? Over small distances he rode in swift

---

[39] Dudley S. Johnson, "Southern Express," 237-8.
[40] Smyth, 63-4.
[41] Gordon, 105-6. Nevins, *Ordeal*, 82-4.

horse-drawn vehicles of many descriptions, with a vigorous ride common to all. The recent introduction of the leaf spring to chaise supports had at least improved the traditional hard ride. Doubtless, too, he traveled a great deal by wagon and on horseback. Over long distances steamboats, often truly luxurious, were extensively available, though prone to many forms of disaster. The best commercial stagecoach was never less than an increasingly horrific form of torture, mile by mile.[42] At least progress was coming to Georgia. By 1861 the state was crisscrossed with more than 1400 miles of railroad track.[43] True, throughout the South a train covering even a small stretch of track tended to initiate a schedule at once arbitrary and erratic. No wonder. Aside from mechanical failure, locomotives of the time were required to take on water every 25 miles, fuel every 50 miles. Southern patrons of the iron horse underwent a nerve-racking education. Their train "was seldom there when the schedule said it would be," but "occasionally it was, and they were amazed and angry when they missed it."[44] Aboard these early trains, moreover, every semblance of comfort came with ghastly disadvantages. Open the windows in the stifling cars, and clouds of soot and cinders blew in. Even by the 1900's, typically, "a first-class coach called a Pullman Palace was dirtier than a hen's roost and its reclining chairs multiplied the varieties of discomfort."[45]

Nonetheless Henry and Ellen Plant, who had grown up in the twilight of the age of the stagecoach, must have looked forward eagerly to their southern travels together. For that matter Augusta gave them a rich life, with its opera and concerts. And, in the course of seven frosty Georgia winters, they took advantage of every opportunity of returning to Florida. They cruised the St. Johns River, broad and smooth and winding, past newly cultivated farmlands—fifty acres free to settlers who could hold their land during the Seminole Wars.

Best of all, for the first five of these years, Ellen Plant was well enough to return every summer to be with their son. A housekeeper was minding the Plant home in Branford. Morton stayed with the Blackstone family and with his Hoadley grandparents in New Haven. When he could, Henry Plant took a few weeks off for these summer trips.

There was business to be done, too, with the Adams office in New York, and he regularly boarded at the Connecticut-owned Judson hotel. His ties to the old days

---

[42] Singleton, "Stages, Steamers, and Stations," 243-57.
[43] Boney, 161.
[44] Ayers, *Promise*, 12.
[45] Dillard, *A Living*, 453.

were strong. Once he found Captain Bart Stone waiting for him in the vestibule of the Judson, his hand on the shoulder of a lad, "Henry, when you were a boy I "took charge of you. Now I know you will do the same for my son."[46] Plant extended his New York business that year until October. Then Ellen's health demanded a return to Augusta and Florida.

Mostly during those seven initial years in the South, Henry Plant was best described as a man "working himself to death." It was easily done, too, given the conditions of train travel in the South and a time when the crack trains of New England traveled at an average speed of 23 miles an hour.[47] When Jefferson Davis would attend his inauguration, he went from his home in Vicksburg to Montgomery, a distance of 350 miles. The historian Paul Johnson notes that the newly elected president of the Confederacy "had to travel north to Tennessee, then across Alabama to Chattanooga, south to Atlanta, and from there southwest to Montgomery, a distance of 850 miles around three-and-one-half sides of a square, on half a dozen different railroads, using [two or three] different gauges."[48]

There was, moreover, an element of intensity to Plant's business trips that precluded what elements of ease and pleasure there might have been along the way. Back then, he was a man who traveled worriedly. He never stayed over, if he could help it, after closing a deal. Always, he went straight back to Augusta. Always back to the upstairs room in the Planters Hotel where, with only temporary respites by the fall of 1857, Ellen Blackstone Plant lay in the critical stages of her illness.

Even with the miracles of modern medicine, the average time from a diagnosis of tuberculosis to death is five years, a death that today will occur while we are under medical treatment. In the 1800s, as in all times before, medical treatment for any disease was rare, even when theoretically available. And dying then was a household affair, done pretty much in the open, and the large part of it from tuberculosis.

Her husband would have made sure that the best comforts of home were available for Ellen Plant in the stately Planters Hotel. Even if he had wished, he could never escape the experience of her suffering. Outside their room, over the years, on his anguished nightly passages up and down their corridor, Henry Plant would

---

[46] Smyth, 54.
[47] Kirkland, *Transportation*, Vol. I, 319.
[48] Paul Johnson, *American People*, 457-8. And Black, *Confederate Railroads*, 9-10.

Two staunch New England traditionalists in a strange land, Henry and Ellen Plant could never make a home for themselves in the South so long as owning slaves was a requirement of housekeeping. As far as we know, they led no social life. Plant's closest business appears to have been other displaced Yankees. Their only child, Morton, had been placed in the care of his grandmother in Connecticut. Surely for Ellen Plant this made for a lonely existence, compounded by the forced confinement of her debilitating illness.

have heard the terrible familiar coughs coming from behind another door, and another, and another. Coughs that were literally tearing their sufferers apart, he would have known too well. And on his journeys, staying in flimsy hotels and boarding houses, he would lay awake, the coughing all around him.

That terrible cough has been one of the persistent sounds of human history. Easily 1,000,000,000 of us have died of tuberculosis since ancient times, but the cough is only one of the disease's destructive elements, and the romantic element at that. Yet it would not be a euphemism to use the literary expression and say, "She died of consumption." The disease consumes its victims. It eats away the vitals, our insides as well as the lungs, tuberculosis attacks the spine, the intestines, the bladder, and the kidneys. Opiates only briefly control the unendurable pain of the ravaging consumption that will continue for months and years.[49]

After long suffering, Ellen Blackstone Plant died on February 28th, 1861, and was buried in Augusta, Georgia. She would be reinterred in Branford, Connecticut, in 1894, daughter of New England to the last. Up in the Planters Hotel for seven years, with only her nurse and her husband's company, it must have troubled her to know that she was dying in a strange land. In the severity of her last agony, though, it probably made no difference that she was dying in an actually foreign land.

After the election of Abraham Lincoln the year before, the seven states of the Deep South—from South Carolina to Florida, from Georgia to Texas—had seceded from the Union and established a capitol at Montgomery, Alabama. Now on February 18th, former U.S. Senator Jefferson Davis stood for induction as president of the Confederate States of America. A few weeks before, on February 1, the City Council of Augusta had adopted the resolution that "the term citizen of the United States be stricken out of the registry oath."[50]

At her bedside, grasping her hand, Henry Plant must have told his wife over and over what this was going to mean for their future. There might be a war coming. He suspected there would be one soon, and this strange land where they'd been living might be destroyed. He suspected that might happen. But no matter what happened, their future was going to be marvelous, marvelous beyond anything he had dreamed of promising her before. He had such an idea! She had only to promise him to stay right here beside him, stay alive, and see it work.

Henry Plant observed a formal period of mourning after Ellen's death. Then, the month after the funeral, he went ahead with the idea. Right away, it worked marvelously, just as he had promised her it would.

Six weeks after the funeral, on the morning of April 12th, the Confederates fired on Fort Sumter. The worst had happened when Ellen died, and now something almost as bad. In Henry Plant's world there was left only the glorious idea, the full realization of the promise he had made.

---

[49] Ryan, *Forgotten Plague*, 5-7, 23-5.
[50] Fleming, *City in Arms*, 10.

~ V ~

Promise in the Ashes

The idea was obvious, but fully obvious, early obvious, to no one but Plant. Otherwise its swift and final application would have been subverted if not prevented. Since at least 1858 he was watching a somewhat juvenile variety of home-grown competition gather potential outside the company. Had "the locals" taken full advantage of the situation in time, at best, Henry Plant's choice of Southern partners would not have been his own. We learn all we need to know about the state of business acumen in the antebellum South when we listen to the clamor of disappointment that arose in retrospect.

What if the wrong person inside the company had caught on soon enough? A directive would have gone out for him to do exactly what he was going to do, modified in company terms. But, in actual company terms, no such order was even contemplated in time to do any good.

The signs were there, plain enough. Everyone who read a newspaper knew what Jefferson Davis meant when he spoke in melancholy but glowing tones in his inauguration address of "the final arbitrament of the sword."[1] Would the consequences of a drawn Confederate sword be any different for the Adams Express Company than for other Northern properties in the South? Possibly. The property part of running an express company was incidental to the know-how part. In the South only Henry Plant had the know-how, and he knew it. Other experienced expressmen knew it too.

---

[1] Davis, *A Government*, 163.

It must have been a problem of reading the signs well in advance and making plans. The Whig Party, which so effectively represented the expansive, nation-binding interests of the Adams Company, had dissolved in 1852 after the almost simultaneous deaths of Henry Clay and Daniel Webster.[2] The Republican Party was up and running two years later—and waiting for Abraham Lincoln. Among the first of the new Republicans was fiery Senator Ben Wade of Ohio. A staunch free-labor advocate, he proclaimed, "There really is no Union now between the North and the South. No two nations on the earth entertain feelings of more bitter rancor toward each other."[3]

The first truly meaningful North-South test of strength came in 1856. Certainly it could not have held more meaning for anyone than Henry Plant, nor been more prophetic. For nine weeks in the winter of 1855-56, Congress suspended all other business during a 133-vote deadlock for Speaker of the House. The Republican candidate Nathaniel Banks of Massachusetts, who had been a child laborer in a textile mill when Henry Plant was a deckhand. For the South, one of the great plantation owners, William Aiken of Charleston, whose family's advice, influence, and investment had played a major part in the fortunes of the South Carolina Canal and Railroad Company.

Quite likely as soon as he arrived in the South to represent the Adams Express in 1854, Henry Plant had been introduced to the SCC&RR's aristocratic president, Elias Horry, and to William Aiken himself. From then on, the former steamship cabin boy and the congressman who owned 1,100 slaves would share many business interests in the Charleston-Savannah-Augusta triangle.

Two years later, the Aiken-Banks rivalry had produced a national emergency, the nine-week-long Congressional deadlock. As distinct from Henry Plant's new interests in the South, where were his traditional sympathies, then? For that matter, where were his company sympathies? Adams Express was totally in the control of self-made, "down-east" Yankees like himself—America's new corporate homesteaders. Appropriately, the express outfits not only rode west with the homesteading momentum of the Free Soil movement; they often supplied the momentum. Banks, the ex-bobbin boy from Lowell, spoke their language under the slogan, "Free Soil, Free Speech, Free Labor, and Free Men." Finally, by a single vote on February 2, 1854, Congress elected Nathaniel P. Banks the Speaker of the House.[4]

---

[2] McPherson, *Battle Cry*, 118-26.
[3] Butterfield, *American Past*, 143.
[4] Butterfield, 143. Derrick, *South Carolina Railroads,* 23, 73-5.

The crisis only worsened, however. Bank's patrician mentor from Boston, Senator Charles Sumner, was an ardent abolitionist. In a speech that spring in the Senate he insulted an elderly opponent, Senator Butler of South Carolina, by depicting him "in the embrace of his mistress . . . the harlot, Slavery." Three days later, the offended senator's nephew, Congressman Preston Brooks, strode up to Sumner on the floor of the Senate and proceeded to "thrash him soundly."[5]

The Southern notion that Washington was rightfully a Southern city was no illusion. A district magistrate fined the perpetrator $300 for the assault which left Charles Sumner a martyr to the abolitionist cause, while overnight, Preston Brooks became the shining example of Southern manhood. Admirers sent him hundreds of canes.[6] In many of the express offices Henry Plant walked into that summer of 1856, he beheld bundles of long slim packages addressed to "The Honorable Preston Brooks, Esq."

Come fall, the Southern District supervisor of the Adams Express Company, with access to telegraph dispatches, would have been one of the first to know how perilously far matters were heading. All at once, to hold onto the possibilities of slavery in "Bleeding" Kansas, South Carolina sent a corps of "well-armed volunteers" to Missouri.[7] And express delivery was the only way to provide delicacies for loved ones at the camp front. Revenues for the Adams Company skyrocketed that season in South Carolina—though only a fraction of what the real war would bring.

—o—

The following year at the annual directors meeting in New York, 57-year-old Alvin Adams stepped down as president. William Dinsmore took over the daily business of running the company, a development highly favorable to Plant. Adams from here out would become a more and more unaccountable force, the classic *eminence gris*. We do know, however, that he kept control of corporate policy in his capacity as permanent chairman of the board. Our leading authority on the early express companies, Alvin F. Harlow, judges that Alvin Adams remained "the dominant figure" in the company he had founded.[8]

---

[5] Craven, *Civil War*, 367-8, 374-7. Davis, *Jefferson Davis*, 252. Nevins, *Ordeal*, 444-6.
[6] Butterfield, 147. McPherson, 150-52.
[7] Cauthen, "South Carolina," 9, n. 20.
[8] Harlow, *Old Way Bills*, 288.

1857 was also the year of the Supreme Court's reactionary Dred Scott decision, which threatened to open the West to slavery. Insistent cries for secession now arose nationwide. The silver-tongued abolitionist Wendell Phillips demanded that the North, the land of "mechanical progress," cut all ties with the "feudal" South.[9] "I am sure you cannot make a nation with one half steamboats, sewing machines, and Bibles, and the other half slaves."[10]

Henry Plant, from the very heart of the land of "steamboats, sewing machines, and Bibles"—from the land that began with Bibles—must have considered this proposition deeply. Over the next four years Phillips toured relentlessly, east and west. In the winter of 1861 he addressed 50,000 people; in written form his speeches reached 5,000,000 more. And every fiery word had its source in Plant's Puritan heritage. John Brown would consecrate himself to the raid on Harpers Ferry at a service in a Congregational church in Hudson, Ohio, a town founded in colonial Connecticut's "Western Reserve."[11] Wendell Phillips put the whole moral dynamic of abolitionism in a few words, "The conviction that SLAVERY IS A SIN is the Gibraltar of our cause."[12]

Surely the directors of the Adams Company read these signs and felt the same economic and moral pressures. But did all of them read and feel equally? Or did one or more have access to better—to inside—information? As we shall see, accusations of collusion would arise and persist. And it certainly was going to be true that with a few of his erstwhile superiors, especially with William Dinsmore and Henry Sanford, Plant would maintain close personal friendships and profitable business associations far into the future.

In any case, we can be sure that in the decision-making process of the Adams Company, Henry Plant was the entire Southern source. Very likely, from 1854, he had reported to vice-president William Dinsmore in the New York office. From 1857 he certainly reported to president Dinsmore. How much of this vital information reached Alvin Adams? How much did Adams need to know? While it appears that the founder kept up a busy schedule of visits to the far reaches of his empire, he is never on record visiting the South. His operative there, after all, was

---

[9] Hofstader, *American Political Tradition*, 151-2.
[10] Hofstader, 150.
[11] Vince, "John Brown."
[12] Hofstader, 144.

his most reliable and capable young executive, who kept to a busy schedule of visits himself.

We can be sure of this much too, based to some considerable extent on the information Henry Plant gave his superiors, Adams Express continued doing business in the South well after the time when other Northern companies had withdrawn their assets and personnel. Soon harsh words were in circulation. In 1860, even the Southern press repeated that the Adams Company was "in league with Secessionists."[13]

Undaunted, Adams Express kept up business as usual in the south, even after December 20th, when South Carolina fulfilled a promise to leave the Union after election of such a "tyrant" as Abraham Lincoln. Six other Cotton States seceded by the end of January—Georgia, Florida, Alabama, Mississippi, Louisiana, and Texas. March 3rd, in his inauguration speech, Lincoln went a long way toward conciliation. But it became clear just weeks later, as the Fort Sumter crisis worsened, that business as usual was soon going to mean business as unusual.

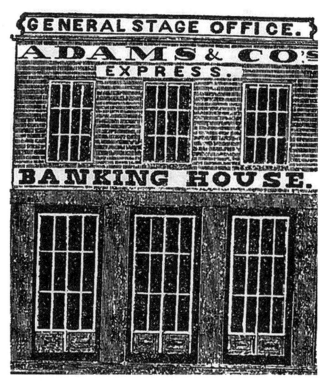

A number of Southern leaders had attempted to quell the mood of defiance that led to secession and was fueling the popular enthusiasm for conflict. Jefferson Davis himself had opposed outright secession. His future vice-president, Alexander Stephens, was warning, "[The people] are wild with passion and frenzy, doing they know not what." In Texas, Governor Sam Houston was deposed when he refused to authorize secession.

---

[13] *Montgomery Confederation* in Dudley S. Johnson, "Southern Express," 224.

"Let me tell you what is coming," said Houston in farewell. "Your fathers and husbands, your sons and brothers, will be herded at the point of the bayonet. You may, after the sacrifice of countless millions of treasure, and hundreds of thousands of lives, at the bare possibility, win Southern independence. But I doubt it. The North is determined to preserve this Union. They are not a fiery, impulsive people as you are. But when they begin to move in a given direction, they move with a steady momentum and the perseverance of a mighty avalanche."[14]

Henry Plant was himself a prime example of phlegmatic Yankee determination and remorseless, incremental energy. What was he telling his constituents? For some years the Adams directors had been seeking his advice through cautiously worded versions of the question—How long can we, should we, hang on? By January and February of 1861, the question had become urgently simple—*How* can we?

In assessing the previous advice that Henry Plant had given, we must include one factor as a constant—he was not staying in the South against his will, nor in any but the most superficial sense because of company policy, much less because of company orders. This central fact of his history is clear, at some point shortly after arriving in Augusta in 1854, Henry Plant resolved to stay in the South for as long as possible.

However badly the North-South political situation deteriorated, he never supplied his superiors with recommendations that would have led to his recall, or any withdrawal of Adams' interests, from the South. By January and February of 1861—during the long days and nights of his vigil at Ellen's bedside—it was too late. By then the great part of the southern district of the Adams Express Company had come to be located in the Confederate States of America. It had come to be located, that is, in a foreign land, hostile to, barely on speaking terms with, the United States of America.

Certainly after the inauguration of Jefferson Davis on February 18th, the manager of the southern district could resolve the barrage of the now insistent questions with a direct answer.—How can we hang on?—You can't. But perhaps I can.

In March the board of directors of the Adams Express Company met secretly with Henry Plant in Louisville, Kentucky. Why there? During the whole decade of 1850s a body of Yankees had doubtless never assembled any closer to the Cotton States. Now it was positively dangerous to do so. Louisville, on the Ohio River,

---

[14] James, *The Raven*, 409-10.

was among the northernmost cities within the Border States, and situated centrally east to west.

Moreover, the man who appears to have been all along Plant's only nemesis on the board was headquartered in Cincinnati, Alfred Gaither, the lame and cane-brandishing, forceful chief of the western division.[15] If Gaither demanded a meeting on his home turf, Plant certainly refused; Atlanta was probably his first suggestion, sure to incite Gaither's wrath. Doubtless the sly and equitable Dinsmore offered Louisville, to the board's clamorous approval. This would have been entirely to Plant's satisfaction. Louisville was the South, and Louisville and Cincinnati were locked in a deadly battle of transportation rivalry.[16] Thwarted but only temporarily silenced, Gaither likely assembled a contingent of anti-Plant directors in Cincinnati, before proceeding down river.

All parties converged on Louisville's best hotel, the Galt House, on the northwest corner of 2nd and Main Streets, near the river.[17] The Sanford brothers and William Dinsmore, the pro-Plant contingent, arrived from the eastern seaboard. Chances are that Alvin Adams came down from Chicago. Just a few blocks up the broad earthen expanse of Main Street, the manager of the local Adams office, Sam Jones, must have watched in amazement as the big shots of the company rolled past in carriage after carriage, each man's face at best a study in concern—at worst, in troubled, often haggard determination.

The exception would have been a widower in black. Henry Plant rode the Western & Atlantic Railway to Chattanooga, the Nashville & Chattanooga to Nashville, and then into town on the two-year-old route of the Louisville & Nashville. Still, he was a veteran of such travel. Doubtless he arrived fresh-faced and placid, if considerably grim. He knew to a certainty that he held a winning hand. At the least, he could profit greatly by simply holding onto his cards. A final agreement might take hours, or days. But the opposition was going to crumble, possibly fold entirely. At the least, while minimizing subsequent hostility, he could afford to wait for the most advantageous degree of the inevitable. The support he could count on—Dinsmore and the Sanfords—would have to play it close to the vest.

By this time Plant had given some pretty clear indications that he had done all the waiting he intended to do, and that he was prepared to act alone. In the exchanges of communication that had produced the Louisville conclave, his opponents had expressed doubts as to the certainty of the impending Confederate sei-

---

[15] *Cincinnati Enquirer* in Neff.
[16] Ross and Wiester. "Development," 235.
[17] *Louisville City Directory, 1859.*

zure of such a complex, necessary, and essentially *neutral* property as the Adams Company. At the initial Louisville meeting these doubts were raised again, raised with a vengeance.

Nine years later, when the matter was in litigation, those present could still clearly recall Plant's stern, aggressive responses.[18] He cited access to powerful allies within the Confederate government, eager to sanction an essentially All-southern transportation agency. But in time of war, did he think he could count on such allies, really, these already rebel gentlemen?—Yes, he did. He was now more than an honorary southerner. He was a Confederate citizen, and he had the proof. He was carrying a Confederate passport.

Then, how on earth could he expect to remain in the employment of a firm dedicated to the principles of free labor and the established, federal union? Why not resign?—Very well, what if Adams Express did try to go it alone, without him, in the South? He was ready right now to start up a point-to-point rival system, using his uniquely acquired special knowledge and his local contacts.

The threat was more than dire. It was irrefutable. If locked in competition on hostile territory with the man who had created and maintained it, the southern district of the Adams Express Company would bleed money by the hogshead, war or no war. The session ended. The directors excused themselves for private confabulations. Henry Plant, strolling along the docks, admiring the steamboats, had time to enjoy at least several choice cigars.

He had known the force of his threat, of course, from the time when secession became an imminent possibility. Back then—in another world, it would always seem, at his wife's bedside—he had recognized the *fortune* of his situation. On a storm-tossed ocean where survivors on bits of flotsam were being swept away, he was left aboard a great and powerful ship—built by his own hands—that was going to remain pretty much intact no matter how the storm raged.

As naturally ambitious as any man, by the time he came to Louisville he had paid a terrible price for the opportunity of a lifetime. When Henry Plant sat down to deal, destiny had taken away the most beloved person in his life on the brink of his triumph. And any rewards he was going to claim would require that he repudiate and possibly sacrifice his beloved birthplace, that he entirely suppress his ineradicable Yankee heritage. His ever-placid demeanor might belie it, but his innocuous *employee* days were over. The drumbeat of the business doctrine that would rule the Gilded Age had begun, "Get all you can, keep all you get."

---

[18] Harlow, *Old Way Bills*, 288.

The Ohio River at Louisville, 1860. Here, on the eve of the Civil War, Henry Plant met with Alvin Adams (inset) and made the deal of a lifetime. For a nominal sum, the young man who had risen through the ranks acquired the entire Southern Division of the Adams Express Company.

Still, he had come to claim the whole of the southern district of the Adams Express Company not at his price, but at a fair price, the best price he could offer. For by the deal made in Louisville Henry Plant put his signature to five $100,000 personal notes. Since it was universally recognized in the South that no one without substantial property in slaves and land could command such princely assets at the stroke of a pen—merely, as it were, on his reputation as an astute businessman—$300,000 was passed as the publicly acknowledged sum.[19]

Probably Henry Plant was back in Augusta by April 1st, in time to witness the most splendid parade ever of the Richmond County volunteer companies. In their glorious regalia, the Clinch Rifles marched "to escort the Oglethorpe Infantry and the Walker Light Infantry to the depot," bound for possible action against Federal

---

[19] Harlow, 288, 302. Johnson, 225.

outposts in Florida.[20] A few days later a large crowd gathered at the depot to hail the officials of the Confederate government. Jefferson Davis appeared on the platform of the train, "in a few burning and eloquent words he electrified them as cheer after cheer rent the air."[21]

Meanwhile a contract had been drawn up. Adams, Dinsmore, and the fiercely limping Gaither arrived in Augusta and came to Plant's office to ratify the sale on April 8, 1861. In Virginia, North Carolina, South Carolina, Georgia, Florida, Alabama, Mississippi, Arkansas, and Texas, the Adams Express Company became the Southern Express Company.[22]

The war finally commenced on April 12th, after months of tortuous political, diplomatic, and military orchestration between the opposing sides. At 4:30 AM, on the misty shores of Charleston harbor, a Confederate battery opened fire. A huge 12-inch mortar shell went soaring into the darkness—came thundering down and burst on the tiny Federal garrison marooned at Fort Sumter Island.

The news reached Augusta on the telegraph wires of the Southern Express. The very next day the Clinch Rifles sent out one of the Confederacy's first formal, official messages, "to thank the Superintendent of the Central R. Rd. and the Superintendent of the Augusta & Savannah R. Rd. for their kindness in passing the company over their roads for half fare on their recent visit to Macon to bid farewell to the Augusta Soldiers. The company paraded with the Battalion and escorted the Washington Artillery to the Georgia Rail Road depot enroute for Pensacola."[23]

The next day, April 14th, the commander at Fort Sumter led forth his bedraggled troops in surrender—ten officers, 65 soldiers, and one New York City police sergeant. The Reverend C.C. Jones of Augusta noted "a kind Providence seems to watch over our Confederacy. Whoever heard of so important and desperate a battle as that at Fort Sumter without the loss of a man on the side of the victors or on the side of the vanquished."[24] And Henry Plant of Connecticut became one of the 7,000 northern-born Georgia residents to accept the kind providence of the Confederacy, and remain.

---

[20] Fleming, *City in Arms*, 13.
[21] Corey, *Confederate City*, 39.
[22] Harlow, 289. Johnson, 225.
[23] Fleming, 13.
[24] Fleming, 14.

―o―

The terms of the 1861 bargain in Louisville—by which a fortunes' worth of Adams equipment, real estate, routes, and privileges were transferred to Henry Plant—remain unknown. The suspicion would never entirely die out that the secret conclave in Louisville amounted to simply this—the Adams' directors created a dummy corporation and made the superintendent of their southern district its "owner." Yet the conspiracy theorists never fully explained how an indisputably independent entity emerged from the Civil War and its chaotic aftermath to become a premier American corporation, lasting fifty years. As Alvin Harlow observes, "The story of the express business is full of mysteries, but one of the deepest and foggiest of all mysteries is that surrounding the organization and subsequent history of the Southern Express Company."[25]

By May 1, 1861 the Adams Express Company signs all over the South were being taken down and replaced by those of the Southern Express Company. On that date Henry Plant and nine associates, all residents of Richmond County, Georgia, appeared before the clerk of the Superior Court of Richmond County and submitted a charter to operate a transportation and telegraph agency under the name of The Southern Express Company.[26] The news of the Louisville meeting soon leaked out. On May 17th the *Augusta Daily Chronicle and Sentinel* announced, "We learn on good authority, that the southern stock-holders of Adams Express have purchased all the property, privileges, and interests of the company in the Confederate States. The new company will, therefore, be organized in a few days, and the business of the company will continue without interruption."[27]

The petition to incorporate the Adams Southern Express Company was approved for a term of fourteen years at the first sitting of the regular court on July 5th. The employees of the new company received this circular the next day.

To Agents and Messengers: Gentleman as you are doubtless already aware through notices in the public journals, the Southern Stockholders of the Adams Express Company, have purchased from their late associates, all the property and interests of said company in the Confederate States, with the right to use the name of "Adams" in their business under the title of Southern Express Company, with the following Board of Directors, viz:

---

[25] Harlow, 288.
[26] Johnson, 225.
[27] *Augusta Sentinel* in Johnson, 225-6.

Edward Sebring, Charleston, S.C.
D.H. Baldwin, Savannah, Ga.
W.P. Chilton, Montgomery, Ala.
H.B. Plant, Augusta, Ga.

The business will be continued as heretofore, and under the same rules and regulations, until otherwise ordered. It is hoped that all the employees will continue to take the same interest in serving the public under the present, as they have under the past organization; and thereby promote the best interests of the Company.[28]

The best interests of the new company in fact required some promoting. In the heady days after Lee's stunning victory at Bull Run on July 21, the Southern Express signs now on display began to excite a small but intensely energetic undercurrent of spiteful envy. The South was going to win. Her true sons and daughters never had needed anything from the North—never had received much of anything except the short end of the same stick used to beat her with. On August 2nd the *Weekly Montgomery Confederation* published a letter claiming that the year before a group of New Orleans investors had attempted to incorporate under the name "Southern Express," only to be thwarted at every turn by the devious Yankee officialdom of the Adams Company. The letter concludes by charging Adams Express with a long history of unscrupulous practices.[29] A few days later both the *Augusta Chronicle* and the *Columbus Sun* offer the criticism that Southern Express "has suspended free delivery of packages to servicemen." This sets off a flurry of op-ed arguments. How will the new company go on paying its employees?

A week later, conspiracy theories began to emerge. A Montgomery daily paper, in a lead article, charged that the Adams Company was using secret titles to retain its capital in the Confederate states, that is it had created a dummy corporation known as the Southern Express Company. A pair of inflammatory letters appeared in the same issue. Perceptive readers immediately recognized them as forgeries, ready, however, to accept the sinister content as standard Yankee operating procedure.[30]

---

[28] Johnson, 226.
[29] Johnson, 226.
[30] Johnson, 227-29.

My Dear P—, [Plant]

If you come across anyone whose influence is worth having, and it can be obtained by issuing them certificates of stock, just let me know, and I will set a lot of clerks to work filling them up. As I have a large lot of blanks on hand, they can be issued in a very short while. This will crimp the style of the dirty rebels in Montgomery, who are trying to rival our company.

I can see by some of your receipts and bills that you have incorporated the word "Southern" into the name of our express; in that you have made a capital hit, and one that is calculated to deceive almost everybody; and people will begin to think that ours is a regular Southern institution. If you can only succeed in pulling the wool over the eyes of some more of your influential citizens, our success will be completed beyond a doubt. For skillful financial engineering we can beat the world.... Yours, etc,

D—, [Dinsmore] President

On the same page was a reply from "P" in Augusta, Georgia, dated May 10, 1861:

Dear D—,

My plan for keeping our line in the South is this: I will *assume* the Presidency and appoint a number of *good Southern gentlemen* as Superintendents, to whom we will give a stated salary, and as they will have nothing to do, I am disposed to think they will allow us to use their names as a guise; we will pretend they have been appointed by the stockholders, and claim it is strictly a Southern Express. Gradually we will get rid of the name Adams altogether in favor of using Southern, although it is humiliating to our pride, I think it best; anything, you know, to make money.

On behalf of its perceptive readers, the *Atlanta Confederacy* reacted promptly: "They both [the letters] bear conclusive evidence of being forgeries; both are the production of one mind—a weak one—and that both are of quite recent origin is palpable."[31] What tipped off the forgery was everyone's esteem for Yankee shrewdness. Down East and New York City businessmen, especially, were much

---

[31] Johnson, 228-39

too sly to correspond so openly. Nonetheless, Southern papers published more letters.

In mid-September a former employee of the Adams Express Company, James McDaniel, was accused of concocting the forgery scheme and jailed. Despite a popular furor—angry mobs came close to freeing the prisoner—a Montgomery judge ordered McDaniel to stand trial for libel.[32]

Especially as the Confederate treasury had started out on empty, by this time the Southern Express Company enjoyed some pretty considerable clout. While the trial got underway, Henry Plant and his friends raised a $100,000 bond "to insure the faithful performance of [their] company as the collecting agency of the revenue department." Jefferson Davis promptly accepted the offer.[33]

Unfortunately further records of the McDaniel case disappeared during the war. Whatever the outcome, however, we can fairly assume that the trial was an ordeal for the defendant. The plaintiff's side was represented by William Parrish Chilton, whose name stood next to Plant's on the board of directors, and who was then a member of the Confederate Provisional Congress. A former state representative and senator, Chilton had been Chief Justice of the Alabama Supreme Court.

Nothing else so serious occurred for the duration of the war. Yet Chilton's prosecution only temporarily put down the often scurrilous, vicious attacks on the Southern Express Company. As Confederate public opinion became a chorus of frustration and finally despair, complaints and doubts would swell to a clamor of damnation. Henry Plant was going to suffer excruciating discomfort.

Of course there was praise, too, plenty of it. Plant's status as a loyal Confederate citizen seems to have been affirmed fairly early. Ultimately and generally, he earned enough praise to last a lifetime.

Often he was justified on the spot. In the spring of 1861 his company was receiving any amount of bad press in southern Georgia. Patriots do not easily renounce their animosities. Sometime that summer the Vigilance Committee of Columbus induced the manager of the local Southern Express office, S.H. Jones, to act as a "mole," and conduct an investigation of his employers. After studying his findings, the Commission reported back to Mr. Jones on October 7th, "Your

---

[32] Johnson, 229.
[33] Johnson, 229.

company being composed of Southern gentlemen, it is worthy of the contenance [sic] you have placed in it."[34]

Thus, at a time when his birthright stood most dramatically against him, Henry Plant had earned the highest recommendation an essentially alien society could bestow. Alien, for he would never be a Southerner no matter how long he was going to live in the South. Especially at the level of being a "Southern gentleman," he would always be moving in a world apart. Rather, scrupulous deportment and reliability made him a gentleman in any society. And thanks to his trustworthiness and his power to contribute, he would merit respect as a loyal citizen of the South all his life.

Most certainly, however, the stern members of the Vigilance Committee of Columbus had not relied only on the report of their mole. A Northerner would scarcely have received such an exalted recommendation without benefit of some impressive references. In any case, President Davis would inevitably take a keen personal interest in the Yankee at the head of his young nation's most vital and essential communication system. It remains in doubt whether Henry Plant met alone with Jefferson Davis on a single occasion; or whether the Confederate cabinet, with Davis present, learned of Plant's interests as represented by counsel. Protocol, quite likely, would require both a private meeting and the formal session. Unfortunately, the whole affair has passed into legend courtesy of the oral tradition.

The popular version goes that during the first months of the war Henry Plant was summoned to Montgomery for an interview with the notoriously high-strung chief executive. He began by confirming Davis's own opinion that secession had been unwise. But, he quickly went on to add, he considered the war much more unwise—knowing he could speak thus frankly. For the president had already heard, here in his office, that the Confederacy was doomed. Every insider knew Vice-President Stephens for a more pessimistic realist even than Sam Houston. Plant would hardly have said anything that strong. Rather, he stressed his total disinterest in politics, and concluded by assuring Davis that his own loyalty to the Confederacy, at this time of her severest trial, was based entirely on economic interests and business associations.[35]

Jefferson Davis may have been the chief dreamer in a nation of dreamers. But he could not have run the risky, competitive sort of plantation enterprise that he had in the Delta without considerable business acumen. He was a hard man to fool

---

[34] Johnson, 230.
[35] Harlow, 289. Martin, 266. Smyth, *Plant*, 57.

to his lean, twitching face. And it would have confirmed his beliefs in the spiritual nature of the whole race of Northerners to hear this Yankee affirm the loftiest form of his civic duty on the sanctity of the profit margin.

Too, from his military days, Davis knew the complexities of large transportation systems. He would have recognized the indispensable value of a man who had single-handedly established and supervised the network that covered the South. From early in the conflict Henry Plant carried a safe-conduct pass signed by President Jefferson Davis, granting him extraordinary privileges of travel, even through lines of battle.[36]

As we have seen, the express agencies had been able to out-perform the U.S. Post Office from the beginning. The Confederate Post Office faced the challenge of attempting to live up to the inadequacies of the old system. Shortly, the Southern Express Company would be entrusted with the shipment of military payrolls and sensitive government documents. In peacetime express agents would have complained bitterly about the extra work. This extra work, however, might earn a military deferment. They struggled heroically to meet schedules and guarantees.

From the outset of its second year the war ground on in all-too evident futility—a process agonizing to both sides, but immensely favorable to the North with its superabundance of industrial, agricultural, and financial resources. By now the fragile Confederate economy had been fairly well pulverized.[37] Merchants were forced to accept payment in kind. Commodities began piling up in Southern Express offices–hay, lumber, eggs, vegetables, molasses, tobacco.

Surely no one at the time had more exposure to the Confederacy's deteriorating infrastructure than Henry Plant, constantly on the move, dealing with one crisis after the other. Shortages of equipment quickly affected every aspect of southern transportation and communication. Any mechanically complex piece of apparatus in Confederate hands was operating on borrowed time. As an already effective Federal blockade tightened, the South became the land where things were literally falling apart. Everywhere he beheld the mortuary sight of dismantled steamboats and locomotives, gutted for their parts.[38]

---

[36] Harlow, 289-90.
[37] Martin, 268.
[38] Fleming, 36-8, 47.

—o—

No wonder Henry Plant's patience and forbearance became legendary. During his years as a Confederate citizen, except for that one colloquy in the presidential mansion, he never had an appropriate chance to express himself about the war. As a Connecticut Yankee businessman he must have had a lot to say.

For in the South the war began opportunistically, even as a business opportunity promising financial rewards. Overwhelmingly Southerners believed that, both in the factory and on the farm, the Northern system of free labor was a cynical hoax, a means of cruel exploitation. Slavery was simply the superior, the enlightened, and the civilized system of labor management. Although chattel slavery had disappeared everywhere else in the civilized world, the future looked bright to zealots in Charleston and New Orleans. They projected the imminent restoration of slavery in the Caribbean—and soon after, a thriving empire of slave-worked plantations, extending from Virginia to the Amazon basin.

And, of course, Southerners welcomed the opportunity of marching off to fight in glorious battles. The news of the easy victory over the Union's puny garrison at Fort Sumter produced a contagion of jaunty optimism. Few doubted that the war was going to last the winter. After the truly magnificent victory at Bull Run, when for weeks Washington lay open to a rebel advance, it might not last the summer. The concept, "lines of supply," was little understood by civilians outside the transportation business. By the end of August headlines were complaining, "Why Don't the Army Move Forward?"[39]

There was plenty of evidence, however, that private lines of supply from home were operating satisfactorily. Letters written by Confederate soldiers at the front rejoice voluminously in the delicacies received via express. The great part of Henry Plant's business week would have been spent at local railroad depots; guaranteeing space and security on baggage cars was the key to keeping his customers happy.[40]

At the Augusta depots in 1861 he became a familiar sight, deferentially but resolutely moving at great haste though throngs of gray-clad soldiers and their stacks of equipment. The mood of the departing men was quietly festive. Outside on the cotton platforms the Ladies Lunch Association had set up picnic tables. A cavalryman wrote to his hometown newspaper, "The noble ladies of Augusta, Georgia,

---

[39] Corey, 42.
[40] Johnson, 231.

have fed every company that has passed through the city. Such deeds of patriotism should be recorded in the history of the Confederacy."[41]

One day, on his way to the depot, Henry Plant would notice a large crowd packed solid against the railings of the graveyard across the street. He must have blanched when he pushed his way through to the attraction—a detachment of Union soldiers on their way to prison camp.[42] Later this became a commonplace sight and the crowds no longer gathered. Then he would see the figures clearly behind the black iron fence, poorly fed, ragged, weeks unshaved and unwashed. For a long while the passing citizens of Augusta took up the custom of doing kindnesses for the prisoners. But it would have been difficult for Henry Plant to have joined in this custom—awkward for him to have so much as crossed the street. He knew there were likely to be Connecticut soldiers behind the fence, men from New Haven.

By early September Federal gunboats were closing in on Fort Pulaski, down river on the Savannah delta. Though marching off to battle could still be a frolic in Augusta, the *Sentinel* noticed the pinch of the blockade, "The people are just now beginning to feel the effects, the hardships, and trials of a state of war. If the war does not end soon, or the blockade is not lifted within three months, we shall have hard times in earnest." By October, "Our markets are nearly bare of starch, soap, oil, tobacco, refined sugar, salt, hay, iron, shoes, clothing and other necessary supplies. We have plenty of corn and flour, rice and tobacco, but very little of anything else." By now hoarding and black-market profiteering were rampant. When Governor Joseph Brown, attempting to raise revenue, placed an embargo on salt, speculators rioted in the Augusta market place.[43]

Basically, though, on those busy fall days of 1861 when Henry Plant left his office at lunchtime and walked down Broad Street, he moved through well-wishing crowds of eager faces. Augusta's cheerful excitement persisted long after hopes for an early occupation of Washington had faded. Whatever shortages occurred in October, new ideas were abundant. The mayor urged the city council to "take some measures to bring it before the Congress of Confederate States shortly to assemble, the advantages which would render it desirable to locate the capital of the Southern Confederacy at or near Augusta. The measure will bring a

---

[41] Corey, 41.
[42] Corey, 43.
[43] Corey, 45.

vast amount of capital to our city to be expended among us, for many years employment would be furnished for large numbers of laborers and mechanics."[44]

Nor was optimism much diminished with the selection of Richmond as the Confederate capital. Already Augusta had employment for any number of laborers and mechanics. Thanks to the war effort, two of the South's most important manufactories were now located in the "industrial zone" just outside the city limits. In a landscaped complex on the seven-mile canal, the immense textile mills of the Augusta Factory were producing 20,000 yards of cloth daily for military use.[45] Nearby, under the supervision of a scientific and military genius, Colonel George Washington Rains, the Confederate States Powder Works had been transformed overnight from a comically inept workshop into far the most superior facility of its kind in North America—the second largest gunpowder factory in the world.[46]

This war-driven prosperity would continue for quite some time. Though easily approached from every direction, the ingenious fortifications of Colonel Rains had made Augusta the Confederacy's most inaccessible city. Still, the travails of the rest of the South had made for an anxious winter. Down river, at Savannah, Fort Pulaski was besieged on all sides. The first action of the City Council on January 1, 1862, was to hire "2 steeplemen solely for the duty of watching on the Bell Tower."[47] The cry "Why Don't the Army Move Forward" had become "When Will the War End?" Anxiety increased until on April 1st the council proposed, "the fire alarm bell of the city be tendered to the government of the Confederate States to be melted into cannon for our common defense."[48] Then came the military reverses at Shiloh and the surrender of Fort Pulaski. Refugee businessmen and workers—with their families—from all over Georgia and South Carolina, deprived of material and opportunities, were attempting to relocate in Augusta. The mayor had written to Robert E. Lee, requesting the action of martial law. On April 16th, on the recommendation of General Lee, Governor Brown approved the request.[49]

All this brought more business than the Southern Express Company could handle. The war effort was requiring the speedy transfer of material and messages

---

[44] Fleming, 18.
[45] Corey, 46-50.
[46] Corey, 50-59.
[47] Fleming, 23.
[48] Fleming, 26.
[49] Fleming, 27.

with ever-increasing urgency. Now, too, this sudden and chaotic migration of a desperate, once-prosperous people, demanding the safe transfer of their valuables. Henry Plant had his hands full, around the clock.

The perception was inescapable, however, that he had his pockets full too. From the first days of the naval embargo, cotton speculators had been operating their own version of the Underground Railroad, making whatever use they could of the freight space theoretically monopolized for express freight. In Virginia, individual small fortunes were being made by couriers willing to risk passage between Union and Confederate lines.[50] Henry Plant and the Southern Express Company were in possession of the documented, guaranteed right to that passage. It comes as no surprise that others eagerly schemed to get in on the bonanza. As far back as the McDaniel case, some Alabama go-getters had successfully lobbied a bill through their state senate granting monopolistic powers to a Confederate Express Company—which never so much as put up a sign.

Strangely, even the name "Southern Express" excited an acquisitive fascination. By December of 1862 members of the same Alabama legislature incorporated an unashamedly titled Southern Express Company on behalf of their own well-heeled colleagues and a consortium of Virginia entrepreneurs. At exactly the same time, the Georgia Senate was about to charter a Southern Express Company of its own. The Augusta *Sentinel* protested vigorously, "There is one thing that does not argue well for the new company—its attempt to take the name of an old, legalized, and responsible company which is working well and giving good satisfaction to the Community."[51] The House of Representatives amended the charter, appropriating the title defunct in Alabama, the Confederate Express Company.[52] But extra space on baggage cars and in depot storage rooms was simply not to be found by the end of 1862. Neither the Alabama nor the Georgia enterprise attracted investors—who would have lost all their capital in the coming year—but who were going to lose it all anyway. Henry Plant's Southern Express would be the Confederacy's only transport agency.

All along there was confidence in the company. The Confederate Post Office claimed all rights to stamped correspondence. This claim was honored, in order to keep the institution functioning.[53] But folks generally preferred, after buying the stamps, to entrust their letters to Henry Plant. In Macon, Georgia, the *Index*

---

[50] Franks, "Drug Supply," 296-97. Jones, *Diary*, II, 60, 80.
[51] *Augusta Chronicle* in Johnson, 231.
[52] Johnson, 231.
[53] Johnson, 230.

advised subscribers sending more than ten dollars to use the Southern Express, "We have found this Company distinguished for dispatch and reliability; and we can recommend it to all who have occasion to remit any kind of articles as a most safe, convenient and quick mode of transportation. Its officials are always gentlemanly, polite and obliging, and the Company is strongly Southern in Character."[54]

—o—

Meanwhile, since the first battles of the war fought in Virginia, Georgia's eastern transportation system was being strained unendurably by a factor disastrous in itself. For now, converging on Augusta in evermore-horrifying numbers, the coffins of the Confederate dead, on the way home for burial.

This, too, as nowhere else in the South, owing to the city's incomparable facilities and tradition of medical care, the wounded converged on Augusta—the wounded massed in Augusta. Since the siege of Fort Pulaski, boarding houses, schools, and hotels had been requisitioned for hospital space. When the Second Georgia Hospital opened in the summer of 1863, the elegant City Hotel on Broad Street, near the offices of Southern Express, was commandeered for an annex.[55]

Day after day, the wounded arrived in agony and exhaustion after terrible journeys by cart and hospital train. Many of them would not recover. A great number who did were amputees, thronging the streets on crutches. Where could they go? Hardly any of them had homes anymore. Always, day and night, the sights, the sounds of suffering.

Families came in from far away to nurse their own. Often quite excellent accommodations were available. But, daily, desperate souls were arriving simply for sanctuary. Soon would commence a torrent of half-starved, terrified refugees scurrying in from all directions—"The Grand Skidaddle."[56] On the same July Fourth weekend, Vicksburg fell to Ulysses S. Grant, giving the Federals full control of the Mississippi, and Lee's proud Army of Virginia was effectively eliminated at Gettysburg. In newly conquered Tennessee, a mighty Union force was gathering under William Tecumseh Sherman. His terrible March to the Sea would aim a swath of destruction and brigandage diagonally through the heart of Georgia, leaving a 50-mile-wide scar that lasted for generations.

Yet so desperate was the management situation in the offices of the Southern Express, and so crucial was the job it was doing, that qualified men could be

---

[54] *Macon Index* in Johnson, 230.
[55] Corey, 65-66.
[56] Corey, 70, 75.

granted leave from the military to assist Henry Plant. Notably a young man from Baltimore, Michael J. O'Brien, who had already served with distinction in the Confederate Navy, was released to manage the Southern Express office in Atlanta—where he remained through Sherman's assault.[57]

For civilians North and South, morale sank to an all-time low during the scorching summer of 1863. General Grant's succession of bloody victories demanded waves of fresh troops. In New York City, two days and nights of anti-draft rioting in July left 1,000 dead in the streets. In Augusta at the end of August, General Pierre Beauregard, who in 1861 had commanded the attack on Fort Sumter, made a special request for "the use of the City Hall for 250 patients." The City Council denied his plea.[58]

By then Henry Plant had taken advantage of his safe-conduct pass for the last time. Appointing A.B. Small superintendent of operations, he left the Southern Express Company in the hands of his eight corporate partners.[59] Soon, though only briefly, he was back home in Connecticut—though years late for the funeral (in January, 1862) of his kindly stepfather, Philomen Hoadley. After so long an absence, his own young son might scarcely have known him.

Perhaps his final memory of the wartime South—of the city then that had been his home for almost a decade, where he had won riches and lost the love of his life—was this, as described by an Augusta matron on August 10, 1863,[60] "(We) stood on the sidewalks and watched 10,000 men march by. Tin pans and pots were tied to their waists, bread and bacon stuck on the ends of their bayonets. Most garments and arms were such as had been taken from the enemy. Such rags we saw now."

---

[57] Johnson, "Plant's Lieutenants," 382
[58] Johnson, "Southern Express," 232.
[59] Smyth, 59.
[60] Fleming, 45.

~ VI ~

Victory in Sight

All the while he was preparing to leave the South, Henry Plant was making plans to return—was taking every precaution to insure his return. His investment in the South went beyond capital. For nearly a decade he had kept up the hard struggle to bring his notion of progress to a stubbornly tradition-bound land. Yet harder than that, to a time-honoring land—a land where, to a Yankee awareness, the pace of life and the structure of institutions exerted a deadening, a deadly fascination on her citizens. True, his own homeland was in many ways tradition-bound but above all time-defying, "go-ahead," progressive. By 1863 he could see the South begin to pay a terrible price for honoring the past not just in terms of respect but absolutely. Her all-consuming honor was proving just that, all-consuming.

What his struggle had produced for the South—in town after town, express office by express office—had yielded a fund of riches which might become a fortune, given another opportunity half as good as the one he had seized in Louisville. He must save what he had from ruin and build on it. The strongest elements of his character, from his New England heritage—duty and ambition—both told him that. And so he fled.

His appearance in Connecticut would be considerably delayed. Ultimately he would arrive from the far north. Even so, he must have given the news well in advance. First, the dutiful son and father, he had been corresponding regularly and of course sending money home. These were hard times in the North as well. Secondly, there no longer existed any remotely direct connections between the Confederate States and the Union. Making the best use of his powers to access routes of travel, booking passage out of Wilmington aboard the steamship *Hansa*, he began his long journey to New Haven by way of Bermuda—by way of a month in Bermuda.[1]

Quite likely no one among his Southern associates knew of his intentions until the last minute, not even his closest and most trusted confidants. With chaos rushing in on every side, why should anyone assume an extra concern? The arrangements he made with Confederate officials may well have involved an exchange of favors. Certainly by the summer of 1863 Henry Plant must have done more than a few. From the time that "Lincoln's Navy" shut down the ports, he had been assuming a rare power to confer benefits. In ways in which money played only a small part, many were in his debt. Medicines, for instance, could only be obtained through the blockade, through enemy lines, by someone with an extraordinary access to delivery services.

Certainly he needed a rest. Ever since coming to the South he had set himself the heaviest responsibilities of work a man could seemingly bear. The war from the start compounded his burden with something worse than weight, with a beleaguering host of daily-new frustrations and complications, and the steady cudgeling effect of ceaseless complaints, recriminations, and demands, demands, demands.

On top of everything else he was prudently stashing away every cent he could put his hands on. Yet doing so, prudently, required some long-headed measures. From the outset the Confederacy's currency problems had been severe. Unlikely, therefore, that he stopped over in Bermuda strictly for his health. Terribly now, the shadow of Appomattox was darkening over the South. He would scarcely be the only bearer of a Confederate passport to spend a month settling accounts at an offshore banking facility.

His affairs at this time, though, must have been extremely complex, well beyond a settling of accounts. Aboard the steamer *Alsa* out of Halifax, he left Bermuda for Canada and sailed past New Haven far out at sea. Of course passages by way of New York and Boston were plentifully available. Obviously his affairs must have been extremely urgent as well as complex. In fact, there were several good reasons why returning directly home was not even a consideration.

To begin with, the problem of depositing his profits had been an essentially ordinary problem. But what about the real bulk of his riches, the Southern Express Company itself? How was he going to securely stash that away? He knew per-

---

[1] Smyth, *Plant*, 59.

fectly well that the war was going to leave every aspect of the physical system in ruins. Still, the property, the property as legal entity, would be there. And when he left, he was its owner. Or was he?

Henry Plant had been grimly aware of this potentially grave uncertainty right along. It was inextricably part of the territory of the deal done in Louisville. A bona fide claim of ownership would be required if he was going to start doing business in the South as before. A less prudent businessman might have nursed long, bitter memories, or scoffed away the wartime complications of those spurious "Southern Express" claims. But Henry Plant, neither an optimist nor a pessimist in the face of adversity, seems to have simply taken another wry lesson in human nature. Future complications might be much greater, much more trying—indeed they would be. Well before making any other preparations for leaving the South, he must have begun to prepare the support and the credentials he would need for his return.

From Bermuda he went to Canada. Henry Plant was urgently in need of some good advice from an attorney specializing in international corporate law. From the first days of secession Canada had been a kind of Switzerland for doing business with the Confederacy. Here the paperwork expertise was available to best insure that after the war his capital in the South remained securely, remained incontestably his.

Moreover, Henry Plant by now had been a Confederate citizen for two years and had done as much as any Southern businessman to aid the rebel cause. To begin to resolve his delicate diplomatic status was clearly going to require a great deal of the experienced legal advice available to him only in Canada.

When he did return to Connecticut, he must have given serious thought to staying for longer than planned. For when he met the current housekeeper of the Branford home, Margaret Loughman, a young Irish woman, he formed a life-long attachment. Margaret was to become his second wife ten years later.

Still, no wonder that he stayed so briefly. Feelings were running strong enough before the war in this part of New England, just on behalf of the anti-slavery issue. Now, neighbors had lost husbands, brothers, and sons. A great many of the young men he passed on the once familiar streets of New Haven were invalids, and would be for the rest of their lives. At least he must have looked in on old Mr. Webb, manager since 1862 of a thriving new business on Chapel Street, the

Adams Express Company.[2] At least he had the time to reassure his Hoadley relatives, to let them know every necessary aspect of his recent activities and his plans—information too risky to include in letters from Augusta. In a few days he was waving them goodbye, sailing for Europe. For ten-year-old Morton, it would not have been enough if his father had stayed until the war ended.

Abroad, he followed the usual itinerary of a wealthy American in Europe, stopping at the best hotels in London, Paris, and Rome. His eyes were opened to what would fascinate him for the rest of his days, the Old World's opulence, the extravagant production of her studios and workshops heaped up on all sides, especially the exquisite, fantastic elaborations of the Baroque and Rococo Ages, still being poured forth in seemingly greater triumphs of ingenuity and refinement.

There were business calls, too. Without the expectation of financial support from Great Britain, her textile mills insatiable for cheap cotton, the South might not have begun the war so optimistically, might not have begun the war at all. The Confederates sent their most persuasive, articulate diplomats to London. English investors developed a lasting interest in the American South that would pay dividends when Henry Plant developed his own lasting interest in Florida.

Most certainly he proceeded to Paris by way of a stopover in Brussels. His old colleague in the Adams Express Company, Henry Sanford, was the U.S. ambassador to Belgium. It had been years since Plant had so much as talked shop with another high-level expressman. Since April 1861, in Louisville, he had not met with, or confidentially corresponded with, any of his former colleagues in the Adams Company. Sanford, on the other hand, had been in constant contact with the likes of Alvin Adams, William Dinsmore, Alfred Gaither, and Joe Hoey. What was more, Henry Sanford knew every detail of the "secret" Louisville agreement.

Two years later when Henry Plant was able to get back to business, he acted decisively to take charge of the Southern Express Company and insure his title to its permanent ownership. We can be reasonably certain that his actions were guided by the advice he took during his stops in Bermuda, Canada, and Belgium.

But how could he get back to business? He was a Confederate citizen. Yankee "Radicals" were already announcing their plans to disenfranchise Confederate citizens and redistribute rebel land and assets among the vast population of newly freed slaves.

---

[2] *New Haven Directory, 1862,* 329.

Then, when Henry Plant attempted to travel from Paris to Rome, French authorities refused to honor his Confederate passport. Was this a surprise? It seems unlikely that such a sagacious student of current events as himself would have been uninformed about a diplomatic policy in effect from the beginning of the war. Certainly the contretemps turned out much to his advantage. In Paris he received a French passport, describing him as a United States citizen with residence in Augusta. He went on to Rome, and then did a brief tour of Switzerland and the Rhine valley.[3]

Far away, in another land that soon would be no more, the tattered, half-starved soldiers of the Lost Cause were fighting their last desperate battles in hills of southern Virginia. Very soon the rebuilding of the South—the building of a new South—would have to begin. Henry Plant crossed the English Channel again, and then the Atlantic. Touching briefly in Canada, he booked passage to New York.[4] His new French passport in hand, he came ashore to the great harbor city familiar from his boyhood, to await the end of the war on native ground.

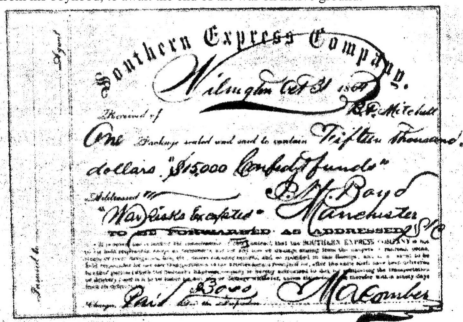

---

[3] Smyth, 59-61.
[4] Smyth, 61.

—o—

Going back to New Haven was still out of the question. His mother could bring Morton down to be with him. Besides, there was plenty for Henry Plant to do in New York, preparing his return to the South. As soon as possible after peace was declared, he must be there, doing business as usual.

Meanwhile, the Adams Express Company had moved into sumptuous new offices at 59 Broadway.[5] Conceivably it might have been a diplomatic blunder for him to call there. Nonetheless, quite inconceivable that he did not contact William Dinsmore, still company president, inconceivable that the two of them did not spend many long hours together in deep and very private confabulation.

At last, Appomattox—April 9, 1865—Lee's Army of Virginia capitulated. A month later Henry Plant was on his way back to Augusta. He went via his original route down the coast by steamboat, Baltimore-Charleston-Savannah. When he had last visited there, Charleston was still a bustling place. Indeed, though reduced by "hardships of war," Charleston was still magnificent in 1863. If he came ashore now, he was in for a terrible shock. After a yearlong siege by Federal gunboats, a few haggard survivors picked their way along deeply rutted thoroughfares, past shuttered stores and empty buildings, and the crumbling mansions of the long-fled gentry. The only sign of the city's legendary high fashions was a bitterly ironic one, the smart uniforms of the occupying Union troops.[6]

He would only have come ashore to stretch his legs. From once-mighty Charleston, Augusta was now a wilderness trek away. Sherman's wreckers had made a special detour through the Carolinas. Most southern railroads simply no longer existed, depots and repair shops were put to the torch, rails were twisted together in bunches, crossties were piled up for bonfires and rolling stock and engines overturned and shattered.[7] The line to Savannah had been destroyed on the March *from* the Sea; in Georgia alone 1,420 miles of track and countless tons of equipment had been destroyed.[8]

But Savannah and environs would be as nearly intact as any place in the South. After liberating over 150 pieces of heavy artillery and 31,000 bales of cotton on December 21st, 1864, General Sherman and his men had accepted the city's polite offer of hospitality, and settled in for the holidays. A few weeks later the famed

---

[5] *Manhattan Directory, 1863*.
[6] Towbridge, *Desolate South*, 272.
[7] Stover, "Northern Interests," 206-7.
[8] Wynes, "Reconstruction" in *History of Georgia*, 232.

marauders marched away like perfect gentlemen, a tribute to their time of gracious living.⁹

And from his association with Manhattan harbor, Henry Plant knew that Savannah had been singled out for special favors immediately after the war. How long before he heard the full report? He would be witnessing similar consequences many times over in coming years. The Savannah historian Edward Chan Seig tells the story well:

> When relief ships suddenly appeared in Savannah harbor with "Welcome Back to the Fold" messages from Boston and New York, citizens were happy to accept the charity, but in a paradigm of the Confederate tragic flaw, many of Savannah's "gentlemen of substance" felt it beneath them to labor with their hands at unloading the needed food. Instead they requested the Union army to furnish the necessary labor. Refusal followed and many ex-slaves were treated to the sight of "Savannah's finest" unloading cargo while women distributed the goods. But there were women in black who never came out on the street again, and there were men who spent the rest of their lives on park benches, muttering to themselves.¹⁰

Meanwhile, Augusta too had enjoyed a favored status—favored by fortune. The war news for November 1864, which Henry Plant perused in the jubilant Northern press, had given him something to worry about. His hometown in the South lay directly in the path of the March to the Sea, and the city was a rich prize, seemingly irresistible. The beneficiary of $25,000,000 in Confederate public funding, the site of some $20,000,000 in warehoused cotton, and the heart of the rebel munitions industry, the city was an attractive prize. On November 24th Sherman's army, advancing on a fifty-mile wide front, flattened Milledgeville to a smoldering ruin. The Union killing machine was poised just 75 miles west of Augusta.¹¹ Then, coming as close as he ever did to a whimsical decision, General Sherman turned sharply south, treating his men to those genteel Christmas holidays in Savannah.

Augusta suffered her most demoralizing damage in 1864-65 from the periodic incursion of "rogues"—renegade deserters from the Confederate armies—lower forms of life even than the hordes of looters, rapists, and arsonists Sherman had

---

⁹ Corey, *Confederate City*, 88.
¹⁰ Seig, *Eden on the Marsh*, 73-4.
¹¹ Corey, 90.

turned loose and fondly referred to ever after as his "bummers." The news from Appomattox reached Augusta on April 22nd. The morning of May 1st, the city's loyal garrison, paid off in worthless money and expecting the Yankees at any minute, helped themselves from the quartermaster stores and soon from the pitiful inventory of the shops on Broad Street.[12]

Two days later a small formal ceremony of surrender took place. The river was cleared for navigation by May 5th and the main forces of occupation arrived under Major General Edward L. Molineux with units from Iowa, Connecticut, Indiana, New York, and Maine. Soon it was obvious that the May Day rioters had done only an amateurish job of looting. Within a few days the conscientious Molineux and his staff had secured for their government $10,000,000 worth of Confederate supplies, $275,000 in specie, and 60,000 bales of cotton.[13]

With steamboats active on the Savannah River again, Henry Plant would be back in Augusta before the end of the month.

Did he join the huge somber crowd that gathered on May 21st to witness the stopover at the Georgia Depot of Jefferson Davis and his staff, under heavy guard? He would have seen a number of the high Confederate officials he had worked closely with, among them Vice-President Stephens and Postmaster John Regan.

In these early days of the peace, acts of courtesy were the rule.[14] Before passing them on to their ordeal before a military court in Savannah, General Molineux entertained the prisoners at a lavish supper. But most certainly Henry Plant would have done his best to avoid an invitation. No one was better informed than he of the coming political clashes that would bring to the South not the interlude of gentle, healing peace that Abraham Lincoln had dreamed of, but a time of harsh retribution. In Augusta, discretion was coming easy even for diehard rebels. Leaving town under armed escort the next morning, Davis raised his hat again and again to a crowd lined up the length of Reynolds Street. A few women fainted, that was all. When General Molineux departed at the end of June, he was able to write home, "The rebels are thoroughly crushed and are now well-behaved. My city is clean and matters are beginning to run smoothly."

---

[12] Corey, 93.
[13] Corey, 93-8.
[14] Corey, 93-8.

The business community would certainly have agreed. From the new city directory, published in September, was this bit of information:

> Stores, whose shelves were then empty, are laden now with choicest goods. Merchants have been North, acknowledging and liquidating debts contracted by them before the war, and have found creditors.
>
> We witness stores undergoing repairs, business houses and dwellings, Phoenix-like, rising out of the ashes. The stores are stocked with goods; the streets thronged with men all proclaiming our city's increasing prosperity.
>
> The flutter of the wheel and the song of the saw on the canal are responded to by the lumbering of heavy drays along the streets, caught up by the ring of the hammer and the clip of the adze at the shipyard, and re-echoed by the same from the shores of South Carolina an unceasing hum—telling us that we live in the midst of an enterprising and industrious people.[15]

Henry Plant must have been delighted to have such an oasis for a base of operations. But Augusta could only be that for him, a base of operations. His business literally took him everywhere else, to the rest of Georgia, to the rest of the South. If stores in, say, the middle of Alabama were ever going to be stocked up with "choicest goods"—and this would take a long time—how were those goods going to travel? Fairly soon during the war the roads had fallen into a sorry state of disrepair. Both the manpower and the money needed for their maintenance had gone to battle. The manpower was now severely depleted by 258,000 Confederate casualties, and the money was gone for good.

Still, bad roads could be traversed eventually. A much worse situation prevailed with the railroad system, the real backbone of the express business. Such as it was to begin with, this backbone had been the Confederacy's obvious handicap.[16] Its 9,000 miles of track amounted to a poorly serviced, rickety, crooked, misaligned system, sawed-off at every opportunity to protect local interests. The North began the war with 22,000 miles of solid track, already under unification to a standard gauge. Nationwide, conflicting gauges had been deliberately set to promote local monopolies along a given line. Moreover, "broken bulk" and the transshipment of cargo from one end of a city to another had meant a good living for a generation of porters, teamsters, inn-keepers, and freight agents.

---

[15] *Augusta City Directory* in Corey, 98.
[16] Gordon, *Passage*, 138. Stover, *American Railroads*, 50-52. Taylor and Neu, *Railroad Network*, 26-55, 77-9.

Twenty years would go by before the South could begin to cope with this problem. Her railways had been pitifully undercapitalized to begin with, ran limited routes, and were laid, in a variety of conflicting gauges, predominantly east-west. It helped a little that the Federal government made short-term credit available to the desperately struggling post-war Southern railroad concerns. The occupation forces, however, immediately put up for auction such "enemy" rolling stock as had survived the war, a turn-around transfer fee amounting to $10,773,000.[17]

The perhaps somewhat over-poetically inspired Augusta city directory may have been music to Henry Plant's ears—briefly. The rolling-stock deal doubtless furrowed his brow—briefly. But an announcement from Richmond, Virginia, in September 1865 captured his attention permanently. Before the war, less than 10 percent of the railroads in the South had any financial connections north of the Ohio River. Now Governor James Pierpont issued an urgent call to Yankee investors, "come to Virginia and help rebuild the railroads of the South."[18]

Was Plant dismayed that the plea went unheeded? Richmond, reduced to rubble now, had always been the northernmost main agency of the Southern, formerly the Adams, Express Company, and traditionally one of the busiest. Nowhere had Union wrecking crews inflicted more damage than on the Virginia railway system. Any improvement in railroad service, anywhere in the South, meant money in Henry Plant's pockets.

Still, a rarity among Southern businessmen, Henry Plant did have money in his pockets, plenty of it. One of his first actions was to produce $500,000, an astonishing sum for that time in the South, and establish the National Bank of Augusta.[19] He named to its board of directors a fellow Yankee turned Confederate, Rufus Bullock,[20] and he appointed to its presidency an old associate from his earliest days in the Adams Company, a man who never had, and probably never did, set foot in Augusta in his life—William Dinsmore.[21]

Of course Adams shareholders took a keen interest in the recovery and success of the Southern Express Company. After all, had the Southern Express been in good running order, the end of the war would have brought a glut of instant riches to Adams agencies along the Mason-Dixon. But again, good running order for the express business depended on a transportation system in good running order. As

---

[17] Stover, "Northern Interests," 207.
[18] Stover, 207-8.
[19] Dutcher, *History of Augusta*, 359.
[20] Foner, *Reconstruction*, 299.
[21] Dutcher, 359.

Charleston after the Civil War—disembarking from New York in May of 1865, such a scene as this greeted Henry Plant when he walked once more through the once proud and beautiful city that had welcomed him to the South in 1855. Twelve years later he bought the railroad that would tie into his Florida-bound tracks at Savannah, and Charleston became the gateway to the brand-new Plant System. Note the northern connection with the Atlantic Coast Line.

his 1871 involvement in "Tom Scott's company" would prove, Henry Plant was now beginning to take an active financial interest in southern railroads. And he would have done so through the agency of his own National Bank of Augusta.

And how else to explain Augusta's sudden prosperity, despite the polite and legally authorized looting of General Molineux? And as for those "Stores laden now with choicest goods," it seems unlikely, in the short and troubled summer of 1865, that Augusta's merchants undertook the arduous journey north "acknowledging and liquidating debts contracted by them before the war, and [finding] creditors." Why go to any such trouble? Word got around quickly about the convenience of the just-opened National Bank on Broad Street, its owner was a likely old friend, Mr. H.B. Plant. Yes, these days he was both an ex-Yankee and an ex-Confederate. Through Mr. Dinsmore, the absentee president of his new bank, Mr. Plant had access to all manner of helpful financial services. Goods ordered on restored credit left the North via Adams Express, arriving in Augusta via Southern Express.

And by Southern Express, goods were arriving. As early as 1860, Henry Plant's company was beating the U.S. Mail delivery, Charleston to Savannah, by seventeen hours.[22]

As soon as he had established his own company-oriented financial institution, Henry Plant recognized the loyalty of his close associates. Subsequent to the signing of the 1861 contract, 588 shares of stock had been quietly distributed amongst eight top officials. According to express historian Alvin Harlow, the new company's owner and president either received, or retained for himself, 500 certificates. The original issue became known only in 1866, when Plant convened the exclusive little group of stockholders for a windfall dividend of 30,000 shares. Harlow adds, "Evidently the war had not devastated the Southern Express Company's property to any alarming extent."[23]

At the same time the company underwent a complete structural overhaul. In extraordinarily short order Henry Plant created two interlocking divisions and one semi-autonomous agency. Yet, he only acted quickly. These initial improvements must have been thoroughly well considered.

First, he authorized a western division with headquarters in Memphis. In doing so he faced a delicate political situation in terms of company politics. The superintendent of the Southern Express was still his wartime appointee, the wily Tennessean A.B. Small, operating out of New Orleans. Clearly the ex-soldier had done a lot to earn his boss's gratitude. In 1866 Plant instructed him to organize their Texas agencies into a separate entity, the Texas Express. As with Dinsmore and the bank arrangement, Small would act as president while Henry Plant simply sat back and owned the company.[24]

---

[22] *Savannah Morning News*, May 15, 1860.
[23] Harlow, *Old Way Bills*, 304.
[24] Johnson, "Southern Express," 237-8.

Henry Plant - Pioneer Empire Builder

His major concern was to streamline the Southern Express. With the vast and distant Texas territory on its own, a lot was still left, and that lot had become much more unwieldy than ever before. All across the devastated South, the war had taken the express out of the express business. Shipments would move by a halting process of delay after delay while repairs were being made—and in some areas, repairs were still being made up to the turn of the century.

Plant's immediate solution was to shorten the chain of command within the company. He created an eastern and a western division, with main headquarters in Augusta and Memphis. To the coveted post of general superintendent over both divisions, he appointed the young man from Baltimore who was going to become one of his most trusted assistants in Florida, Michael J. O'Brien. In addition to the Texas operation, A.B. Small ran the New Orleans agency. The other main offices Plant had set up in the 1850s remained as before—Charleston, Montgomery, Richmond, Vicksburg, Atlanta, and Savannah.[25] At just this time Morton Plant, now a tall, handsome youth of sixteen, had graduated from the Russell School in New Haven. Morton was looking for a job. His father placed him at the heart of the exciting western division, in Memphis.[26]

Henry Plant's main problem, though, was his claim to ownership to the company, which continued to haunt him. Well after the reorganization had proved a brilliant success, matters came to a crisis. Three disgruntled Adams stockholders, the Einstein brothers, after years of agitation, brought suit in New York State in 1869. A legal document explains their position that "certain notes they held were for the *bona fide* sale of the property in the southern states at the commencement of the war. The defendants contend that the notes were a mere cover for the property, and that the Southern Express Company stock, really amounting to a large sum should be accounted for." Furthermore, they claimed "that many of the stockholders believed, upon information which they claim to have received from directors and agents of the company, that the transfer, through Plant, to the Southern Express Company, was merely an arrangement to prevent confiscation."[27]

The plaintiffs went on to allege that ever since the Louisville deal, the Adams Express Company's New York office had been receiving secret reports from its "dummy" partner in the south. In evidence, one of the Einsteins submitted that no

---

[25] Martin, "Henry Bradley Plant," 270.
[26] Mueller, *Steamships*, 136.
[27] Harlow, 301.

less an important Adams official than Edward Sanford had told him to his face, at the races in Saratoga, that the Adams and the Southern were one and the same, and that the Southern had the potential to be "the bigger money-maker." Another brother claimed to have learned from board member I.W. Babcock that the Adams held interest in the Southern to a minimum value of $2,000,000. Another brother had evidently come to Augusta to do a little detective work. A teller at the National Bank had revealed that, to his certain knowledge, the Southern was an adjunct of the Adams, under a surreptitious arrangement "to evade the Confederate authorities and protect the property during the war."

In terms just as certain, the clerk would disclaim this statement before the Supreme Court of the State of New York. The proceeding dragged on for almost five years. Plant, the Sanford brothers, Hoey, Babcock, Dinsmore and a host of Adams officials ultimately appeared. In sworn testimony, they denied the Einstein charges categorically, in every detail.

Publicly, the Sanfords stated their belief that Plant's original notes—$500,000—were settled. On his own behalf, Henry Plant testified that in 1861 he had instructed the Adams treasurer to withhold dividends on his Adams stock, at interest, in payment of the Louisville sale. In the words of Alvin Harlow at this point, "Mark the richness of the express bonanza." From his Southern profits of 1867-68, Plant paid himself $80,000, the next year, $307,936. By 1869 there had been applied $395,486 in stocks and dividends on his behalf. With accrued interest, Plant's payments now came to $782,916.66. So, in settling their accounts, the Adams Company presented Henry Plant with a check. He had overcharged himself $506.42. Harlow comments, "Fancy buying a half-million dollar property on notes and paying for it, with more than 50% added for interest, in eight years!"[28]

The defendants were unable, however, to introduce a shred of documentary evidence to support their allegations. All the original company records in the South had vanished during the war, and the plaintiffs made the telling point that the Adams directors had accepted Plant's IOUs in lieu of cash and even in lieu of a transcript. Then, just when everything might have sunk into a quagmire of legal uncertainty, Henry Sanford produced a copy of the Louisville contract, "a Memorandum and Bill of Sale," and swore to its authenticity. After careful examination, Henry Plant testified that, yes, this was identical to the agreement signed in his Augusta office on April 8, 1861. William Dinsmore and other members of the original Adams team concurred.

---

[28] Harlow, 301-02.

Alvin Harlow's verdict was simple, "Without suspecting the defendants of wholesale perjury, the court could do nothing else than reject the petition of the Einsteins. But suspicions of chicanery cursed the minds of many Adams stockholders forever after. For, down to the time of their absorption by Railway Express during World War I, a peculiar harmony existed between the two companies, amounting to an affiliation. In every city in which they both did business, their offices were in the same building, their freight and money shipments usually handled in the same big room. Often the same wagons were used, the names of companies being painted on the sides of each."[29]

Without the Edward and Henry Sanford's public support, without Henry Sanford's timely discovery of the 1861 agreement, the Einstein matter might have very considerably stymied the ambitious plans that Henry Plant was making in the 1870s. Had he begun thinking seriously of Florida at this time? Chances are that he had. Pacing the pleasant byways of Albany's judicial district, chatting with Henry Sanford, he must have taken in quite an earful on the subject of Florida's agricultural potential and its crying need for transportation facilities. For his friend had acquired quite a unique education.[30]

The intellectual, frail, ever-restless Sanford was quick to leave the diplomatic corps after the war. Taking from now on the honorarily-bestowed title of General, he was obsessed with the tropics. His time in Belgium had made him one of King Leopold's many minions, dreaming of African treasures. His later life would be consumed by this dream, with his ill-advised American Congo Exploration Company.

In 1868 Henry Sanford made his first warm climate "money" move. He bought a coastal South Carolina cotton plantation in the heart of Southern Express country, 100 miles east of Augusta, halfway between Charleston and Savannah. The next year he went deeper south, investing in a yet more tropical product, a sugar plantation in Louisiana's Cajun country. Within two years these ventures were floundering. Cotton and sugar are among the world's most labor-intensive crops, and Henry Sanford was among the most absent of the world's absentee landlords. He was to run through a stupendous fortune simply on the basis of eagerly investing in an immense, complex project—then, after a brief period of chagrin over its failure, more eagerly running off to buy another.

---

[29] Harlow, 303.
[30] Fry, *Sanford*, 87-111, 112-32.

Shortly after the Civil War, Florida became the "most advertised state in the Union." Dismayed, but determined to recoup his losses in South Carolina and Louisiana, Sanford paid a visit to America's tropical frontier, to the wild country below St. Augustine. In the year of his most crucial testimony on Plant's behalf at the Einstein trail, in 1870, he went as far south and into the interior as the Kissimmee Valley. Here, the old hunting lands of the Seminoles had become the open-range fiefdoms of cattle barons. When he returned home to Philadelphia, Henry Sanford was the enthusiastic owner and promoter of 12,547 acres of Florida real estate. Even by the standards of Florida real estate at the time, these were 12,547 miserably under-cultivated, under-populated, and commercially inaccessible acres. Or, perhaps, miserably under-cultivated and under-populated because they were commercially inaccessible.

—o—

The land Henry Sanford had selected lay in territory long familiar to Henry Plant. In the days of those annual visits to Florida for the sake of his wife's health, he and Ellen had sojourned extensively along the rustic plantations of the interior waterways. The proposed new city, Sanford, would be situated on the eastern rim of the shallow Kissimmee Valley, on the shore of Lake Monroe, at the source of the meandering and mighty St. Johns River.

From the time he had come to Augusta, Plant had been regaled with tales of fabulous wealth waiting for the man who could lay a transportation route to Florida, bringing the tropical foodstuffs of the Caribbean to the markets of the northeast.[31] Indeed, in Savannah the possibility of developing a port in the fever-ridden little town of Tampa had been discussed. The astute Colonel John S. Screven, postbellum president of the Atlantic & Gulf Railroad, described the massive peninsula on Georgia's southern border as "the great wharf-head which nature has constructed between the Atlantic and the Gulf of Mexico."[32] The dreamed-of route meant, simply enough, railroads. During the mid-1850s, railroads were being built in Florida, some 531 miles worth by the time of the Civil War.

Railroad financing in Florida, however, had always been a tricky proposition at best. The territory entered the Union in 1845 with a modest award of 500,000 acres for development. But with the federal Swamp and Overflowed Lands Act of 1850 came a stupendous bonanza of 22,000,000 acres. Immediately, all the most desirable sections of this property, particularly its vast tracts of lumber, could be

---

[31] Corey, 29.
[32] Anew and Lee, *Historical Record*, 147.

offered as "land grants" to initiate transportation projects. But, as well, under the dubious rationale of opening the interior highlands to cultivation, the state began converting its newly gifted public wetlands into collateral for the bonds of antebellum railroad and canal companies. After the Civil War these companies were hopelessly in default to northern banks. In 1855, David Levy Yulee, offering the bonds of his cross-state Florida Railroad as collateral, purchased $105,000 worth of iron rails from a New York firm of which Francis Vose was a partner.[33] Now Vose was leading other creditors to a New York court, seeking back interest and principal on the defaulted bonds. The court promptly issued the "Vose Injunction." Until settlement of the claimants' suit, this stern decree prohibited Florida's government from using any of its land whatsoever to underwrite future development.[34]

Practical-minded dreamers such as Henry Plant knew it would take a miracle to break this impasse any time soon. There was also the great likelihood that, if awarded their collateral in the course of further litigation, the bondholders would simply exploit the railroad's resources on behalf of their long-overdue profit. But such a committed promoter as Henry Sanford dreamed all the more desperately of an immediate solution. True, canal builders and steamboat men promised great things. At best, though, their help would be cumbersome. The potential tons of perishable produce, packed in Sanford's new city, bound for New York and Boston, required the modern miracle of locomotion at speed, the gleaming miracle of railroad track.

Throughout peninsular Florida, in empty sales offices on forlorn main streets, lesser promoters than Henry Sanford also dreamed of the miracle that would bring the gleam of iron rails to the edge of their towns. But new railroads meant land grants, and land grants meant paying off the state's long-term creditors, arrayed behind the hated Vose Injunction. Only an infusion of cash, that mighty elixir, could end the decade-long stalemate that had made Florida the one state in the union without even the promise of significant railroad construction. Then.[35]

None of those dusty main street promoters were aware of it when the possibility of the miracle began to peek forth. In the mid-1870s a supremely ambitious young Philadelphian, a member of Henry Sanford's social circle, stood poised to inherit

---

[33] Shofner, *Nor Is It*, 115.
[34] Tebeau, *History of Florida*, 277-8. Williamson, *Gilded Age*, 47-51.
[35] Derr, *Paradise*, 87-9. Tebeau, 278, 280-81. Williamson, 73-8.

an immense fortune. He was about the same age as Henry Plant's son, and his name was Hamilton Disston. His father, Henry Disston, an immigrant blacksmith, had perfected the manufacture of tools, especially saws, and items of military equipment just in time for the demands of the Civil War. With his bedridden father's blessing, young "Ham" was pleased to visit Florida at General Sanford's behest, ostensibly to fish for the famed lunker black bass in Lake Monroe. That was in 1877, the year the city of Sanford became an official place name, and the year before Hamilton Disston inherited one of the great American fortunes.

In Florida in those days, you caught the fish of your dreams. But gazing out on the scrublands and jungles and watery reaches of south Florida, Hamilton Disston was himself caught by a dream. It was the biggest dream of all, the dream of finding and creating vast treasures on earth—the dream of empire. By the light of a lantern in a tent, what maps had the ever-eager Henry Sanford unrolled for him?

Over the next two years Hamilton Disston kept himself busy, back home in Philadelphia, unrolling his own maps of Florida and pondering the question of how to make Florida pay dividends. The problem was there, on the all too-flat surface. Indeed, the problem was simply that, surface. There were no mountains to assail, no gorges to span, no mighty rivers to bridge, only a vast and unimpeded flatness, mere distance. Conquer distance and Henry Sanford's agricultural community would expand and proliferate. Property values would then go sky-high in the Kissimmee Valley. But as it was that expanse of that undeveloped region, beckoning and fertile, lay landlocked in terms of moving the potential treasures of its husbandry.

Already Sanford had the dream of building a railroad west from his base on Lake Monroe into the heart of the Kissimmee Valley. The line would run though Orlando, a dusty little cow town, and terminate at Kissimmee City, a central location that would become a thriving metropolis, that is, provided it became the transshipment point to the great urban markets far to the northeast. Going west, wasn't Henry Sanford land locking himself yet more securely?

Gazing down on his maps in Philadelphia, the young heir saw the solution. Southeast of Kissimmee City lay what amounted to a "veteran" harbor on the Gulf of Mexico. From the beginnings of the central Florida cattle kingdoms, Punta Rassa, on Charlotte Harbor, had been the embarkation point for beef-on-the-hoof, bound for Cuba. Now Hamilton Disston contemplated a "Kissimmee Valley and Gulf Railroad," terminating in Port Charlotte. From there, steamships would carry citrus and iced-down vegetables around Key West and up the Atlantic Coast.

Still, all that was going to take time and the time would have to be ripe. It wasn't going to be just a matter of forking over the money and walking off with, say, a million acres of public domain. There were already hundreds, probably thousands, of homesteaders—squatters—throughout the region. And powerful political voices would oppose the sale of one tremendous block of state land to a single interest, even if that would remedy the Vose impasse.

Besides there was a much bigger, older, potentially richer dream to be realized. An empire was there, seemingly, for the taking. The first white man to explore the Everglades, Buckingham Smith, in 1848, had come away with a vision of everything but an ecological wonderland. After all, "ecology" was a hundred years in the future. Rather, Buckingham Smith came away with a vision of an Everglades empty of water and glades; of an Everglades drained to the bottom, exposing organic muck fourteen feet thick. Smith imagined a panorama of ten-acre yeoman farms, each worked profitably by a family owning one slave. His 12,000,000-acre Everglades reclamation project would become a Jeffersonian Utopia.

Now, late in the 1800s, the technology was available to do the job, and do it without opposition, without limits on its application, without any significant possibility of public outcry. Moreover, the belief was universal that the Everglades should and would be drained. No one dreamed of the gigantic machines and the hordes of laborers needed to farm a horizon-wide panorama of exposed muck, much less of the gigantic corporations required to do so profitably. Like ecology, agribusiness lay far in the future. As it was, Disston's engineers were going to come perilously close to pulling the plug which would have flushed millions and millions of gallons of fresh water forever into the Atlantic, causing one of the greatest ecological disasters of all time.

With a good-faith show of capital, the march toward empire, the march toward Utopia, could now begin. Hamilton Disston had been meeting with a group of friends from the start—and doubtless Henry Sanford would have added some names of his own to the list. In 1879 the Disston group filed for incorporation as the Atlantic and Gulf Canal and Lake Okeechobee Land Company.

The Atlantic and Gulf Canal Company? Where had the railroad gone? By now Hamilton Disston had been treated to awesome demonstrations of modern technology—colossal dredges that scooped up swampy muck by the ton and heaved it aside. Once these monsters had done their work on the woefully disorganized waterways that fed the western Everglades, steamboats could transport agricultural products from Lake Monroe to Port Charlotte via the Kissimmee River, Lake Okeechobee, and the Caloosahatchee; then by sea through the Florida Straits and up the east coast. A grander enterprise by far than running a railroad!

—o—

At these tidings Henry Plant's practical-minded Florida dreams must have taken on a new life or, at least, an added glow. He would have been one of the first to know that Hamilton Disston had accepted Henry Sanford's invitation in 1877. He would have been pleased to learn that the fabulously wealthy young man had been "caught" ever since. If the Disston money came to Florida, those tight-fisted folks holding the Vose indentures—with interest, now well over a $1,000,000—just might have their due at last. Then Florida and all its promise would be opened up to transportation investments. For that matter, the whole of the South was in greater need than ever of connections to the factories and markets of the north.

And who knew more about these possible connections than Henry Plant? Surely Henry Sanford asked him about young Disston's proposed steamboat route. Down the Kissimmee, across Lake Okeechobee and into the Caloosahatchee, then on to Key West and up the coast? Was that the best way to reach the markets of the north? Well, Henry Plant was taking more trips up north than ever, was even looking into the possibility of a home in New York, on Fifth Avenue. He had married Margaret Loughman in 1873. His son was twenty-one that year, and terribly keen about anything nautical. When they had the leisure for it, he and Margaret and Morton would relish such a long and colorful and circuitous journey.

Later, if Hamilton Disston did make the kind of contribution that would satisfy Francis Vose, if next year Florida put a pro-railroad man in the governor's mansion, and everyone knew that William Bloxham, leading the Democratic revival, was such a man—well, that would be the time for good friends to sit down together and quietly discuss the situation, very quietly. It all depended on where Disston was going with his money, and how Bloxham did in 1878. Already Henry Plant had some definite ideas of his own about the best way to reach the markets of the north from the promising state of Florida.

~ VII ~

On the Brink of the Dream

Right until the very end of the 1870s, Florida continued to languish in much the typically pristine conditions that Henry Plant had encountered in the winter of 1853. Then he and Ellen, with their guide, the daughter of a Seminole chief, had almost been required "to spend an uncomfortable night in the woods." To investors, a land of promise perhaps, but a land of stubbornly distant promise.

True, between 1860 and 1880 the population increased 90 percent, but this would bring the total figure to only 225,000, spread over an immense area, some 58,000 square miles. And what of the age's refinements, the gaudy saloons, the opera houses, and the pleasure parlors, such as the little mining towns of the Wild West might occasionally offer? To all but the most determined travelers—especially to well-heeled travelers—Florida remained a frontier in depth.[1]

Here, by and large, the coming of civilization had labored to produce, instead of towns, mere settlements, each one a monotonous repetition of pioneer discomforts. In 1877 Henry Sanford spent the night in the best accommodations to be found in Palatka, the crown-jewel community of the interior. He was almost eaten alive by fleas.[2] Henry Flagler, the man most famously credited with civilizing Florida, also visited in 1877. As Plant had 24 years earlier, he set out to bring his tubercular first wife to a life-saving climate of warm, pure air. The Flaglers left New York harbor in February, bound for Savannah and Jacksonville. And

---

[1] Shofner, "Renewal" in *New History of Florida*, 249-65.
[2] Fry, *Henry S. Sanford*, 96.

appraising Jacksonville's primitive facilities, Henry and Mary Flagler were every bit as much dismayed as Henry and Ellen Plant had been. But unlike the adventurous Plants, they went no further. In fact, they returned by next passage to their marble parlors in wintry Manhattan.[3] Flagler, the son of an impoverished county clergyman, had grown up a harder way than Henry Plant, but he was still dismayed at the primitive conditions in Jacksonville. And, given nearly a quarter century, Jacksonville had improved!

On January 22nd, 1912, eighty-two-year-old Henry Flagler had this to say when the first train from New York arrived at the southernmost city in the US via his Key West Extension:

> On the first day of December 1885, we commenced the digging of the excavation for the foundation of the Hotel Ponce de Leon in St. Augustine. At that time St. Augustine had a population of from 1,500 to 2,000 persons. There were but 12 houses on the line of the railroad between Jacksonville and St. Augustine. There was no house, no habitation between Jacksonville and what is now East Palatka. Ormond may have had 150 inhabitants [and] Daytona 150 [while] Rockledge existed, [but] only practically existed.
>
> The 66 miles between Palm Beach and Miami were practically an unbroken wilderness. I traveled over it riding behind a mule and a cart, fortunately that had limber springs under the seat. Palm Beach had three houses, two families living in two of them and an old bachelor in the third house. Coconut Grove perhaps had three or four houses—nothing south of that. Today there is a very large population and that whole country is filled with an industrious, prosperous people, and thousands of comfortable homes exist where only desolation existed 25 years ago.[4]

In 1897, near the end of his life, Henry Plant would be able to make a similar claim for the stretch of territory between Jacksonville and the Gulf of Mexico. Working apart, Plant and Flagler would reach and grasp the land of distant promise.

—o—

The year that both Henry Flagler and Henry Sanford happened to come to Florida was a particularly dismal one for the state's future in terms of investor confi-

---

[3] Chandler, *Henry Flagler*, 86-9.
[4] Chandler, 257-8.

dence—for its reputation as a well-run, progressive, and, above all, *auspicious* social enterprise. Compounding the seemingly permanent crisis over the Vose Injunction, the State Treasury had closed the year 1876 by repudiating $4,000,000 worth of bonds sold in Europe. The Territory of Florida, at the end of the Whig Era in 1842, had defaulted on $3,900,000 in bonds—also sold in Europe.[5] Thus Florida entered 1877 still very much the same resolutely rough-hewn, backward, ill-omened social enterprise that it had been when Andrew Jackson chased out the Spanish in 1821.

Indeed, in every Southern state the future from the year 1877 looked particularly fraught and ambiguous. The end was drawing near for the massive social experiment known as Reconstruction, and the garrisons of Union troopers, maintaining martial law for better than a decade of tight Federal supervision, were marching away. *The Battle Hymn of the Republic* was heard for the last time in even the worst die-hard corners of "the damned rebel" South. But here for once Florida—less than fully damned—had been in the vanguard, earning relief from military occupation in 1868. Nothing had come of the plan to confiscate and resettle the Black Belt plantations with freedmen and Union veterans.[6]

The truth was that the state's backwardness paid certain dividends during and after the Civil War. An adequate transportation system would have brought conquering Union armies to the central highlands. Near the end of the war General John K. Johnson estimated that, over any six-month period, Florida ranchers were capable of feeding 250,000 men. In addition, Florida farmers were supplying the Confederacy with oranges, lemons, sugar, syrup, peas, corn, and potatoes. As it was, Federal attempts to penetrate the interior were defeated at every turn by a dashing captain of the infantry, J.J. Dickison, and his necessarily motley forces. The Union Navy bombarded such pesky backwater smuggling havens as Tampa. The Union Army settled for uncontested occupation of the major port cities of Pensacola, Cedar Key, Fernandina, and Jacksonville.[7]

Still, when measured by the Confederacy's socio-economic criterion, the ownership of slaves, Florida had become a promising locality at the time of her secession. In 1860, slave-owners made up one-third of the population. The peculiar institution, however, was virtually confined to an arc of cotton-growing land in the northern part of the peninsula, the Black Belt—"a virtual barony that centered

---

[5] Williamson, *Gilded Age,* 15.
[6] Wynne and Taylor, *Florida,* 118.
[7] Patrick and Morris, *Five Flags,* 56-62. Taylor, *Rebel Storehouse,* 66-132.

on the territory's newly minted capital city of Tallahassee"—home to 70 percent of all the slaves in Florida.[8]

Long before facing the reality of defeat, everyone in the South was urgently aware of living in a different world. Better than three million slaves had been set free. Many, understandably, were enjoying a self-proclaimed and seemingly open-ended holiday Then, in the weeks after surrender, Florida joined her sister Deep South states in a series of assumptions, and of policies, which were at once naive and brutal. The first and most naive assumption was that the surrender of the southern armies would provide automatic readmission to the Union. In short, business as usual. By then, in the late spring of 1865, the fields must be made ready for planting. Especially, in a shattered economy, for the planting, and the raising and harvesting, of the great cash crops, cotton, tobacco, indigo, rice. Southern state governments quickly enacted legislation, the infamous Black Codes, intended to put the freemen back in the fields under the barely disguised conditions of slavery.[9]

The administration of President Andrew Johnson was stubbornly pursuing Lincoln's policy of patient reconciliation. It has been widely assumed that in the hands of Lincoln himself, the policy would have worked. But the old order responsible for the Confederacy was savagely entrenched. And the Radicals of the Republican Party were determined to extirpate what they perceived to be the cause of slavery in America, southern feudalism—the aristocratically ruled social structure of the South. Moreover, even before the outrage of the Black Codes, the Radicals were committed to a moral crusade *beyond* Appomattox. Their leader, Senator Thaddeus Stephens of Pennsylvania, had sworn to literally "trample out the vintage." His original program called for the outright confiscation of rebel wealth. The plantations would be divided into 40-acre plots and put up for sale to freemen at ten dollars an acre.[10]

Leaving his deathbed to come to the Senate in the attempt to impeach Johnson for opposing Reconstruction, Thad Stephens advised, "Strip a proud nobility of their bloated estates; reduce them to a level with plain republicans; send them forth to labor and teach their children to enter the workshops or handle a plow, and you will thus reduce the proud traitors."[11]

---

[8] Rivers, *Slavery in Florida*, 11. Williamson, 22.
[9] Kolchin, *American Slavery*, 209-10, 220-21.
[10] Foner, *Reconstruction*, 63-77, 276.
[11] Butterfield, *American Past*, 186-88.

But in Florida no such "proud nobility" existed in any numbers. The struggling, 1,000-acre plantations of the Black Belt hardly qualified as "bloated estates." The majority of Florida's successful farmers, natural opponents of the plantation system, owned no slaves. They were exactly plowmen, many of them fitting precisely the Jeffersonian ideal of the sturdy yeoman settler. Other settlers, in the wiregrass country and deep in the piney woods, certainly owned no slaves, and subsisted well below the level of even the plainest of "plain Republicans."

The days of Radical rule in Florida would be numbered when, in the early 1870s, the Black Belt plantation owners, the yeoman farmers, and the poor whites found common cause. This political alliance created a new Democratic Party and would finally bring Henry Plant, the investor, to Florida. Until then, as everywhere in the fallen Confederacy, the Reconstructionists had their will with the state's social structure, turning it precisely upside down, "putting the bottom rail on top."

Across the South, unrepentant Confederates were stripped of their rights. Newly enfranchised black voters became a potent political force. Yet the former slaves, as the condition of slavery, were largely illiterate, and almost as politically illiterate. Quickly, actual civil power devolved to a disorganized but effectively ruthless tribe of northern and southern opportunists, carpetbaggers and scalawags.[12] The long-term sorry consequence of their rule was a tweak to the psyche of loyal white southerners, promoting the pathological entrenchment of an already unhealthy tradition of racial bigotry.

The immediate sorry consequence of the carpetbagger invasion, however, was economic, and affected transportation systems particularly. Big-money swindlers descended on every southern state—and no big-money scam emptied a state treasury quite so quickly as a railroad scam.

When Henry Plant began taking an interest in southern railroad investments in 1871, was it any help that the crowned king of the Reconstruction con men was a tall, stately Connecticut Yankee? No other carpetbagger approached the brazenness of Hannibal I. Kimball, who managed to take over four of Georgia's seven war-scarred railroad lines and siphon off the public funds intended for their salvation.[13] Folklore would have it that the only way to avoid this former carriage-

---

[12] Shofner, 249-65.
[13] Stover, "Northern Interests," 209. Stover, *Railroads*, 99-100.

maker's charm was to stay out of the room, even the courtroom. In the face of Kimball's devastating *bon homie,* angry victims simply fell victim again.

In the course of building the Southern Express, Henry Plant had met more than his share of flimflam artists. These were easily brushed aside. He could regale the barbershop crowd with their downfall. But after the war, how was he to dismiss Hannibal I. Kimball of Connecticut, the president of four railroads? Yet he needed to maintain his distance from Mr. Kimball, and needed to make the distinction of his own Yankee credentials publicly clear, if he ever hoped to make himself a factor in the railroad business of the South.

While a tricky enough balancing act to deal with on the ground, Henry Plant was required to deal with it on the high wire, as it were. For Kimball practiced his slippery arts in friendly alliance with Georgia's first, soon-to-be notorious governor of the era of carpetbaggers and scalawags, Rufus B. Bullock.[14] This same Rufus B. Bullock had become one of the original high officials of the Southern Express Company in 1861,[15] and in 1865 Plant had appointed him to the board of directors of the National Bank of Augusta.[16]

Arriving in Georgia from New York State in 1859, Bullock became a lifelong resident—hence, no carpetbagger. But neither was he a scalawag, purely speaking. To the heightened regard of his associates in the Southern Express Company, he had served with distinction as a Confederate officer in the Quartermaster Corps. After the war, however, he unhesitatingly cast his fortunes in with Georgia's radical Republicans, the political wing of the Reconstruction interests.[17] Still, Rufus B. Bullock was regarded by his enemies as no worse than a "scamp" even in the bitterly fought governor's race of 1868. With overwhelming black support, he edged out a revered Civil War hero running on the Democratic ticket, General John B. Gordon.[18]

Before long General Gordon would develop railroad interests that were to coincide directly—on paper at least—with those of Henry Plant, and possibly with those of Henry Flagler too.[19] If he had wanted to make a quick fortune and retire to Branford, what could have been easier for Plant than to get in on the railroad bonanza during the two years of the Bullock administration?

---

[14] Foner, Reconstruction, 386.
[15] Foner, 299.
[16] Dutcher, 359.
[17] Cashlin, *Story of Augusta*, 301.
[18] Foner, 332. Wynes, *History of Georgia*, 212-13.
[19] "Great Southern Railway."

Nothing better illustrated his commitment to fiscal responsibility and to the people of the South. Right along, and for years to come, he would conceal an avid interest in railroads and he would play no part in politics. In that respect the requirements of his balancing act were perfectly clear. Through the early 1870s, railroads in Georgia were politics—the politics of exploitation, retaliation, and favoritism.[20]

—o—

Perhaps the key to Henry Plant's survival in the South while hanging onto his Yankee identity had always been a resolutely blind eye to politics. The key to his success though, had been a preternaturally bright eye for the long-range prospect and for the speck of that misty disturbance in an otherwise cloudless future which signals the brewing of a horrific storm. Or now, in his immediate future, twin storms, twin disasters.

The first was the certain and, in many ways, tragic doom of the support and the aims of Reconstruction. All through the Confederate period there had been pockets of Union loyalists in the South. Many of these were stern folks who vigorously opposed the true disloyalists, the scalawags. As well, they cooperated with the best legitimate efforts of Reconstruction, defined as "the movement" of its day. For some Yankees had come south not to enrich themselves, but to enrich others, that is to foster the ultimate benefits of abolitionism. Old Dixie would not experience such a flood of northern idealists again until the civil rights crusades of the 1960s. As a result of the work done before 1877 by people of good will, a few of the most outrageous plans of the bigots, such as to maintain a school system wherein "the Negro receives only the crumbs from our table," were at least mitigated.

Henry Plant's interests were economic, however, and the main legacy of Reconstruction in the South, he could see, was going to be economic rapine. But what of looting's opposite, investment? In 1864 Virginia's governor had issued a desperate call for northern capital. That call was still ringing. By early 1871, Tom A. Scott, president of the Pennsylvania Railroad, had assembled a group of fellow Yankee investors committed to the recovery of southern railroads. The group's only passably southern member—by virtue of his time spent as a resident of Augusta—was Henry Plant. Their plan was to buy up and consolidate the ruined and fragmented

---

[20] Wynes, 207-37. Stover, "Northern Interests," 210.

railroad system between Virginia and Georgia with a view to long-range development.[21] The wisdom of the "southern" member would have reinforced the agenda. Those now associating themselves with short-term developments had best prepare themselves, well, to be around for the short-term. Even a man with all the good luck of Rufus Bullock had not won the 1868 election by that much, had he? The stormy after-effects of Reconstruction would be around for a long, long time.

There was bound to be another storm too, larger, and of greater if briefer intensity. Every day, in his office at Southern Express, and in hotel lobbies and dining rooms, Henry Plant listened to wild and true tales of Reconstruction's boondoggles. But news came, too, of real-world accomplishments. Despite mismanagement and outright pillage, railroads were being built—740 miles of new track in Georgia by 1872. It was now possible to make the trip Washington-Jacksonville in 2-1/2 days. And in Florida, no less, under the promotion of a well-known politico, David Levy Yulee, 140 miles of track had been laid and were almost ready for use.[22]

Putting the two together, the boondoggles and the accomplishments, one had to ask, "Where was the money coming from?" With access to the telegraphic messages pouring into and out of New York City every day on the lines of the Adams Express Company, to say nothing of the actual "finance" itself being transported—a shrewd enough person knew well enough—from the banking empire of Jay Cooke, the ultimate big-money operator. Given a kind of telescopic bright eye for economic bad weather, one also knew that, in the summer of 1873, just a speck now, the worse storm of the century was out there on the horizon.

It struck on a Tuesday, September 18th, ever after, Black Tuesday. The House of Cooke collapsed in one swift rush. On Wednesday, across the continent, banks were barricading their doors against mobs of angry depositors. By the end of the week, in cities and towns everywhere across the USA, shops and businesses stood empty. Soon the Panic of 1873 would go global, and would last for years.

The big express outfits weathered the storm far better than most.[23] The volume of business declined drastically, true. But the minimal confidence stayed alive that, in the USA at least, lemonade stands would open up on the Day of Judgment.

---

[21] C.K. Brown, "Security Company," 159-62. Stover, "Southern Empire," 30-37.
[22] Hoffman, *Great Railroad*, 36.
[23] Harlow, *Old Way Bills*, 300.

In the USA, somehow, goods and communications would still move steadily through the catastrophes of war and the least euphemistic of economic "downturns."

Nowhere, though, were times harder than in the South, and desperate times produce desperados. So tempting were coffers at the Southern Express offices that branch managers had to literally fight back a recurrent a crime wave to stay in business. The Texas Express had become a prime target, too, for would-be robbers. By 1873, agency's business had proliferated so rampantly across the Lone Star State that president A.B. Small took charge full time, moving from New Orleans to Houston and relinquishing his superintendent's duties with Southern Express. Two years later, when Small died suddenly, Plant took his place as president. He would continue to manage the company as a separate branch until 1880, when Texas Express was officially merged into the Southern Express Company. By then Henry Plant was focusing his attentions increasingly on the southeast, ready to make his move into into Florida.[24]

> **NOTICE**
>
> Sundry attempts have been made to Rob the agents and managers of funds entrusted to the company for transportation; and inasmuch as it is believed by the management that SIMILAR ATTACKS are likely to be made in the future, it has been determined to require all agents and messengers, when in charge of property belonging to the publis, TO ARM THEMSELVES with REVOLVERS and other means of PROTECTION in order to DEFEND THEMSELVES and said property; and should such defense result FATALLY to the WOULD-BE ROBBERS the company will undertake to protect such messengers or agents from the consequences of their justifiable act and SUITABLY REWARD THEM FOR THEIR SUCCESS. BE WAKEFUL! BE WATCHFUL! BE VIGILANT!
>
> Michael J. O'Brien
> General Superintendent
> Southern Express Company
> December 18th, 1875

When the time came, the express business was going to help him make that move in more ways than one. Besides being an unfailing source of revenue, Southern Express was a source of lasting good will. In bad times the company was often the closest thing the hard-pressed people of the south had to an angel of mercy. When yellow fever epidemics struck coastal Georgia in 1876, Savannah and Brunswick would have been isolated save for Plant's decision to bring in supplies and medical aid—free of charge. And it was hazardous work, in the fever zone. Expressmen reported to the area on a volunteer basis. When one young husband died, Plant set up an endowment for the family. Donations were given in the name of Southern Express after the epidemic had passed. For such works Henry Plant would receive the first of the many gracious public testimonials that would honor him for the rest of his life. The company as well might benefit directly. In

---

[24] Johnson, "Southern Express," 226.

Brunswick, for instance, the city council rescinded all Southern Express's taxes and fees for 1876-77.[25]

—o—

Twelve years before, the most casualty-producing battlefield war in human history had ravaged the Deep South, leaving in its wake uncounted civilian casualties. "The March to the Sea" was a fifty-mile-wide mobile atrocity passing through the heartland of Georgia, led by a supreme master in the arts of organized terror and destruction—along the route, charred and bullet-riddled buildings were still common well into the 1910s. To make matters just a little worse for Georgia's railroads, the cotton crop had failed at a critical time. That was in 1871, when the Yankee investors, headed by Tom Scott of the mighty Pennsylvania, began hunting for bargains in southeastern railroad securities.

Among American executives of the time, Tom Scott was matched only by Henry Flagler for innovative corporate planning. ("Henry Flagler had all the ideas that started the Standard Oil Company," recited John D. Rockefeller, under federal indictment.) The Southern Railway Security Company, chartered in Pittsburgh by Scott's shadowy operatives on March 22, 1871, was thirty years ahead of its time, a purely holding company.[26] In its own best words, "The object and purpose of this organization is to secure the control of such Southern railroads as may be essential to the formation of through-lines between New York, Philadelphia, Washington City, and the principal cities of the South, by the ownership of the capital stock of said companies, by leases, and by contract relations."[27]

Right up to Black Tuesday, 1873, how could anyone miss, bargain-hunting for railroads in the southeast? An awesome brain trust had been gathered into "Tom Scott's Company." In terms of power, behind Scott stood the wealthy flour merchant, banker, and philanthropist from Baltimore, Benjamin F. Newcomer, who was a founder of the railroad that was evermore steadily dominating the route between New York and Charleston, the Atlantic Coast Line.[28] Others, who sat on the SRSC board, presided over by James Roosevelt of Hyde Park, New York, were George W. Cass, Pittsburgh; J.D. Cameron, Philadelphia; Morris Jesup, NYC; and Henry Plant, NYC.[29]

---

[25] Johnson, 238
[26] Brown, 160-70. Stover, 30-37.
[27] Brown, 169.
[28] *Baltimore*, 165-69.
[29] Hoffman, 23-5.

Though congenial fellows, so astute a group of financial thinkers never expected to take a bath together. But they would. Their financial statement for May 1, 1873 lists liabilities to the tune of $8,269,084.65. The Southern Railway Security Company proposed to stay afloat on a $3,000,000 bond issue, but had no takers. Hastily Scott came to the rescue with a series of cash advances and credit schemes. Then his stockholders formed an Investigating Committee to announce that the "illegitimate direction given to the funds and credit of the Pennsylvania Railroad cannot be approved."[30]

Henry Plant, though, would take a lesson. Within a few years he thoroughly discussed his plans with trusted friends, particularly with Henry Sanford and with his recent bath-mate, Benjamin F. Newcomer. These two joined him in forming the Southeastern Investment Company, chartered in Connecticut. There would be eight more original members, reflecting the founder's background and values—three New England businessmen; three Southern businessmen; and two family members, Plant's step-brother, H.P. Hoadley, and Ellen Plant's older brother, Lorenzo Blackstone. With headquarters at 12 West 23rd Street in Manhattan, PICO would be a company of doing, not holding. A close observer reported, "Mr. Plant and his friends have money to invest. When they decide on a thing to do, build a piece of railroad for instance, they figure out what each one is to pay and send in their checks for that amount. They have no bonds, no debts, and no interest to pay. They build railroads to operate them."[31]

As for the Southern Railway Security Company, all records after 1873 have disappeared. Its liquidation proceeded slowly, as slowly as possible, and was not complete until 1878.[32]

—o—

Later in life Henry Plant would be unable to resist the lure of membership in another prestigious brain trust, the seemingly omnipotent Richmond and West Point Terminal Company, but from his experience with "Tom Scott's Company" he had developed a keen ear for the sound of running water. Given a second chance, he would absent himself in time, just before one of the most ruinous baths in American economic history.

Basically the 1873-78 experience reinforced his instincts in two important areas, geography and financial management. The Southern Railway Security Company

---

[30] Brown, 167.
[31] Johnson, "Plant and Florida," 119-20.
[32] Brown, 169.

had gone broke chiefly due to a stubborn investment in building a line between Charlotte and Atlanta. This attempt had violated the company's original intention, which was to concentrate on the coastal corridor. To Henry Plant's mind from then on was the maxim "if you were going to build a railroad in the south, whenever possible build it on the north-south axis." And build it yourself. Another SRSS violation had been the first principle of a holding company, to eschew "operations." But, in the South, pure financial management obviously would not hold up. If he was going into the railroad business, he must find someone he could trust to take charge of operations—to stand beside him in the daily business of running the railroad. No doubt he had already found that person well before 1878.[33]

In the early 1860s, Henry Stephen Haines had been the general superintendent of a railroad line between North and South Carolina. Born and raised in Nantucket, Massachusetts, he could easily pass for a Connecticut Yankee. But his parents were Southerners. During the war Colonel Haines had been in charge of maintaining military transportation service in the Carolinas. Only a handful of top-level railroad men had anything to compare with the breadth of his experience. He could lay track, run an engine, mend a boiler, issue a payroll, and balance the books—all in the same morning. What was more, no one dreamed that his title might be honorary. Colonel Haines was a leader of men. No matter what their conditions had been or were, men working under him worked hard, worked fast, and made no mistakes.

After the war Haines took on the resurrection of one of Georgia's leading basket case railroads, the Atlantic & Gulf, which had begun in 1847 as the Savannah, Albany & Gulf. Originally intended to connect Georgia's coastal and southern regions with New Orleans via Pensacola and Mobile, its far more modest claim to glory had been to provide access to the Gulf of Mexico, from a terminal at Bainbridge, down the Flint River to Apalachicola. In the tumultuous Reconstruction years, while rebuilding the 250-mile-long original line, Haines contrived to keep a trickle of short-distance revenue coming in. In 1868, he persuaded management to purchase a branch line connecting directly with the plantations of the Florida Black Belt, and rebuilt it too.

Henry S. Haines was not a man to boast. But he had given the Atlantic & Gulf Railroad six years of the hardest work he knew how to give. Come the start of 1871, he pretty well told everyone in the transportation business in Georgia to stand aside. He had brought the dead back to life, his miracle was coming. Then the cotton crop failed.[34]

---

[33] Kennedy, "Running a Locomotive," 86-93. Johnson, "Plant's Lieutenants," 388-9.

Still, he hung on grimly for six more years, even through the Panic of 1873. During those years there were no improvements, no replacements, hardly even any repairs, properly speaking. Just cannibalizing the junkyard, more solder, more wire, more rope and twine. On April 22, 1878, the Atlantic & Gulf Railroad went into receivership. Everyone associated with running the company left with their pockets turned inside out. First mortgages had soared to $2,710,000; second mortgages, to $1,400,000. Claims were on file for broken contacts, unpaid bills, missing property, assorted damages. Laborers' liens alone amounted to $100,000. And before the battered old line could be auctioned off, accountants and lawyers submitted their bill for closing the books, $251,000.[35]

The sale was held in Savannah on November 4, 1879, at twelve noon on the steps of the Custom House. At mid-morning spectators were already milling about on the sidewalk. By 11:30, more than six hundred had gathered. Had anyone ever seen anything like this before? But where was he? Where was he? Then, just moments before a marshal stepped forward to read the public notice, broad-shouldered Colonel Henry Haines appeared and at his side, a pleasant, calm, purposeful gentleman in a black frock coat. The crowd parted to let them through. When Colonel Haines started forward, the calm-looking gentleman restrained him, pleasantly. The doors had opened and the marshal, Captain Anderson, now stood at the top of the steps. As Anderson began to read aloud, in his clear and distinct voice, many kept their heads turned and their eyes on Colonel Haines's companion. Some were still whispering his name, though everyone knew of him—Mr. H. B. Plant of the Southern Express Company. Everyone knew that Mr. Plant had come to buy the railroad. Soon his attorney, Judge Walter Chisholm, joined him.

Captain Anderson announced:

> In accordance with the decree of the United States Circuit Court, the railroad running south from the city of Savannah to Bainbridge, with a branch to the Savannah River, a branch to the tracks of the Central Railroad and Banking Company and the Charleston and Savannah Railroad Company [sic] and a branch to Live Oak, in the state of Florida; together with all depots, wharves, lands, buildings, structures, rolling stock, property, privileges and franchises thereunto belonging or in anywise appertaining, the same being known as the Atlantic and Gulf Railroad, its property, franchises, and equipments.[36]

---

[34] Covington, *Plant's Palace*, 48.
[35] Johnson, 119. Knetsch.
[36] *Savannah Morning News*, November 5, 1879.

Another report from the *Savannah Morning News* continued:

The sale was then commenced, the first bid being $50,000, which slowly, and with increased bids of $25,000 each, built up to $275,000, the bidders being confined to Mr. H.B. Plant and Captain John McMahon. When $275,000 had been reached, Captain Anderson dwelt for some time and it was thought that it would possibly be knocked down at this figure, when an additional $5,000 was offered and the bid was declared to be $280,000. It then ran up to $290,000, $295,000, and finally $300,000. At this juncture Gen. A.B. Law, one of the attorneys in the case, stepped forward, Marshal Anderson retiring slightly, and read the following for the information of the bidders.

Inasmuch as the decree requires that any bid of $300,000 or more, the sum of $300,000 in cash, or its equivalent, shall be paid by the bidder before the property is knocked down to him, the last bidder is required to have a conference with the receivers and their counsel for a few minutes, during which time the bidding shall be suspended.

After a brief absence the gentlemen returned the last bid being $300,000. Captain Anderson dwelt on this bid some time, and finding there was no prospect of an increase, closed the sale at that figure, Mr. H.B. Plant becoming the purchaser. The amount obtained under the circumstances, we learn, is considered a fair figure.

We understand that Mr. Plant [and friends] had secured most of the outstanding second mortgage bonds, and hence there are few holders of the latter concerned in the sale. We learn that during the last summer Mr. Plant [had] purchased a large quantity of these bonds in New York, some being bought as low as ten cents on the dollar.

From the *Savannah Morning News*, November 11, 1879:

The property of the Atlantic and Gulf Railroad Company having been delivered by receivers on Tuesday last, as previously stated, to their successors, the Savannah, Florida and Western Railway Company, the President, H.B. Plant, issued his first general order, announcing that Col. H.S. Haines, general superintendent, would at once take charge.

From the *Savannah Morning News*, December 4, 1879:

ATLANTIC AND GULF RAILROAD NIGHT EXPRESS
Leave Savannah daily at ... 4:30 PM
Arrive at Jessup at 7:00 PM
Arrive at Thomasville at 8:35 PM
Arrive at Albany at 10:45 AM

> Arrive at Live Oak at 2:00 AM
> Arrive at Tallahassee at 7:00 AM
> Arrive at Jacksonville 7:50 AM
> Palace sleeping cars run through to and
> from Savannah and Jacksonville.

—o—

Two conflicting theories attempt to account for this, Henry Plant's first railroad purchase.[37] According to one, he simply intended to make a quick profit on the second mortgage bonds; then Colonel Haines talked him into staying. According to the other, Plant had secured support well in advance from someone who shared his own habitual enthusiasm for the long haul, the New York financier Morris K. Jesup.

In either case, following the auction, Plant's major partner in the sale, the City of Savannah, was in court vigorously defending the validity of the transaction. When the trial wound up quickly the City's favor, coastal Georgia's north-south railroad, the Savannah & Charleston, immediately entered the courtroom and declared bankruptcy.[38]

Henry Plant had his eye on those proceedings, most definitely. He had placed an order with a Wilmington, Delaware, shipyard for an iron-hulled steam packet grossing 288 tons, the *H.B. Plant*, a side-wheeler destined for service on the St. Johns River.[39] Down on Lake Monroe, Henry Sanford must have been clasping his hands together. By steamboat to Jacksonville and Savannah, by rail to Charleston—halfway there!

Then, what had Henry Plant's main actions been, on acquiring the Atlantic & Gulf? First, to authorize an initial stock offering of 20,000 $100-par shares and to claim 19,482 for himself.[40] Next, to appoint Judge Walter S. Chisholm vice-president and invite his old friend Henry Sanford to join the board of directors. Finally, to change the name: the Savannah, Florida & Western.[41] And from then on, his major concern with respect to running the railroad would be simply this—running

---

[37] Covington, 48. Hoffman, 24.
[38] *Savannah Morning News*, December 6, 1879.
[39] Mueller, *Steamboats*, 187-88.
[40] Hoffman, 55.
[41] Johnson, 122.

it to Florida. Ever afterwards he would proclaim this intention, and its fulfillment. Ten years later, the first of the two fabulous Plant System Special Cars 100 would carry the name of the Savannah Florida & Western.[42]

—o—

Obviously the "Night Express" to Florida entailed going the long way around. On the "Fast Mail," the 115 road miles between Savannah and Jacksonville via the Live Oak connection became 375 roundabout miles, entailing four different railroad lines. Why not a more direct route? A possible route existed on the drawing board, via Waycross, Georgia. And Henry Plant already had a firm foothold in Jacksonville.[43] On December 23, 1879, he capitalized the six-mile-long Jacksonville Street Railway, with its fifteen double-platform cars, at $20,000, and appointed Henry Haines its president. In 1880 Plant began conferring with Drs. Folks and Lott whose East Florida Railway Company held the charter from Waycross to a spot on the St. Mary's River directly across from Jacksonville. Before the year was out, he purchased this charter. For some time Florida citrus growers, such as Henry Sanford, had been petitioning the state legislature for trans-border railroad rights. Oranges traveled great distances poorly in horse-drawn wagons. Unfortunately for the future of the citrus growers, powerful interests, principally the steamboat lobby, had long discouraged railroad activity anywhere near the state line. The Atlantic & Gulf's route to Live Oak had been a Civil War "military necessity."

Developments in Tallahassee had been promising, though, as of 1879. A bill had passed authorizing an east-west connection with the grandiose Texas & Pacific Railroad Company. Consideration was being given to an even more grandiose plan, hatched in Georgia—a coastal railroad to Key West! With, as a bonus, an east-west branch line, from Palatka to Tampa.[44] But by now the steamboat lobby had been buttressed by populist elements of the resurgent Democratic Party. The leader of these "white wiregrass" Democrats was a charismatic and hardheaded state senator, Wilkinson Call, destined to be the sharpest thorn in Florida politics for many years. A repentant Whig, Call implacably opposed all forms of land grants.

---

[42] Beebe, *Mansions on Rails*, 166.
[43] Hurst, *Magic*, 105. *Jacksonville City Directory*, 1887. Mann, *Rails*, 66-7. *Orderboard*, 7. Phillips, *Cotton Belt*, 359-61. Taylor and Neu, *Railroad Network*, 43.
[44] Corliss, "Overseas Railway," 4.

But in the crucial 1880 campaign for governor, Florida's voters would choose the pro-railroad "Bourbon" Democrat, William Bloxham, a plantation owner and Civil War hero. Well before he took office, Bloxham was actively working to settle the Vose Injunction. Soon—secretly—he would be packing his bags and traveling to Philadelphia.

While on the south shore of Lake Monroe, on January 10th, 1880, ex-President General Ulysses S. Grant lifted a ceremonial shovel of dirt. Shortly thereafter, Henry Sanford helped build a little narrow guage railroad to the "empire city" of Kissimmee.[45] Insiders now had good reason to believe that Sanford's dream might be coming true. If young Hamilton Disston were to acquire substantial acreage in this region, generous land grants would be in order.

Governor William D. Bloxham took office January 4, 1881. The same winter, Colonel Henry Haines was laying track south, from Waycross, Georgia. And that spring Henry Plant bought the bankrupt Savannah & Charleston Railroad at auction for $320,000.[46] This sum included the securities of the company through the participation of other well-known railroad financiers who received shares in the new company, the Charleston & Savannah. In addition to Plant himself (400 shares), the beneficiaries of this arrangement were W.T. Walters (225), Morris K. Jessup (125), Thomas K. Jenkins (125), and B. F. Newcomer—Plant's old friend from the earlier watery experience in "Tom Scott's Company"—(200).[47]

By this time Newcomer, in alliance with his fellow Baltimore railroader, W.T. Walters, who had formed the Atlantic Coastline Company, a syndicate that would take over where the Southern Railway Security Company had left off.[48] They invited Plant and Jessup to join them as trustees. Soon Henry Plant sat on the board of a number of ACL mainstays: the Northeastern Railroad Company, the Richmond & Danville, and the Wilmington & Weldon—this last with S.M. Shoemaker, his colleague from the Adam Express years. The Atlantic Coast Line's insightful historian, Dr. Glen Hoffman, notes Plant's future "participation in the financial control of the Coast Line roads."[49]

Dr. Hoffman adds:

> Henry Plant was aiding Walters and Newcomer in their efforts to cement the Coast Line roads into an effective trunk line from Richmond

---

[45] Pfeifauf, "Local Railroads."
[46] Hoffman, 56.
[47] Hoffman, 43, 56.
[48] Hoffman, 45-6
[49] Hoffman, 54.

to Charleston; and they and Jessup were helping Plant to extend a system of connecting roads below Charleston into Georgia and Florida. Walters and Newcomer retained predominant voice in the roads north of Charleston; Plant assumed control of acquisitions south of Charleston. Continued cooperation was assured, however, by Plant's large interest in the Northeastern, and by Walter's and Newcomer's heavy investment in the Charleston & Savannah. The route to Florida was financially interlocked at Charleston.[50]

—o—

By now this new member of America's railroad royalty had accepted delivery of the steam packet *H.B. Plant*, and stationed her in Savannah harbor.[51] Margaret had been occupied with furnishing their stateroom for some time, and now they settled into what would become a semi-permanent maritime residence. Right away, life aboard an elegant steamboat suited Margaret down to the waterline. As for young Morton, he was in heaven at last.

Whereas, the steamboat people figured the *H.B. Plant* for a hedge bet in case the legislature turned down the cross-border railroad permit. Mr. H.B. Plant was often to be seen in Tallahassee. These days ever at his side was a young lawyer down from Georgia. His name was Robert Erwin, and he would be at Plant's side pretty much from then on. Their affinities went way back. Born in Savannah in 1854, Erwin had taken himself off for some Connecticut Yankee exposure at Henry Sanford's old school, Trinity College in Hartford. Back home, he was good enough to be asked into partnership with Judge Walter Chisholm.[52]

When the Florida legislature did deny the permit, though, in the winter of 1881, did Plant so much as notice? He seemed more calmly determined than ever. Over on the panhandle, the Southern Express Company had raised its tariffs 60 percent. Protests were spreading like wildfire. Plant left it all in the capable hands of the newly appointed district manager, M.J. O'Brien.[53] He was busy himself on the outskirts of Jacksonville with Henry Haines, who was building what looked like a huge dock on the St. Mary's River and laying East Florida Railway track toward it. Then they were building something on the other side. Why, it looked like another big dock, wearing iron trestle like a bonnet. Come April, the old-timers on the waterfront were shaking their heads in somber earnest. Might be the grounds

---

[50] Hoffman, 57.
[51] Mueller, 187-88
[52] Johnson, "Plant's Lieutenants," 384-5. Mueller, 6.
[53] Johnson, "Plant and Florida," 122.

for official complaint pretty soon, a hazard to navigation, if they kept building like that, into the river. Overnight the "docks" joined and track was laid across. From the Jacksonville *Floridian*, April 26, 1881:

"At twenty-five minutes past noon yesterday, the track-layers on the Waycross-Jacksonville Short Line met on the north side of Boggy Bottom, about six miles from Callahan and 25 miles from Jacksonville, and the last spike, a solid silver one, was driven, which completed the long desired all-rail short line. At 3:42, the first passenger train passed over the new connection, and, at four o'clock, the President's car passed over. Two solid Magnolia crossties, in which are driven eight brass spikes, mark the connection at Boggy Bottom."

VIPs in Florida and Georgia received engraved invitations signed by H.B. Plant and H.L. Haines:

Dear Sir: The management takes pleasure in notifying you of the opening of this line through between Charleston, Savannah, and Jacksonville. You are respectfully invited, with the privilege of being accompanied by a lady, to take a trip over the East Florida Railway and its connections between Charleston, Savannah, and Jacksonville, at any time that may suit your convenience during the next thirty days. Please present the enclosed pass to the conductor.[54]

Florida was now on the East Coast railroad corridor. In December of 1882, the famous new "fast mail," the Atlantic Coast Line's train No. 40, could bring you from New York to Jacksonville in 36-1/2 hours.[55] The great authority on the history of Florida railroads, George W. Pettingill, explains the consequences of what had been the strategy all along, "The soundness of Mr. Plant's reasoning was obvious the major portion of the traffic-flow shifted northward from the state by rail, rather than follow the eastward route through Jacksonville, which entailed an ocean connection with the cities of the North."[56]

By now Henry Sanford's community on Lake Monroe numbered more than 1,000 and boasted America's southernmost inland sportsmen's hotel. One fine day

---

[54] Hoffman, 58.
[55] Hoffman, 58.
[56] Pettengill, *Florida Railroads*, 64.

When paved roads lay far in the future, only the coming of the railroad could bring prosperity to the vast agricultural region between Jacksonville and Fort Myers. It was more than a dream of glory that Henry Plant's railroads might come across the state line from Georgia. It was a matter of survival.

out on Lake Monroe, a guest caught 140 pounds of lunker black bass. And the promises had just begun:

FLORIDA for
Tourists, Invalids, and Settlers
containing
Practical Information
regarding
Climates, Soil, and Productions, Cities, Towns, and People;
The Culture of the Orange and Other Tropical Fruits;
Farming and Gardening; Scenery and Resorts;
Sport; Routes of Travel, Etc., Etc.

Three miles from Sanford is Belair, the special grove of the General, a fine estate of one hundred and twenty-five acres, all fenced and under the highest cultivation. Here are thousands of orange, lemon, and lime trees, and pineapple plants, including every known variety of these, and hundreds of other foreign and native tropical plants, fruits, and shrubs. A visit thither is very interesting, and a cordial welcome is extended to all.

Indian corn, sugar cane, cotton, tobacco, rice, strawberries, cabbages, tomatoes, watermelons, and all garden products yield immense crops in the soil around Sanford.[57]

—o—

On February 26, 1881, Hamilton Disston signed an agreement with trustees of the State of Florida.[58] At the top of a daunting list of commitments, he would drain a large part the Everglades at his own cost in return for 12,000,000 acres of the exposed land. Henry Sanford had already covered his wager and was negotiating with buyers in London. No matter. On May 27, Florida's specially appointed land agent, Samuel Swann, sent a telegram from New York to his superiors. He had secured an $110,000 binder from a British syndicate prepared to pay forty-cents an acre for 1,000,000 acres of public land. Still, no matter. No matter that Swann had worked on his own for months and was out some $40,000 in salary and expenses. Even as his telegram reached Tallahassee, Governor Bloxham was returning from a clandestine trip to Philadelphia. On May 30, he let the state trustees know that before leaving he had instructed Attorney General George P. Raney to draw up a contract—and here it was! Signed by Hamilton Disston! Four million acres at twenty-five cents an acre. What with Sanford's extra bet and Swann's unpaid work, the long-hated Vose Injunction was now better than doubly dead.

—o—

A life-giving miracle occurred across Henry Plant's corner of the Southeast in the years 1881-83.[59] In the opening round of a major revival of railroad construction, the Savannah, Florida & Western struck out toward the Florida panhandle. From Climax, Georgia, a branch led to the Chattahoochee & East Pass Railway; another to the L&N's east-west oriented railroad, the Pensacola & Atlantic. Both junctions provided access to the Gulf down the Flint River to Apalachicola. Next, creating the Live Oak & Rowlands Bluff Railroad, Plant headed due south into

---

[57] Barbour, "Florida for Tourists."
[58] Williamson, 74.
[59] Johnson, "Plant and Florida," 226. "Orderboard," 7. Turner, *Short History*, 59. Turner, *Southwest Florida*, 9-10.

Florida, toward the Suwannee River. From there, at Rowlands Bluff, his steamboat, *Cato Belle*, offered freight and passenger service to Cedar Key. At the same time, in ever-renewed pursuit of his master plan to reach central Florida's Gulf Coast region by an all-rail route, he aimed an extension from Dupont, Georgia, toward the territory below Gainesville, ambitiously naming it the Live Oak, Tampa & Charlotte Harbor Railroad. Progress in this direction, however, quickly generated a major conflict of interests. The Florida Southern Railroad, under the direction of wealthy New England businessmen, was at work on a line, Palatka-Gainesville-Ocala. The genial "Southern Yankee," however, soon turned what might have been a long-time acrimonious dispute into a highly rewarding collaboration. And since the new concord would leave Lake City without a southbound connection, a special branch was built, Lake City-Fort White. When the tracks appeared to terminate ten miles south of their town, the citizens of Brooksville contributed $20,000 to insure an extension. Two years later, in 1885, with Plant at the helm, the South Florida Railroad built a line from Chubb (later Lake Alfred) to Bartow. This move facilitated a connection with the Southern Florida Railway, still mired in its attempt to reach Port Charlotte. And when Henry Plant did eventually acquire the Florida Southern outright, its young president, Franklin Q. Brown, would become one of his closest associates. Born in Chicago in 1854, Brown had graduated high school in Massachusetts.[60] A fabulous destiny awaited him in what would soon be the all-inclusive Plant System.

Henry Plant himself was going to spend a good part of 1881-82 traveling through the lands of the Disston Purchase. Quite a territory. What with the Everglades deal, the young man could lay claim to nearly half the state. The 4,000,000 acres he had bought outright formed an equilateral triangle that virtually was central Florida. To Plant's mind the choicest side of the triangle had to be the 250-mile-long western one, running from Marco Island in the south to above Tampa Bay. At least when he came to inspect the western area of the Disston Purchase in the summer and fall of 1882, that stretch would receive the best part of his daily buggy rides—going from town to town, ever cordial, always ready to meet with the local property owners, merchants, and community leaders. They all had their plans for betterment. They all knew he could help. They all had some big dreams they wanted him to share in.

His own dream he had always kept to himself—that old schoolhouse dream of treasure lands, far to the south. He had dreamed it often, stowing cargo for the Commodore. He had seen its reality, in miniature, during his days in the store by

---

[60] Johnson, "Plant's Lieutenants," 385.

the Long Wharf with old Mr. Washington Webb. He had often heard the dream spoken of, though by dreamers only, from his first days in the South, opening up the Gulf of Mexico and the Caribbean, bringing to the great cities of America and Europe "a desirable and immense trade, the fabulous and inexhaustible riches of the Great Amazon Valley."[61]

He had the means now, financial and otherwise. Cooperation with the Atlantic Coastline was producing an abundance of opportunity for all concerned. PICO, the Plant Investment Company, became fully operational in 1882. In April of that year he had signed a contract with the Pullman Palace Car Company to provide the latest line of sleeping and parlor cars for the Plant System.[62] He knew the main line was nearly complete. He was within just a few vital connections of establishing a southern terminus. When he found the right place for that terminus, for that all-important ending, he would make the old dream new, make it a reality. Then he could share the dream.

---

[61] Corey, *Confederate City*, 29.
[62] Hoffman, 59.

~ VIII

Deadline Railroad

The afternoon and evening of December 1, 1883, the citizens of Tampa held a gala banquet to honor Henry Plant at their one appropriate hotel, the Orange House—though more a boarding house than a hotel. They were celebrating what looked like a certain sure thing, Plant's gamble on the seven-month-deadline completion of the railroad link that would turn their dreary village into a great city. Somewhat astonishingly, according to record, Henry Plant never set foot in the most important locality of his financial career until he arrived for these festivities. Just as well, perhaps. In 1876 the poet Sidney Lanier had boarded at the Orange House for three months. He dismissed Tampa as "the most forlorn collection of one-story houses imaginable."[1]

The whole of settled Florida was little better than a "forlorn collection of one-story houses" in 1853, the year that Henry and Ellen Plant stopped over in Jacksonville. Though by Eastern standards a frontier outpost, the hardscrabble port on the Atlantic had been more than a settlement. Certainly Jacksonville was "connected."

Whereas Tampa, 120 miles southwest across a forbidding wilderness of swamp and scrub, seemed doomed to remain forever a settlement, altogether undeveloped and isolated, a tiny frontier of its own within the frontier. In that same year of 1853, a traveler forced to stop over had this to write home about, "Tampa is a small town, inhabited by the most worthless population in the world. They seem

---

[1] Sidney Lanier in Covington, *Plant's Palace,* 51

to be, well, the refuse of creation. Three or four lawyers, as many preachers, three stores—half a dozen grog shops, and these live on each other. I do not believe there is a dollar per head among them. They hate the sight of an honest man."[2]

Henry Plant prided himself on being an honest man. The location chosen for the Gulf Coast terminus of the Plant System railroads stood to benefit enormously. What had been Tampa's appeal?

Most likely, to begin with, Tampa had not been even a remote consideration. The obvious choice was simply too overwhelmingly the obvious choice, Cedar Key. Whenever it may have been that Henry Plant began giving serious consideration to a railroad link to the West Coast of Florida, Cedar Key, in terms of shipping and commerce, was the West Coast of Florida.

A tantalizing 180 miles of track stretched diagonally southwest across Florida from the Atlantic toward the Gulf, a stretch of track originally aimed at Tampa, indeed named with Tampa in mind. In the Rail Road Act of 1853 the state legislature proposed a line running from Fernandina, just north of Jacksonville, to "some point, bay, arm, or tributary of the Gulf of Mexico in South Florida." Subsequent legislation would be more specific. The Internal Improvement Act of January 1855 authorized a line to run "from Amelia Island on the Atlantic, to the waters of Tampa bay, in south Florida, with an extension to Cedar Key."[3] Subsequently David Levee Yulee obtained a charter for this line, naming it first the Florida Railroad, later Florida Transit.

This pair of pro-railroad bills, with exclusive emphasis on a southwest diagonal, had been assured passage thanks to the support of United States Senator David Levy Yulee, also the vice president of the Fernandina, Tampa & Key West Railroad. The last words in the operative phrase of the Internal Improvement Act must have held a particular and appealing fascination for him, "with an extension to Cedar Key." The Yulee family owned a significant portion of the island.

And a particular fascination for the tantalized citizens of Tampa, but an altogether unappealing one. For as the tracks of the railroad emerged from the dense scrub and tall pine woods of highland Florida and approached the Gulf, suspicions grew in the hungry little town 80 miles south that the Cedar Key "extension" was going to mean the Cedar Key "conclusion." Indeed, after some swift work in 1858, a mighty trestle spanned the bay waters to the island. Senator Yulee promptly arrived at the port to inaugurate a terminal for his railroad. Just as

---

[2] "Notes" in Canter Brown, "Tampa and the Railroad," 13.
[3] Brown, 13.

promptly, he proceeded to issue its bonds under a new and Tampa-less name, the Florida Transit & Peninsular.

When the news reached Tampa, the grog shops emptied. A wild and disheveled mob gathered on the sandy lot outside the courthouse. Before the night was done, they danced around a burning strawman that wore the familiar high collar and waistcoat of Senator David Levy Yulee.[4]

Whenever it was that the idea of a railroad connection to the Gulf of Mexico entered Henry Plant's mind, and he gazed on a map of Florida, he must have thoughtfully traced the route of the Florida Transit & Peninsular over and over again. If an investor wanted to find a going proposition that hadn't gone anywhere, look no further. But was the FT&P ever going anywhere? In the words of a later Tampa partisan, it had become "David Yulee's plaything." His other toy was the South Florida Railroad. Governor Reed offered the company a generous allotment of state bonds to establish a line between Waldo, near Gainesville, and Ocala, then on to Tampa. After laying a few miles of track in 1871, Yulee lost interest, or his nerve. Ultimately he declined to pay the $250 delivery fee for the bonds, which languished for two years inside a Jacksonville express office.[5] Meanwhile, the FT&P was languishing, too. In 1880 its books showed a loss of close to $112,000.[6]

On April 25, 1881, completion of the Waycross Shortline began a reign of dread, if not yet terror, in the boardroom of the FT&P. In his customary genial manner, Plant wrote David Yulee twice over that summer, attempting to interest him in the possibility of a steamship service between Cedar Key and Key West-Havana. Pointedly, however, he received no reply. To Yulee and his associates, Plant's presence in Jacksonville cast a shadow all the way across Florida to the Gulf. Yet a positive atmosphere prevailed when the two rivals met on November 1, 1881. By friendly arrangement, their rail systems would coexist side by side for the time, and even interchange passengers and freight.[7]

Popular legend has it that subsequent negotiations produced a conclusion far more favorable to the Plant System. A seemingly compliant FP&T lease prepared for Henry Plant's signature would give his railroad access to all David Yulee's

---

[4] Grismer, *Tampa* 128, 152. Harner, *Promoters,* 22-3.
[5] Shofner, *Nor Is It*, 251-2.
[6] Johnson, "Florida Railroad," 296
[7] Johnson, 299-300.

transportation facilities at Cedar Key. But the crucial issue in the transaction became clear only at the last moment: the Plant System might have access to all the Yulee facilities right up to the depot—and hence the port—at Cedar Key.[8]

Now, according to that popular legend, occurred the exception to a lifetime record of perfect equanimity. Plant erupted. "I'll wipe Cedar Key off the map! Owls will hoot in your attics and hogs will wallow in your deserted streets!"

News of the failed Cedar Key negotiations must have spread fairly rapidly. A number of potentially superb harbor facilities were situated further south, and soon Plant was giving serious consideration to three localities, Tampa, Bradenton, and Port Charlotte. In Bradenton two local businessmen, Warburton Warner and John S. Beach, envisioned a terminal on a tiny part of the Disston purchase, Snead Island, at the mouth of the Manatee River. Warner and Beach made the arduous journey to the offices of the Disston Land Company in Jacksonville and on November 23 bought 43 acres on Snead Island. Other local businessmen began to buy land there, too.

Henry Plant visited Bradenton in the winter of 1882-83 to look the situation over. Apparently, though, he would entertain the notion for a Snead Island terminal only if the investors agreed to put the whole island up for sale quickly, and at a reasonable price. Warburton Warner and John Beach must have scrambled desperately to persuade their real estate "partners" to seize this momentary opportunity.[9] But the deal fell through. Bradenton went on to enjoy a sleepy and countrified existence for almost another century.

During these early years of the 1880s, however, two opportunity-filled events would combine to create a development crucial to the future of Florida and the Southeast. The first was this. Sometime late in 1880 or early in 1881 Henry Plant and Henry Sanford, those two old friends and business associates, rode together by train from New York to Florida. A crisis was confronting each man, and the two crises neatly interfaced. The potentially thriving agricultural community Sanford had founded still lacked any adequate connection to its markets. Plant was being stymied in his master plan to provide a national, and even global, transportation system for Florida's produce. Clearly the two ambitious men had a lot to talk about.

We know of the entire development through the recollection of a bright young man, James Ingraham, who had come down to be a partner in Sanford's orange grove business in 1880. Almost immediately the bright young man, who liked

---

[8] Grismer, 171
[9] Warner, *Singing River,* 15

nothing more than an awesome challenge, began performing life support on the South Florida Railroad Company.

Ingraham recounts that[10] in February or early March of 1882, he and General Sanford were strolling down Bay Street in Jacksonville. Suddenly the general drew him up and nodded toward someone approaching on the other side of the street. Henry Plant, wearing a long black broadcloth coat and silk hat, drew near. Taking Ingraham's arm, Henry Sanford began crossing the street. "That is a man I think you ought to know," he said. "I rode with him on my last trip down from New York."

They all shook hands. "Mr. Plant, I'd like you to meet Mr. James E. Ingraham. Mr. Ingraham, this is Mr. Henry Plant."

Plainly the Gulf of Mexico connection had been uppermost in Plant's mind. His first words to James Ingraham were, "So you are the young man who's building a railroad from Sanford to somewhere in the south of Florida."

"Yes, Mr. Plant, we have a little narrow gauge railroad there and we feel quite proud of it. We expect to open that railroad to Kissimmee shortly—sometime early next week—and I should be more than glad to have you and your friends come down and be our guests at the opening."

Early the next week on the tree-shaded shore of Lake Monroe, Henry Sanford and James Ingraham, with their business partners, and all their wives, stood gathered together on the new city dock. Out on the dimly gleaming pale expanse, beneath a satiny plume of black smoke, a crisp white shape materialized. In a blast of snowy steam, its whistle blew them a greeting. It was the side-wheeler *H. B. Plant*, out of Jacksonville early that dawn.

They had been hearing the ritual steady call of commands drift across the water. Now, abruptly, the loud jangle of engine bells, abruptly silenced and slipping a little sideways, in all its tremendous power, the broad and suddenly towering vessel glided soundlessly toward them, only moments away from crushing the dock to splinters. Then the great wheel reversed with a roar, tossed and churned the water to a bulging fury. The ship's whole immense bulk quivered and suddenly subsided. Gliding by inches now, soundless again, the 228-ton structure of steel and timber bumped gently to the dock. Deckhands made the hawsers secure.

---

[10] Ingraham, "Mr. Plant," 27

Meeting the six-month deadline kept the *Henry P. Plant* as busy as its namesake hauling cargo desperately needed on construction sites and bringing fresh workmen, many of them with special skills, likewise desperately needed

While wavelets clambered about the pilings, the gangplank came down. Greeted by the little crowd ashore, Henry Plant, Margaret, Colonel and Mrs. Haines, and half a dozen guests disembarked.

James Ingraham recounted what happened next:

We boarded a brand-new train consisting of a parlor car, coach, and baggage car—the crew having blue uniforms and white gloves. Mr. Plant was visibly impressed with the outlying country, and after returning from Belleair called a conference, at which he asked, "What can I do for you, Mr. Ingraham, on this railroad project?"

"If you will give us connection on your river steamer, and secure for us through representation as to tickets and rates, I should be greatly obliged," I replied. Continuing, I said that it was my ambition to extend the railroad on to Tampa, and put on a line of steamers to Key West and Havana.

"Do you think your stockholders would sell an interest in this property?" to which I replied, "If you can see your way to purchasing, say, a three-fifths interest in the property, extending it to Tampa, eventually putting on a line of steamers, I am sure they would."[11]

And, after a stockholders meeting in Boston, such were the stipulations of the contract signed between officials of PICO and the South Florida Railroad.

It was as well this had been a gala excursion. Anyone exploring the region southwest of Kissimmee, especially anyone dreaming of a transportation empire between the Gulf of Mexico and the St. Johns River, would have been greeted by an ominous sight—a fifteen mile length of gravel and weeds extending straight through the wilderness—an abandoned roadbed exactly intended to connect the Gulf and the St. Johns. This corridor of desolation was the precariously owned property of the Jacksonville, Tampa and Key West Railroad. Early in 1882 the JT&KW had started grading the line from a point east of Tampa.[12] The work must have been underway even during Plant's timely meeting with Sanford and Ingraham in Jacksonville.

The JT&KW's major interest lay in the northern part of the line between Jacksonville and Sanford. Unfortunately their Tampa-Sanford charter had been a fatal golden apple, its stem a self-destructing fuse, still sizzling. The land-grant benefits were as generous as any ever offered at 10,000 acres per section. In the abortive attempt to claim these millions of acres that would have financed all the rest, the JT&KW had just about gone broke. Now, in the spring of 1883, the provision for completing the east-west line would expire in January of 1884.[13]

Accounts of what was to follow make the assumption that Henry Plant found out about the JT&KW's land-grant provision at some unspecified time after he bought the South Florida Railroad. Naturally he then preferred to obtain and use the lavish JT&KW charter, instead of the SFRR's, to build the Tampa-Sanford railroad.

Henry Plant obtained the Sanford-Tampa charter, by quit claim deed, from the negotiating officials of the JT&KW on May 4, 1883.[14] This transpired two months after his verbal agreement with Ingraham to purchase three-fifths of the SFRR. But why suppose that it was only during this "afterwards" that he became aware of the JT&KW's activities and benefits, and that he suddenly acted to

---

[11] Ingraham, 28.
[12] Grismer, 172.
[13] Brown, 16. Johnson, "Plant and Florida," 122.
[14] Grismer, 172.

improve his position then? So there is much to say that Plant and his PICO partners were making a series of impulsive and essentially uninformed decisions. In the light of all other Plant-PICO decisions, it seems far more plausible to view the SFRR and the JT&KW transactions as critical points in a pre-determined strategy. After all, was that lucky encounter on Bay Street in Jacksonville entirely fortuitous? On their train ride down from New York, Henry Plant and Henry Sanford doubtless took the opportunity to enjoy some rewarding discussions, and do some deep thinking together.

Early in 1883 Plant authorized negotiations between PICO and the JT&KW. Concerns vital to both parties were at stake. For the already thriving PICO, the lure of vastly increased profits and prominence, indeed total dominance of transportation systems in southwest Florida and throughout southern Georgia and Alabama loomed, while for the nearly bankrupt JT&KW, survival appeared to be at hand, at least temporarily. Soon a deal was arranged whereby PICO would finance the northern end of the JT&KW line, creating a source of seemingly suicidal competition for its steamboats in the St. Johns region. But, unperturbed, Henry Plant had clearly made some far-reaching plans. On May 4, 1883, he met with Alfred Parslow and paid $30,000 for the Tampa-Kissimmee franchise.[15] PICO officials had already begun drafting contractual arrangements for the creation of a major transportation facility in Tampa.[16] To other investors, and railroad men and engineers outside PICO, the deal looked like a reckless gamble at best. The seven-month deadline, to complete 74 miles of track, was going to be unbeatable. Surely, the word was, Henry Plant had missed by a long way his chance to buy the golden apple. He had paid a lot of good money for all that was left of it, the self-destructing fuse, burning fiercely now.

Meanwhile, the man Plant counted on to beat the deadline for him, Henry Haines, had been keeping fit. He was just east of Pensacola, "on loan" to a former CSA cavalry officer turned Florida railroad man, Colonel Willaim Chipley, supervising his own chosen team of skilled workers and a large gang of convict labor. News of the JT&KW deal reached Haines in his private railroad car, and by May 7, he had made preparations to bring his crew, minus the convict labor, to Tampa.[17] Obviously there would be no need for laborers right away. A shovel couldn't be lifted until the best line for the route had been selected. Haines sent his

---

[15] Grismer, 172.
[16] Brown, 16. Grismer, 173.
[17] Covington, 53.

experts into the field to join a crew of engineers, surveying under Captain Bill Kendrick's direction along the fifteen-mile JT&KW roadbed east of Tampa.

Indeed, in terms of labor, in terms of actually working on the Sanford-Tampa connection, the seven-month deadline amounted to a six-month deadline. All the equipment and supplies needed to start and finish the job on day one had to be amassed and made available without fail on the site of day one—tools, heavy equipment, material, and plenty of foodstuffs, fodder, and fresh water. Especially fresh water, since men and mules and oxen would be working all day in eighty- and ninety-degree weather.

Then day two, day three, day four. Each day's job site becomes a new "end of line," dependent on the previous day's work. Essentially the situation required a system of advancing supply depots. We might suppose that after a little serious planning everything would go like clockwork, and with a great deal of experience and hard work and good luck it might. Even so, the job sites could only be connected by freshly cleared trails, ready to become quagmires under every tropical cloudburst. Haines, of course, was scheduled to begin construction during the months of Florida's heaviest rains. Then, too, the men and animals that did the hauling were no stronger than forged chains and wooden axles. Mobile repair shops followed the supply depots. An approach to anything resembling Haines's previous records of progress put blacksmiths and wheelwrights to work around the clock.

The end-of-line situation meant a severely restricted workspace. Ordinarily, construction can be speeded by putting more workers on the job. Building a railroad with 19th century technology, however, meant that only a limited number of workers could be assigned to actually advancing the tracks.

Henry Plant was ready with two solutions to defeat this part of the deadline. The first was drastic. He would dearly have loved to build the railroad in standard gauge. But doing so would require more workers, more equipment, more time. He shouldered the expense of making the conversion later and went ahead with narrow gauge. Then, using his commonsense, he doubled the number of track-advancing workers by proceeding simultaneously, east-west and west-east, from railheads in Tampa and Sanford.

Both railheads could be serviced by water. In Savannah and Jacksonville supplies from New York, Baltimore, and Boston were already being warehoused, were piling up on the wharves. Day after day, at docks in Boston and New York, ships take on cargo labeled "PICO - FLORIDA." Orders for iron rods and heavy chain, kegs of nails and rolls of wire, and always for more and more rails and spikes, had been placed throughout the Northeast.

On July 5, PICO officials met with the Tampa City Council to sign a contract for the rights to a depot on the banks of the Hillsborough River at the foot of Polk, Zack and Twig Streets. The contract offered concessions so thoroughly favorable to PICO as to be a later source of political embarrassment and included a full waterway access on a five-year lease at $30 a year.[18] At its next meeting the council formally bestowed the JT&KW's southern franchise on PICO. Ten days later, on July 16, teams of skilled workers had been assembled. From the riverfront at Polk Street commenced a roar of noise—of hammering, sawing, shouting and general knocking and crashing—that would be ceaseless for weeks. Every manufactured item needed on the western extension had to come up the Hillsborough River. Everything depended on building the depot immediately. Then, on laying the tracks that would bear a locomotive and its freight of materials west, to immediately return and go west again. Every day, further and further west.

Already, though, Tampa had been experiencing a glut of human beings, animals, and material. Everything substantial had to arrive by sail brought on schooners and brigs out of New Orleans, Mobile, Pensacola, Cedar Key. All day, for weeks, stevedores piled up immense stacks of timber in the vacant lots by the river. The local sawmill, Jack Thomas & Son, had been geared up to meet an onslaught of demands, and guaranteed all the work they could handle for the next six months. Teamsters on mule wagons clattered down the dusty roads into town, ready to haul the hundreds of thousands of crossties to the end-of-line on the western extension. And from every point of the compass an army of cardsharps, whores, and pickpockets converged on the suddenly overcrowded little city. At night, gypsy peddlers camped on the streets, unprecedented mountains of garbage accumulated, dog packs roamed, scavenging animals multiplied, and raw sewage clogged the gutters. Long after the carpenters were done at the depot, the din of hammers and saws filled the increasingly insect-busy and malodorous air. Rows of gimcrack saloons, restaurants, lodging houses, shanties and stables appeared, hastily assembled by roving journeymen. And everywhere, everywhere, were large and small tents of gray canvas—temporary homes that remained for years. Tampa would be one of the great American boomtowns of the 1880s well before the railroad was nearly complete.

---

[18] Brown, 16.

And naturally the boomtown fever was catching. A typical case explained the overnight existence of the village to be known as Plant City.[19] Its founder, Judge Henry L. Mitchell, would become Florida's 16th governor. In 1858 Mitchell had been a leading promoter of the Florida Central & Peninsular Railroad, intended to complete the Tampa connection thwarted by David Yulee's treacherous "diversion"—only to be thwarted again by the Civil War.

As a youngster, Henry Mitchell had often hunted on a farm belonging to the John Thomas family, thirty miles east of Tampa. Now, in June of 1883, Henry Plant was aiming his railroad out that way. Somewhere east of Tampa, he would need a main supply depot and somewhere east of Tampa, in the same place, a major north-south spur. Tinhorn speculators could name you the spot, but a boom time meant that lots of folks would lose their money listening to such operators.

Quietly that summer, Judge Mitchell bought up forty acres of Thomas land, and in October, fifteen more. In early November surveyors arrived to plat that part of the former Thomas farm for a township. An announcement followed that the area was to be the site of an important north-south spur and the main depot for eastbound supplies. At first this suddenly bustling corner in the wilderness called itself simply, "End-of-Line," while waiting for a more distinguished inspiration. When it came, Henry—and especially Margaret—Plant would forever grimly ignore the abrogation of the family name, remote from the likelihood of fashionable possibilities.

Henry Mitchell's knowledge of the Tampa-Sanford route seems to have come on authority for which he was grateful. His town's east-west thoroughfares would be named for Plant System railroad officials, Mahoney, Reynolds, Drane, Haines, Ingraham, Renfro, Warren. After leaving the bench and the governor's office, Henry Mitchell became a corporate attorney with the Plant System.

Even for insiders, though, the route's progress was far from an exact science. Initially, work on the eastern extension went much more efficiently and rapidly than anything the Tampa end could hope for. Between Sanford and Kissimmee, SFRR trainmen kept the rolling stock rolling. Possibly not a drop of dew had been allowed to settle on those recently constructed tracks.

In mid-September, Jacksonville's *Times Union* reported what must have been an oft-repeated event, "The steamer *H. B. Plant* left for Sanford yesterday with every stateroom filled with passengers. Besides she carried up a large number of laborers for the South Florida railroad extension. She was also loaded down with

---

[19] Bruton and Bailey, *Plant City,* 84-87.

freight."[20] A locomotive patiently hissing steam and a chain of empty cars was waiting on south shore of Lake Monroe to take the laborers and supplies straight to the west end of the track.

James Ingraham and Henry Haines were typical of the men who built America, from down on the ground, out in the fresh - if often smoky - air. Largely self-educated, both mastered complex aspects of engineering, accounting, and the management of men and material. Life-long, they applied their skills tirelessly to the urgently required, grandest, and most challenging projects they could find. Meanwhile, the contributions of the stalwart and *ready* Plant system workmen were no less valuable.

—o—

The western end was nearly ready for its own full-scale assault on the deadline. On September 1, a schooner carrying the components of two locomotives arrived in Tampa Bay.[21] The heavy crates, unloaded onto smaller vessels, were taken

---

[20] *Jacksonville Times Union* in Mueller, 191.
[21] Mormino and Pizzo, *Treasure City,* 78.

ashore and dragged up the riverbank at the Polk Street landing. There, the foundation of the depot was solidly in place, and round-the-clock work commenced, assembling the first engine.

The work took nearly four days. At last, in the early hours of September 6, the graveyard shift tightened down the last bolt. Then resin-rich logs blazed up in the firebox, a flaming dance of scarlet and black. The water, cool at night in a maze of coiled brass tubing, heats, stirs, circulates and soon feeds the great vertical piston cylinders with explosive steam.

The engineer was ready. Wearing heavy leather gloves against the touch of hot steel, he mounts the cabin, sets himself at the controls and gently tests each one. A needle climbs the black numbers on a dial; when it pushes the red, he eases forward a lever. Instantly the whistle-pull cord dances a jig. His gloved hand takes it. Abruptly, and appropriately by the dawn's early light, what will be recorded as a mighty blast, in reality a mighty toot, arouses the citizenry.[22] Appropriately, too, each morning and throughout the day, for the first time, work at either end commenced and continued with the same clangorous, unabating shock. Each work crew, fully manned and fully supplied, was kept moving at one speed—full-steam ahead. And all the while it must have seemed that Colonel Henry Haines had become fearfully capable of appearing on both work sites at once, more driving and exacting than ever.

Through the terrible heat of the tropical September, east west, west east, with equal purposeful fury, the graded and graveled roadbed surged forward, and the crossties and tracks went down. But how to find, in time, and hire enough men to clear the brush and dig the ditches along the line? To cut the network of roadways that will connect the line with the countryside? Daily, within earshot and sight of the workers on the track—though a sight to be shunned—crews of convict laborers, in chains and under the lash, moved in the wilderness. The infamous convict lease system, was at work.[23] Keeping unskilled laborers on the job was management's most persistent headache in a time when the toil of an ordinary day meant bone-crushing exhaustion, and when a paycheck meant an alcoholic binge. But absenteeism was a contradiction in terms under the convict lease system. In a prison camp run for profit, bed-rest sickness did not exist, any more than compassion among the guards. A sick convict was easier to replace than a sick mule, and

---

[22] Winter, "Hell in Harness," 8.
[23] Mancini, *One Dies*. Powell, *American Siberia*.

a much greater burden to the system. Malingering was never more than an irritant. The foremen carried heavy whips and were experts in their use. The life-crippling threat of the turpentine camps would take care of the hard cases. Thus was the life of a prisoner caught up in this sytem.

Unless severe weather intervened, only daylight regulated the convicts' hours on the job. The implements of roadwork were deadly weapons. At the end of each task, the pickaxes and shovels, axes and brush cutters, would be counted and stacked, or laid in wagons, under the strictest supervision of the day.

Obviously, no necessity of a deadline would be worth the risk of marching a detachment of even "disarmed" convict laborers through the wilderness in the dark. The hired workers, however dead on their feet, might continue to lay track well into the night under lantern light and the illumination from the locomotive's headlamp. But at the sound of the supper whistle, the guards formed up their exhausted workers, counted them, and connected long chains through the ankle shackles. Shotguns ready, they herded the shuffling figures, awkward at first, along rutted-out pathways to the stockade.

They all know where they are going, its direction. They could hear the stockade from far off. A long wail followed from the kennels there when the whistle blew, and filled the woods with a heart-melting sweetness. Even while it lingered, though, an ever-louder cacophony of yelping and howling arose—and now the clashing of wire and wood—the bloodhounds, always nearly breaking loose. The pack could pull down and half kill a running man in seconds. The guards' own dogs answer, lurching against their leashes, but there was no whip for these.

They come to a clearing. The stockade looms ahead in the failing light. The ravishing crude odors wafting from the cookhouse competed with the fearful stench of the latrines. A tall gateway opens. They push through into the crescendo of the howling and barking, that only the new men heed. Then, instead of food, more formations and counting. Finally, too weary for speech, leg irons chained to logs, the convicts hunker down to a lantern-lit supper of salt pork and collards, black-eyed peas, cornbread and molasses; then quickly unfastened and marched off; to be fastened down again and locked up inside stifling barracks, alive with insects.

Because it required a special act of the Florida legislature in 1915 to exclude whites from the leasing system, we can assume that both black and white convicts were at work on the Tampa-Sanford railroad. Women, black and white, were eligible for other forms of labor under the system. But quite likely the stockades, and the actual work gangs, were segregated.

Certainly segregation was the policy among hired laborers. And, to judge by an incident that the media of the time held up as a classic example, separate was not equal. In August, far out on the eastern extension near Bartow, a crew of black workers walked off.[24] Or, put more accurately in the terms of the time, they "jumped their obligations by running away." If white workers had taken this recourse, they would have simply—in the terms of our time—walked after they jumped. Aside from the hardly cost-effective expense, the pursuers would look foolish, trying to chase down white laborers dressed like everybody else in an all-white rural area. On the other hand, escaped black workers were literally marked men. The Bartow escapees must have been extremely desperate and extremely resourceful, for they managed to elude capture for nearly twenty miles.

Henry Plant was a scrupulous manager and he may have had a fleeting knowledge of such an event. It only insignificantly affected the progress of his railroad, a routine item in a routine report, doubtless from Haines. Typical of the matters requiring Plant's full attention was the J.B. Gordon affair, which, if insignificant in itself, could have delayed progress dangerously short of the deadline. He had to deal with something like that himself, immediately.

The man who had almost been Georgia's governor in 1868, Civil War hero John B. Gordon, toured Florida in 1877 on behalf of the Lost Cause. He had been invited by those struggling plantation owners, the Black Belt "Bourbons." At their head was another Confederate hero who would be Florida's governor four years later, William D. Bloxham. For William Bloxham and his friends, unfettered railway expansion, *soon*, meant the survival of their way of life. General Gordon returned to his home state, promoting the cause of Georgia-Florida railway connections.[25]

Now, suddenly in the fall of 1883, in the midst of Bloxham's successful campaign, Gordon re-introduced himself to Florida with claims to a franchise on the line to Lake Monroe prior to the JT&KW's. The claims were valid for a 126 mile Palatka to Tampa line, part of a highly ambitious enterprise to reach Key West and Havana, which Gordon would actually begin in Georgia the next year. By this time the deadline was in the offing. If all went well, Plant was going to beat it. Suddenly, deeds and surveys in hand, the general arrived in Tampa, commenced building a wharf on the Hillsborough River, and poised himself before the courthouse. The threatened legal wrangle might set back work on Plant's railroad several crucial days, even a week. Promptly, Henry Plant anted up the nominal sum

---

[24] Brown, 17.
[25] Williamson, *Gilded Age*, 64, 67.

and settled. John Gordon went his way, though continuing to promote his Florida railroad schemes for several years thereafter.[26]

—o—

Of course men of lesser ambition were getting rich too. Cattle drovers from the highland followed the railheads, butchering steers on the spot at the end of the day's work.[27] Daily, shopkeepers and peddlers sold out their wares and celebrated, or came home, early. If housewives were paying twice what they had before to put food on the table, their husbands were bringing home the money to pay for it and lots more besides.

At the same time many essentials were scarce, naturally. The first three months of the railroad's construction coincided with the sun-scorched "winter" of the growing season in south-central Florida. Produce vanished from the markets as soon as it arrived. Anybody with a wagon and an animal to pull it was in business. Farmers worked until it was too dark to see, clearing new fields. Florida dairymen paid top prices at Georgia auctions. Drovers brought horses from Texas, mules from Alabama.

Though obviously the pace of the boom might level out, everyone could be pretty sure that the prosperity was permanent. Indeed, if you believed what they were saying about Henry Plant, another boom was on its way. A speaker honoring him at a banquet in Leesburg proclaimed, "He will make the desert bloom and build the banquet palace of Versailles on the banks of the Hillsborough River."[28] And why not believe it? With ease, Plant was proving the naysayers wrong. By mid-November the railroad was clearly closing in on the deadline. On December 1, He arrived for the "ultimate" banquet at the Orange House. Though with help from a horse and buggy across an eighteen-mile incomplete stretch, he rode in from Kissimmee across his own fresh crossties, on his own bright steel rails.

And at least this much was done. On December 10, Mr. Henry M. Drane, "Agt. Plant Investment Company," announced partial service over twenty miles of narrow gauge.[29]

Leave Tampa ... 2:00 PM
Arrive Plant City ... 3:30 PM

---

[26] Corliss, "Overseas Railway," 4. Grismer, 173. "Great Southern Railway." Jones, "Early Days." Shofner, 253-4.
[27] Grismer, 173. Patrick D. Smith, *A Land Remembered*.
[28] Smyth, 109.
[29] Pettengill, *Florida Railroads,* 77

Leave Plant City ... 8:30 AM
Arrive Tampa ... 10:00 AM

Flag stations: Bunch's, Coe's Mill, Bakers Old Camp.
All freight must be prepaid.

By this time 2,000 men were at work on each end of the line. On the morning of January 22, 1884, from either end of a trestle over a marshy creek, the two railheads were coming together. This was at Carter's Mill, about thirty miles east of Tampa, near Lakeland. Within a few short hours, the men could see the whiskers on each other's faces. Soon it was done. They drove the last spike. They had beaten the deadline by just sixty-three hours.[30]

---

[30] Mormino and Pizzo, 78.

~ IX ~

STRIVING TO THE END

That year, in October 1883, when haste was his watchword, Henry Plant scarcely had time to observe one of his most remarkable achievements, his sixty-fourth birthday. Today, in our part of the world, such events are no longer extraordinary. But from pre-historic times to the dawn of modern medicine, the average lifespan remained constant at forty-five. Only ten percent of the population, clergymen for the most part, would see sixty-five and beyond. Then, during the Industrial Revolution, the high priests of finance would begin joining this privileged statistic. Curiously, the corporate executives of the express business were particularly long-lived.

From 1884 and onward, though, birthday tributes to "the founder" became progressively grander occasions. Organized under Margaret's lavish direction, these would be celebrated for him in tremendous style, quite beyond the possibility of mitigation, attended by crowds of friends, well-wishers, associates, employees. And every year more of these in every category.

Up to now, all this time, his life had been the life of an ambitious young man. In terms of anyone's ambition, it had been a life remarkably free of disappointment. As an executive, his career had been one long steady ascent. He had only known striving, striving and achievement. He could have put the striving behind from 1884. After all, the simple life suited him. What could possibly beat life aboard Special Car 100, life aboard the *H.B. Plant?* And in 1884 he added the *Margaret*, a grand vessel set to cruising an assortment of waters off Tampa Bay, running a busy schedule down the Manatee River to Bradenton, then out onto the Gulf and on to Fort Myers.[1] With his grand scheme realized, with his dream come true, his last years might have been a time of luxurious ease. Certain significant developments, such as the extension of his north-south railway connections, were simply waiting to fall into place—waiting to fall into his hands. And with even this end to striving, he might have been a little more successful.

Henry Flagler's business career had faltered ruinously at one point, only to rise steeply—spectacularly.[2] Brought up much closer to poverty than Plant, he too had been a bright child intended for the clergy. Instead of going to sea, however, Henry Morrison Flagler married into a prosperous family on the Ohio frontier. There as a diehard teetotaler, he invested wisely in a distillery, and more wisely converted his profits into a Michigan salt works. And he did this just on the eve of the Civil War, when the best means then for preserving meat would turn salt to gold. But peace ended the bonanza too quickly for his calculations. Thirty-six now and busted in Cleveland, he ran into a man ten years his junior who sold him on the possibilities of a highly speculative new substance, "rock oil." Flagler, as suddenly inspired as he was lucky, and despite his record as a business failure, talked his wife's uncle into the $100,000 investment that made them partners in John D. Rockefeller's refinery.

In December 1883, about a year after General Sanford introduced James Ingraham and Henry Plant to each other, Henry Flagler passed through Jacksonville. He was making all possible haste. His wife of thirty years had died shortly after their abortive attempt to spend a winter there and now remarried to a young actress, Flagler was on a delayed honeymoon and had promised his bride a few weeks in historic St. Augustine. But not much haste was possible. If going south, one waited on the banks of the St. Johns River for a ferry. Once on the other side, a narrow gauge railroad headed off to a woodland stop somewhere near St. Augustine; then on by buggy.

This was the first real vacation of Flagler's life. He was easing himself out of the oil business. To his bride's utter delight, he extended their stay through March. During this time, he was captivated by a unique vision of what St. Augustine could be and how he could make the dream a reality. Back home, Henry Flagler met with America's most innovative architects, Thomas Hastings and John Carrere. In the first week of December, 1885, hundreds of laborers and artisans set to

---

[1] Mueller, *Steamships*, 145-9.
[2] Akin, Flagler, 1-133

work building a luxury hotel in St. Augustine which in its comforts and grandeur would far, far surpass all others in the South, indeed, all others in America. When the couple returned two years later, a thoroughly adequate luxury hotel had opened. Other wealthy northerners were wintering in St. Augustine. The trip down from New York took a week.

At the end of the month Flagler bought the little railway out of Jacksonville. He began converting it to standard gauge and extended the tracks to a depot near the hotel site. He also ordered a drawbridge erected across the St. Johns River. Soon, with a connection to Henry Plant's line from the north, passengers could ride from New York to St. Augustine in the same car.

When the Ponce de Leon Hotel opened January 10, 1888, the Flaglers, of course, arrived straight through by private railroad car. Other millionaires followed in their rolling palaces—a parade of wealth which became an instant tradition. Carrere and Hastings had designed a masterpiece exactly to the Gilded Age's demanding taste for the spectacular. In a perfect compromise between the enduring and the ephemeral, walls of coquina-packed cement four feet thick ascend serenely in tiers of intricate loggias and balconies to an irregular skyline of Venetian campaniles. Inside, two miles of carpeted corridors and 450 guest rooms, furnished in rosewood and walnut; at the end of each hallway, bath and toilet facilities. For all guests, the supreme luxury of semi-private indoor plumbing!

The Ponce de Leon was a smash hit from that first season that Henry Flagler had to add a number of "offspring" in the neighborhood. He began buying sites for other hotels down the coast and running his trains further south, even to the most desolate regions, to West Palm Beach and the Miami River. Especially for his hotels, it was going to be one smash hit after the other.

How well hotels and railroads went together was no secret. In 1885 Henry Plant, too, was conferring with architects. His plans were—at this stage—less grand than Henry Flagler's. But they were every bit as innovative. Since 1882 the *H.B. Plant* had been the mainstay of "The People's Line" on the north-flowing St. Johns River.[3] The river, traditionally the domain of an elegant winter visitor, Count Frederick DeBary, was a vital link in Plant's ambition to reach the Caribbean. The shrewd aristocrat recognized the benefits of doing business with a newly crowned railroad prince. Both men saw cooperation as the key to the future, as the following notice indicated:

---

[3] Mueller, 189

Henry Flagler's lavish Ponce De Leon Hotel opened in 1885—a smash hit. Henry Plant's arguably more lavish Tampa Bay Hotel materialized six years later. But by this time the East Coast had a lock on the big money crowd, and the Tampa Bay Hotel became an expensively decorated white elephant. It wasn't easy keeping up with a "Friend" like Henry Flagler.

Carrying the U.S. Mail — Double Daily Through Line — Elegant Sidewheel Steamers *Frederick DeBary*, Captain W.A. Shaw; *Geo. M. Bird*, Captain G.J. Mercier; *Rosa*, Captain Jon. J. Amazeen; *Anita*, Captain C.H. Brock; *H.B. Plant*, Captain J.W. Fitzgerald.[4]

Increasingly from then on, bound on business or pleasure, passengers arrived in Jacksonville via Plant's Waycross Shortline and proceeded on his People's Line up river to Sanford. The operation had become so efficient that the town's several lodging houses were sleeping guests two and three to a bed. Sanford was destined to become the railroad's headquarters and home to an impressive depot, to extensive rail yards and repair shops, offices, warehouses, and a hospital.

The year chosen by Henry Plant to accomplish all this began sadly. In 1886, after a lifetime of robust health, the family matriarch, Betsey Bradley Plant Hoadley, took to her room with the onset of winter. She died on January 20, at age eighty-six. After the funeral Henry Plant, now sixty-seven, returned to Sanford, blueprints in hand, and ordered work begun on a main-street hotel. It would be the second largest building in town. Immediately afterward he built an office complex that occupied the whole adjacent block, and, henceforth, the area was known as the Plant Investment Company Block. Plant had chosen a local architect, W.T. Cotter, and approved, surely after consultation with Margaret, a remarkable set of designs.

The structure dominating the "PICO" Block was appropriately impressive. Two L-shaped stories of brick and stucco, outlined by a plain cornice and surmounted by a somewhat severe-looking four-cornered dome, dominated the sklyine.[5] For the Pico Hotel, however, Henry Plant must have encouraged Cotter to take his inspiration from the new rage of the day, the mysterious "Near East." For such inspirations surely piqued Plant's interest whenever he went to his office on 23rd Street in Manhattan. Close by, the Grand Masonic Lodge of New York had opened its portals. Its members, the Ancient Arabic Order of Nobles of the Mystic Shrine, regularly came marching up the street in red fezzes and flowing silk trousers.[6] Yet, after bricklayers had been at work for months, onlookers surmised that, yes, this was something a Connecticut Yankee would choose, traditional red brick, in the stodgy colonial style. But then—the workmen finished off the windows in ogee and horseshoe arches. But then—a massive facade of peaked crenel-

---

[4] Mueller, 187-201
[5] "Sanford - Historic Downtown."
[6] Harner, *Promoters*, 25.

lations and a tall corner tower from which arose a bulbous dome striped blue and yellow: the palace of a sultan, with rooms to rent. And the railroad from the dock could bring you right to the lobby.

—o—

When the hotel opened in 1887, though, Plant was busy far afield, acquiring what would prove to be a modest foothold in Alabama railroads, purchasing an under-construction outfit, the Alabama Midland Railway.

Complete three years later, this gave him a 175-mile-long connection from the SF&W depot in Bainbridge, Georgia, to Montgomery. There, to provide a switching route through city streets, he authorized what was to be the shortest railroad in the Plant System, the 2-mile-long Montgomery Belt Line Railway.[7] And, from headquarters in Sanford, he soon had his hands full at the far end of the line. In September disaster struck in Tampa, a yellow fever epidemic, the worse in the town's history. When cold weather brought relief, Henry Plant brought his own relief over the first six months of 1888 in the form of a $1,000,000 "Port Tampa" project.[8] First his engineers put a drawbridge over the Hillsborough River and extended the tracks of the South Florida Railroad almost 10 miles into shallow Tampa Bay. Ships could finally begin to load and unload in volume, quickly. Next, every able-bodied survivor for miles around went to work on a tremendous multi-purpose wharf that, when finally completed, jutted better than a mile out into the bay. Here, on the ocean side, ships came to berth next to freight cars, with cargo cranes in between. Likewise passenger trains had immediate access to ships of the Plant Line, providing direct service to Mobile, Key West, and Havana. This was all done by the first part of June, and that was by no means the end of Plant's plans for Tampa.[9] In 1886 the Plant System had begun moving south of the Sanford-Tampa line with the narrow-gauge Florida Southern extension to the orange groves at Bartow and on to the cattle town of Arcadia on the Peace River. For nearly a year Plant and his lieutenants debated the options of a terminal on the Gulf. Finally, in bitter disappointment to a number of promising candidate communities—especially Ft. Myers—they chose the most economical route, to Charlotte Harbor. And by the time the Florida Southern reached its terminus in 1888 at hitherto insignificant Punta Gorda, Henry Plant had prepared a more than adequate site for the celebration: a magnificent three-story, 200-room hotel.

---

[7] Dozier, *Atlantic Coast Line,* 30.
[8] Harner, 24-5. Pettengill, 78.
[9] Covington, *Plant's Palace,* 69-70. Turner, *Short History,* 62.

The year 1888 provided a yet greater cause for celebration. Morton, now thirty-seven, was finally settling down. He had wed Nellie Capron of Baltimore that spring.[10] Though half Morton's age, the pretty young woman was serious-minded. She would make a good mother.

But over in St. Augustine that spring, someone else was celebrating, counting his receipts. If Henry Flagler had his way, Tampa would remain a little southern cousin of Chicago and Cleveland: a workingman's town. On the east side of the Hillsborough River, in a tribute to the influx of railroad passengers, one Jerry T. Anderson had erected a two-story structure and named it the H. B. Plant Hotel. Its claim to fame would be "central heat," a wood stove in the middle of the upstairs hall.[11] The city fathers knew that what Tampa needed was not just another big hotel. What Tampa needed was a hotel so big it would leave the Ponce de Leon eating dust. And Henry Plant wanted it too.

The matter had been under consideration. In 1887 Plant told his PICO partners, among them now Henry Flagler: "Very well, gentlemen, if you do not agree with me that the hotel will benefit the railroad and the community, I will build it as a personal investment." And this he very shortly would do, committing $2,500,000 for starters.[12] Yet what had the issue been, exactly?

The partners had backed the construction project on Lake Monroe, and they had no objection to owning hotels. Two years before the inauguration of the Ponce de Leon, a magnificent resort facility on the traditional American rustic model had opened in Winter Park, on the route between Tampa and Sanford. The Seminole Inn featured its own streetcar line, steam heat, a bowling alley, and a yacht basin. In the winter of 1888 Henry and Margaret Plant joined such luminaries on the guest list as the Duke of Sutherland, George Pullman, George Westinghouse, Charles F. Crocker, Ulysses S. Grant, and Grover Cleveland. Before spring, the Seminole Inn joined the growing properties of the Plant System.[13] Meanwhile, in Tampa, land was available, and the locals were more than cooperative. James Ingraham met with a committee of the city council on February 2, 1887, to discuss a half-cultivated piece of property across the river from the town hall. Meanwhile, far to the north along the Savannah-Charleston line, the renowned New York

---

[10] Martin, "Morton Plant" in *American Biography,* 328-29
[11] McLaws, "Plant,"8. Johnson, "Plant and Florida," 124.
[12] Harner, 25.
[13] Covington, 58.

architect, John A. Wood, was putting the finishing touches on a lavish hotel in Brunswick, Georgia. A year later the local newspaper noted, "The fountains in front of the Oglethorpe are now in running order and throw up a tiny spray to beautify the scene" and added, "Mr. Plant and family, with a few friends in tow, reached the city by special train."[14] Soon Wood was in Tampa to approve the proposed site. On May 10, 1888, the mayor and the council met with Plant and generously agreed to three conditions—to build a bridge across the river, to promote a good-faith $100,000 bond, and to keep taxes low on the hotel property: never more than $200 annually.[15] Immediately thereupon Henry Plant swung into action.[16] He paid $9,800 to the Heydens, the family farming on the other side of the river, for fifteen acres of their "wilderness." To get to town the popular "Doc" Heyden, a self-certified dentist, had been crossing the river in a skiff. Now a gang of black laborers began grading for a spur line from the main rail yards. Port Tampa had already been fully operational for a month. By the last week in May bushwhackers were attacking the dense jungle of oak and palmetto that might have eventually become an orange grove. On July 26, 1888, Henry Plant laid the cornerstone for his hotel. Already 1,500 barrels of shell had been excavated from an Indian mound to the south and were being barged down the Alafia River. Brick was on the way from Green Cove Springs. An order placed in New York at $1.75 a barrel for quality "Brooklyn Bridge" cement exceeded the supply. The next best deal was for German-made Portland cement, shipped over from Hamburg at $3.00 a barrel. Plant ordered that steel rails and wooden ties, salvaged from the conversion of his Florida railways to standard gauge, be used to reinforce the supporting walls. Up the Hillsborough River the huge steam-driven saws at Dorsey's Mill were snarling out planks and beams by the ton: lumber for scaffolding; for temporary offices, shelters, storage sheds, and stables; for a kitchen and an infirmary. Initially, eighty men were set to work digging and laying the foundation at a weekly payroll of $1,000.

For Henry and Margaret Plant there had been only one man they could trust with their plan, only one man with the genius to design and execute their stupendous dream house, and that was J.A. Wood, architect extraordinaire. Probably Wood's talent for the unusual had first come to their attention in Thomasville, along the Brunswick & Western route. Likewise J.A. Wood knew of Henry Plant.

---

[14] *Brunswick Advertiser*, March 9, 1888.
[15] Covington, "Tampa Bay Hotel," 6-7.
[16] Rogers, *Thomas County*, 135-48.

There had been quite a stir in that part of Georgia when PICO acquired the line in 1884:

A Big Railway Transaction

Mr. H.B. Plant has purchased the Brunswick & Western Railroad. This will give the Plant syndicate control of about 900 miles of railway. Mr. Plant is a bold, but at the same time, a cautious man. He is, it is said, backed by an unlimited amount of capital. With remarkable foresight he has laid his plans and extended his lines to make his system impregnable. He has done much toward developing the latent resources of this part of the South, especially in Florida and Southern Georgia.

Thomasville Times
August 30, 1884

In Thomasville, Wood's sumptuous Piney Woods Hotel had been a center of attention since 1881, and the elegant Mitchell House since 1886.[17] And surely before commissioning the architect of their future home, the Plants had inspected his Mizzen Top Hotel, not far from New York City, in Duchess County. In its flair of ornamentation, exhausted only by budgetary restraints, the Mizzen Top amply displayed the Oriental fascinations of the day.[18]

As soon as construction began, Wood—spelled only occasionally by his trusted assistant, W.T. Cotter—was on the job around the clock.[19] Indeed, he would have huge bonfires lit at night and invite the public to share his ongoing wonderwork. Thanks to Plant's "unlimited amount of capital," and with six acres of his own to build on, this highly imaginative designer would be freed from any and all restraints. Nor was Wood by any means simply a dreamer. Like Henry Haines, he was a highly respected "driver of men," soon supervising a 500-man workforce. And when the local labor pool, such as it was, proved difficult to motivate, he went out himself and recruited youngsters, instructing them in specialized skills. On the job, some became expert brick masons. One, Fred J. James, went on to enter the A.I.A., and became president of the State Board of Architecture.

"Leave it to Wood," Henry Plant told everybody. "He knows what I want. He will get it right. Leave it to Wood." Especially when it came to problems of any sort, Wood's was the final and often the only word. And when it came to improvements on an already daring design, to "improvisations," who was there to question

---

[17] Rogers, *Thomas County*, 135-48.
[18] Covington, 59.
[19] Braden, *Architects*, 271-3. Browning, 89. Mclaws, 8.

him? Thus, happily putting everything in the capable hands of John A. Wood, architect and magician, Henry Plant went off with Margaret to Paris in the summer of 1889.

Officially they were members of Florida's delegation to the great international exposition of that year. PICO had contributed $15,000 worth of displays on the natural resources of the South, and Henry Plant was invited to run up the first American flag to fly from the brand-new Eiffel Tower. Later he whispered to an American reporter, "In fifteen years the condition of the steel in this structure will necessitate its demolition." [20]

Principally they were on a shopping spree for the hotel. They would bring back forty-one freight cars full of European treasures, furniture, tapestries, paintings, statuary, and—music lover Henry Plant's personal favorite—a colossal steam-powered music box. On the way through London they chanced on one of the great carpet bargain buys of all time, some 30,000 yards of gorgeous blue and red ceremonial carpet presented by Sultan Abdul of Turkey to Queen Victoria on her wedding day. But the red dragons on a blue field, sacrosanct emblem of the British monarchy, had precluded its use on the floors of the royal British household. [21]

Everything would remain in storage for another year at least. The Tampa Bay Hotel was still far from complete. But it did now awesomely occupy its place in the "jungle." With the architect for a guide, Henry and Margaret had the pleasure in 1890 of showing Vice President Morton Levi and his daughters around the construction site one quiet Friday afternoon in March.

The enormous scaffold-covered structure, spanning nearly 300 yards from wing to wing, would vary between five and three stories high. While workers with caps doffed stood idly by, quite a considerable expense with the payroll at $1,000 a day, the party approached cautiously through a new kind of wilderness, a forest of gigantic, elaborately fretted forms in woodwork. Whenever they looked ahead, great arched apertures gazed back on them, the openings for the huge front windows, triumphs of the bricklayer's art.

Telling always what was to be, John Wood led them up the broad marble steps to the sweeping verandah. The largest forms of fretwork would be its facade. Then, into an airy and as yet empty rotunda supported by slender, tall granite pillars which he mysteriously invited them to count, thirteen. This would be the

---

[20] Harner, 25.
[21] Covington, "Tampa Bay Hotel," 12.

lobby. From here a spacious central corridor ran east and west, into the dimness of the far wings. All the resources of modern technology were being applied to insure a perfectly fireproof and sanitary environment. As the steel-beamed walls arose, teams of the best steamfitters and plumbers from all over the country had been installing mazes of pipes and tubes. In a vast improvement over the Ponce de Leon, there would be a minimum of one bathroom per three rooms. For a number of the choicest suites, entirely private bathrooms!

Back outside in the wilderness of woodwork again, the master builder had everyone turn around and look up. His magical hands danced in the air. In the Arabian Nights, the months of the calendar were thirteen. There above the tallest trees, up in the blue sky, larger than horses, larger than elephants, would rise thirteen gracefully pointed silver domes, each bearing a silver crescent moon. Finally—and this was exceedingly mysterious—spider-strung from high poles, lines of thick fiber-covered copper wire reached the building. A wonderful wizard had come to live in Florida. When the hotel opened, Mr. Plant would bring him here by steamboat. At the touch of the wizard's hand a power would flow through the lines. Instantly, all at once, inside and out, the whole immense building would be ablaze in lights.

By the end of that year all 511 rooms of the hotel were ready for occupancy— the largest dwelling in the world to be illuminated by electricity. That first season 4,367 guests would register. Most of them arrived by train, disembarking to the rear of the hotel, amid exquisite gardens of tropical foliage.[22]

Inside, all the fabulous treasures brought back from Europe had found a home: A stupendous artwork in bronze and marble now dominated the rotunda, went soaring up into it, a pastoral subject in the style of the contemporary Baroque. Its entry had required the best efforts of eleven moving men using block and tackle. Elsewhere, in salons and parlors and reading rooms, furnishings attributed to the Versailles of Louis XIV and Marie Antoinette, to the chateaux of Louis Philippe and Napoleon, the households of Mary Queen of Scots and Queen Victoria. Throughout, 110 mirrors from Florence and Venice, and countless ornaments from the old-world workshops of Germany and Spain. And all this variety and opulence made a hit. A guest wrote home, "Oh, what a pleasure it is to feast from the table service. They bring you your beef on a bit of French porcelain, your

---

[22] Harner, 25.

salad on an old Vienna plate, ice cream on a saucer designed by Maurice Fischer, and coffee in a Wedgwood cup."[23]

Each year, especially after their trip to the Orient in 1897, Henry and Margaret Plant would add to the collection. The hotel became a Gilded Age art museum where people could spend the night: It was a museum of natural history, too. The Plants were cruising the Caribbean now at every opportunity, and brought back boatloads of trees and plants for the hotel's magnificent conservatory and its many gardens and groves. To supervise and embellish all this, they imported France's famous landscape architect, Anton Fiche.[24]

Most of all, the hotel was a resort. You could be fully occupied around the clock with pleasant, exciting, relaxing activities, and never have to leave the grounds. A sixteen-piece orchestra played every evening. In 1896 the Casino was built on the banks of the river. Here popular entertainments were presented. Otherwise, in the Gay Nineties in wide-open Tampa, there would have been no need for a "casino." Within the hotel, on the sub-floor sixteen feet deep, were a rathskeller, billiard parlor, and barbershop. The staff, from bootblacks and chambermaids, to chefs and the head housekeeper, were expertly trained or simply the best in their fields to begin with. The pastry cook was from Delmonico's, the baker from the Manhattan Club, while the groundskeeper was the renowned horticulturalist, Thomas Hayden. Then, in a supreme coup, the impeccable Mr. J.H. King, prince of hoteliers, had been enticed away from the Ponce de Leon.[25]

Outside, tennis, horseshoes, and that craze just taking hold in America, golf, was available. Henry Plant was already passionate for the new sport. He had been introduced on the courses of Long Island, and young Morton was taking it up in a big way. Otherwise, what could be more pleasant than just strolling the miles of winding pathways, under laden fruit trees, past banks of flowers, while skilled gardeners did their silent work and peacocks paraded? You might enjoy four-footed companionship as well. Henry and Margaret Plant were great dog-lovers—Margaret favored the small breeds of the Far East. The Tampa Bay's brochure rightfully claimed that for its half-acre kennel under shade trees offered "the most complete dog accommodations of any hotel in existence."[26] For the real sportsmen of the day, when organized sports were in their infancy, there was the great outdoors. In Tampa Bay, and up and down the coast, the fishing was simply abun-

---

[23] Covington, 62-3. 65, 66. Nolan, *Fifty Feet,* 113.
[24] Browning, 89. Covington, 63-4. Mormino and Pizzo, 88.
[25] Covington, 64.
[26] Covington, 66.

dant. A day's catch could be overwhelming. And the vast and sprawling suburban area of today's Tampa was then an untamed region of wetland, meadow, and forest, teeming with game. Led by professional hunting guide Arthur Schleman, only the most ambitious expeditions need venture beyond a seven-mile radius of the hotel. On one such typical venture, Schleman conducted Mr. and Mrs. G.W. Berger to Braidentown (Bradenton) where they joined the pioneer family of the Garrett Murphys. In five days their hunting parties bagged 321 quail, 147 snipe, 82 ducks, 48 doves, ten plover, one rabbit, one deer, and an uncounted assortment of squirrels, sand hill cranes, pink curlews, and white and blue egrets. Within the "urban" perimeter G.W. Berger achieved a record single-day, one-man bird kill: 283 snipe and plover.[27]

The hotel officially opened with a glorious grand ball on February 5, 1891.[28] When Henry and Margaret Plant awoke the next morning, in their apartment on the east wing, they must have been suffused with triumph. And the feeling doubtless continued, and grew, all that season and well into the next. In the major national publications, the hotel received reviews that went over the top, even for the time, in effusive, lavish praise.[29] But too soon it became irrefutably clear that Flagler's success on the East Coast would be the only Gilded Age grand success of its kind in Florida. He was running his Florida East Coast Railway further south. He had the traffic. When he opened a pair of gigantic hotels, in West Palm Beach and Palm Beach, the Inn and the Breakers, he doubled and redoubled his pull on its flow.

ROOMS, $5.00 DOLLARS AND UPWARDS PER DAY

ROOMS WITH BATHS EXTRA; ALSO, EXTRA FOR DOUBLE ROOMS OCCUPIED BY ONE PERSON.

HOURS FOR MEALS

BREAKFAST 7 TO 10,   DINNER 6 TO 8,
LUNCH 12 TO 2,   TEA 8 TO 10

HOURS FOR CHILDREN AND SERVANTS
BREAKFAST 7 TO 9   DINNER 12 TO 1   TEA 6 TO 8

GUESTS ARE EARNESTLY REQUESTED TO IMMEDIATELY REPORT ANY INCIVILITY OR INATTENTION ON THE PART OF SERVANTS OR THE HOUSE.

J.H. KING, MANAGER

Guests at Victorian luxury hotels preferred keeping to the regime of their own orderly households.

---

[27] Gibson, "Sport Hunting."
[28] Covington, 65.
[29] Smyth, *Plant*, 183-203.

Within a few years the Tampa Bay Hotel would become, sadly, a spectacular loser. Many of its problems, too, were inherent. A number of the architect's costly inspirations turned out to be strictly last minute, and the project went $500,00 over budget. For instance, after improving the ballroom with several ornate non-blueprint fireplaces, Wood suddenly realized that it was too late to install chimneys. And, owing to unchecked calculations, the two central minarets suffered water damage and crumbled from within, extensively damaging the roof.[30]

On the American continent there had never been seen before a white elephant nearly so colossal or so day-to-day expensive. The Tampa Bay Hotel was Henry Plant's mammoth, bedizened baby, though. To the last, he would say that she was worth it to him, just to sit in the rotunda of a late afternoon, listening to tunes from a prodigious German pipe organ, the grandest of all his European treasures.

Henry Plant would not be dismayed, however, and in his overall career as an innkeeper would be notably successful. He acquired and improved already profit-making hotels in Punta Gorda, Fort Myers, Kissimmee, and Ocala. Partly to end a rivalry with cross-bay upstart St. Petersburg, he instituted major improvements in the neighborhood.[31] To insure first class service to his favored locale west of Tampa, in the village of Belleview, just south of Clearwater, Plant undertook control of the hitherto erratically running Orange Belt Railway, renaming it the Sanford & St. Petersburg Railroad. By 1895 he began building the all-wooden Belleview Resort Hotel, overlooking the Gulf. It would feature a bicycle track and its own fire department. His nephew, C.E. Hoadley, relocated from New Haven and to spend years supervising improvements. Something on the order of the world's largest country house, the Belleview opened in 1897 and became both a "millionaire's playground" and an instant and steadily popular family resort.

In the summer of 1895, from the *Jacksonville Times-Union:*

The Plant Investment Company, with its well-known judgment and energy, has recently undertaken an entirely new departure.

The company is now having built [in Philadelphia] a first class iron steamship, 225 feet long [and] she will have four separate water-tight compartments, in fact she will be practically fire and water-proof. The motto of the Plant Investment Company in this case is, "Safety first, comfort second, speed third [Yet with] a guaranteed continuous sea speed of nearly seventeen statue miles per hour, [this] is said to be the fastest ship

---

[30] Covington, 64.
[31] Arsenault, *St. Petersburg*, 83. Horgan, *Pioneer College*, 95. Johnson, 125.

Henry Plant - Pioneer Empire Builder

of her kind built in the United States.

The steamship is to run from Tampa via Key West to Havana. The distance is 387 miles, and she will make semi-weekly trips. The present time between Tampa and Key West is twenty-six hours, and the mail is taken by another vessel to Havana, so that it now takes about forty-eight from Tampa to Havana.

The vessel will be placed on the route early in the fall and the managers have no hesitation in saying she will be a first-class vessel in every respect, and the most costly ship of her size in this country.[32]

On the morning of October 27, a party of twenty-five left New York in Special Car 100 for the launching.[33] Those present with the Plants for the occasion included Henry Sanford, Colonel Haines, Hamilton Disston, and Governor George English of Connecticut. Margaret did the honors, declaiming, "I christen you the *Mascotte*, hoping that you will prove all the name implies."

Within a year her hopes were answered. The *Mascotte* carried from thirty to fifty first-class passengers, and space was in such demand that a companion ship was ordered, "larger and better." On her second trip, the *SS Olivette* better than cut in half the old time from Tampa to Havana—22 1/2 hours! The demand and the possibilities were wide open. In 1895 when Vincente Ybor Martinez led the exodus of cigar manufacturers from politically overheated Key West to what he hoped would be a milder climate for management in Tampa, Henry Plant sent his new steamships to help out. They returned, their cargo holds and even their staterooms stuffed with choice tobacco.

With these swift, efficient, and capacious ships, Plant became the first man to make that old dream come true, of tapping the resources of the Caribbean. He was the first, as well, to add an all-important, up-to-date resource—tourism.

Mascotte & Olivette

Southbound
>
> Leave Port Tampa 9:30 p.m. Monday and Thursday
> Arrive Key West 8:00 p.m. Tuesday and Friday
> Leave Key West 9 p.m. Tuesday and Friday
> Arrive Havana 6 a.m. Wednesday and Saturday

Northbound
>
> Leave Havana 12:30 p.m. Wednesday and Saturday

---

[32] Jacksonville *Times-Union* in Mueller, 22.
[33] Mueller, 23-9.

> Arrive Key West 7:30 p.m. Wednesday and Saturday
> Leave Key West 10 p.m. Wednesday and Saturday
> Arrive Port Tampa 2:30 p.m. Thursday and Sunday

During the summer the ships went north and operated a passenger service between Boston and Bar Harbor. Through regional lease and purchase the Plant System soon acquired a number of serviceable steamships, notably the *Halifax* in 1893. A regular route quickly developed between Canada and the tropics, and Henry Plant grew determined to rule these waters.[34] He kept his steamship agency in Boston open the year around. The Plant System was a New England business, too. And now, traveling alone, he more and more frequently left the Fifth Avenue home for New England, for Connecticut. In 1894 he had directed the reinterment of Ellen Blackstone Plant's coffin from Augusta to a magnificent gravesite in the Branford cemetery.

By this time, how apparent to their closest friends was a certain distinct estrangement between Henry and Margaret Plant? Certainly it was not publicly apparent. The age's criteria of decorum demanded in any case a formality of distance between husband and wife. Their religious differences had perhaps always been reason enough for time apart. Henry Plant reaffirmed his Congregational affiliation by appointing his New York pastor, the Reverend G. Hutchenson Smyth, his official biographer. Margaret had forged close associations with the Catholic community in Tampa.

Above all else, though, Henry Plant had a new cause for striving. After eight long years, he was a grandfather. In 1895 Nellie Capron Plant had given birth to a fine baby boy, Henry Bradley Plant II.[35]

In April of that year the old cabin boy ordered no expenses spared on the design of a "super ship," *La Grande Duchesse*. Visiting the yards during construction, he stubbornly insisted on a radically innovative power system—destined, in his lifetime, to an unending series of embarrassing and costly failures.[36]

Still, undismayed. The Tampa Bay Hotel would triumph yet. He had the resources to hang on. Money poured in from the other hotels. Money poured in from the Texas Express and, now that all Florida was booming, more profusely than ever from the Southern Express. As for the *Duchesse*, a little more tinkering would prove him right yet. The rest of his waterborne business more than made up

---

[34] Mueller, 121-4.
[35] Martin, "Morton Plant,' 329, 29.
[36] Mueller, 124-6.

for her little troubles. He had steamboats on the Flint River bringing wares and lumber and produce down from Columbus, Georgia to Apalachicola.[37] The *Halifax*, during the winter, was put on schedule to Jamaica.[38] The *Margaret* was busy all summer on the waters of Long Island Sound. For the Florida season, she was joined on the Manatee River schedule by another side-wheeler, the *Kissimmee,* and the twin-screw *Tarpon*.[39] For the hotel guests, these ships were available for fishing and picnic excursions, out on the Gulf to Egmont Key and Anna Maria Island:

> With her three spacious decks the *Margaret* affords her passengers ample space for promenading and dancing. The upper deck, upon which stands the pilothouse, is equipped with benches and cushions. The second or middle deck is the Falcon, which is covered with canvas for dancing. An orchestra of eight pieces ... has been engaged to furnish the music of every trip. On the lower deck is the cafe where meals and drinks are served. No drinks will be served outside the bar. No females will be allowed on board unless accompanied by a male escort.
>
> There will be separate accommodations for colored persons.[40]

Henry and Margaret Plant often joined these excursions themselves. Famously, after a cantankerous confidential meeting between Plant and Flagler in the winter of 1893, the two men and their wives took advantage of the *Halifax's* first trip out of Port Tampa. They sailed on Thursday, February 16, and spent most of Saturday on Nassau, arriving in Kingston early Tuesday.[41] Flagler had started his own Florida East Coast Steamship Company—but nothing to match the Plant Line. After three days in Jamaica and a two-day voyage back to Tampa, all was well from then on. In a correspondence of brief notes, the two addressed each other as "friend Henry." Six years later Henry Flagler would be an honorary pallbearer at Henry Plant's funeral.

——o——

Did anyone tell him to slow down? It stands as reminder of how hard Plant must have driven himself on behalf of the Adams Express in the 1850s, and to establish the Southern Express in the 1860s, if he twice required "rest cures" back then. In

---

[37] Mueller, 165-85.
[38] Mueller, 27.
[39] Mueller, 144-9.
[40] Mueller, 148.
[41] Mueller, 29.

the 1890s, when he was seventy, he took his typical rest in the form of shifting his attention to a new endeavor. After announcing his retirement from railroad activities in 1895, what was there left to do in that field? The greatest railroad warhorse of them all, Colonel Henry Haines, had retired the year before, to travel in Europe In 1896.on the last day of May and first day of June, in two long shifts of frantic labor, a mighty army of workers had converted the entire Plant System, and every mile of hobgoblin track in the South, to standard gauge.[42] Then the JT&KW had given up the ghost, and the Sanford-Jacksonville route came into Plant's hands, as he knew it finally would.[43] As of 1886 the whole line was under consolidation from Charleston south, and you could ride from New York to Tampa without changing cars.[44]

Meanwhile, land grants per mile of successful Florida railroad construction had normally been 3,840 acres. At the time the founder made his announcement, when Florida and Texas led the nation in bestowing real estate upon the railroads, the holdings of the Plant System via land grants alone made for a comfortable nest egg:

South Florida Railroad   72,428 acres
Jacksonville, Tampa & Key West   1,474,129 acres
Florida Southern Railway   2,655,482 acres
PICO (various)   95,329 acres[45]

And while these awards were made in "blocks" along alternate side of the track, each award was chosen from prime territory, rich in mineral, timber, and agricultural possibilities, not necessarily adjacent to the track. The Plant and Flagler Systems depended on whole communities of farmers coming to settle in Florida. Promotional literature appeared all over Europe. A principal source of railroad revenue would be supplies coming south and produce going north. Everyone was going to get rich growing citrus; that is, until countless small-time investors lost everything in the big freeze of 1895. On the grounds of the Tampa Bay Hotel that year, $30,000 worth of rare tropical foliage drooped in sere, withered ruin.[46]

There was another crimp in the working out of Henry Plant's dream for Florida's West Coast, less crucial but of much longer duration.[47] Access to the Tampa Bay

---

[42] Stover, *American Railroads,* 144. Taylor and Neu, *Network,* 79-81.
[43] Murdock, *Central Florida Railroads,* 18.
[44] Pettengill, 78.
[45] Ayers, 45. Harner, 25.
[46] Covington, 67.
[47] Herr, *Louisville & Nashville,* 76-83. Hoffman, 125-6. Klein, *History of the L&N,* 316-321

region via Jacksonville and Sanford left something to be desired for potential Midwestern guests. From 1888 Plant had been attempting to link together a "West Coast Route" toward the SF&W line between DuPont and Waycross, with a major railroad center—warehouses, repair shops, and hospital—northwest of Gainesville, in the new resort town of High Springs. It was here that the Plant System's most usual railroad operated, the Barr's Tram Railway, a 27-mile-long consistently profitable logging operation. By 1893 SF&W workers had laid 22 miles of track southward from High Springs, and the Florida Central & Peninsular granted trackage rights for the remaining distance to Dunnellon. Service on the "West Coast Route" commenced on January 1, 1894.

The key to the Midwest's mightiest flow of passengers and freight, however, lay further west: the north-south lines of the Louisville & Nashville in Alabama. In 1890 PICO consolidated its majority interest in the Alabama Midland Railroad, running 175 miles between Bainbridge and the major L&N connection at Montgomery.

Overall the early 1890s would be years of methodical expansion.[48] For already the success had been dramatic. In 1885 customs receipts at the Port of Tampa had amounted to $75; five years later—$100,000. After the Gold Rush to California and the Oil Rush to Pennsylvania—the Phosphate Rush to Florida. This valuable source of fertilizer had been discovered near Port Tampa in 1882, but kept secret while a local company bought up the land. Henry Plant was quick to get in on the transportation end of phosphate mining. In 1889 he extended the tracks of the SSO&G into the mineral-rich area around Homosassa. By 1891 his major gateway to the Homosassa phosphate lands, the Silver Springs, Ocala, & Gulf Railroad Company, had nearly completed an extension linking Inverness to Lakeland. Here in 1892 the Plant System would absorb the Winston Lumber Company, whose logging tracks ran to the super-rich Pebbledale phosphate territory. Four years later, towering gravity elevators—such structures as would not be surpassed until Cape Kennedy—were in place at Port Tampa.

—o—

Otherwise, times were going to be terribly hard for the country through the early mid-1890s, and for the transportation business especially. A lesser man than Plant might well have thrown in his hand right then. True, he would have looked awkward doing so, for he was in the tub again with his old bath mates, Henry Sanford and B.F. Newcomer. In 1888 they had accepted an invitation to serve on the board

---

[48] Derr, *Paradise*, 121-3. Johnson, 124. Mueller, 19-21. Nolan, 83, Turner, 65.

of an irresistibly promising venture, the Richmond and West Point Terminal Company. This corporation was the brainchild of one Mr. John C. Inman of the Tennessee Coal, Iron, and Railroad Co. For a long time John Inman had been waging an extension of the Civil War by other means. His ingenious financial arrangements had earned him the title, a "Southern carpetbagger on Wall Street," and his confidante and corporate attorney was Patrick Calhoun, grandson of John C. Calhoun. Immediately, the two used the prestige of their new directors to leverage a $7,500,000 loan and buy the badly deteriorated Central of Georgia Railroad. Young Calhoun had earlier fought a duel to obtain a railroad, and this deal would be called an "outright swindle." The Central of Georgia continued to deteriorate. Where had the money gone? After seven fat years, the Richmond Terminal Company went broke, making a major contribution to the worse depression in twenty years, the Panic of 1893.[49]

Things got so bad that, to save itself from bankruptcy, the U.S. Government came to J.P. Morgan, hat in hand. It was a sign the pinch had eased when Henry Plant retired from the daily business of running his railroads. It may also have taken that long to shake himself dry.

Only the L&N's great president, Milton H. Smith, contributed so much to Southern railroads. Little else remained to be done to improve the Plant System.[50] A writer for a small magazine might have complained in 1885 about riding "fifty-eight miles over the bump-along Savannah, Florida and Western. It is the roughest and bumpiest on the face of the earth." An old story. In southeast Georgia, SF&W had long stood for "Stop Frequently and Wait." In all ages the best passengers have been stoics. A wry commonplace at this time in the Southeast: "There are two way to get from Savannah to Jacksonville, rail and water. And whichever way you take, you'll wish you had taken the other." Of course comparisons are relative. Some outfits earned reputations for smooth running from the start, such as the freight-hauling Florida Midland Railroad—Lake Jessup to Ocoee, Apopka to Rock Springs—acquired in 1896.

That same year a writer for the nation's most important magazine had this to say about the heart of the operation:

> The Savannah, Florida, and Western Railway, known as the Plant railroad runs from Charleston through Savannah to the Chattahoochee River and to Jacksonville, with branches to Albany, Bainbridge, Gainesville, and Brunswick, and has a steamship line from Tampa to Key West and

---

[49] Woodard, *New South,* 122-3.
[50] *Louisville Truth* in Rogers, 114. Turner, 64.

Havana. It combines over 800 miles of track under the single masterly administration of Mr. Plant. The policy of the management has been comprehensive, far seeing, and sagacious. No dividends have been paid, but the whole profits have been invested in extending and perfecting the system. It is one of the best-equipped railways in the Union, and handles the large winter travel to and from Florida admirably. It has made new connections, opened up new industries, tapped fresh regions of trade, and created remunerative businesses. Its iron tentacles have penetrated and gleaned the orange-laden realm of Florida.[51]

The connections of these "iron tentacles" worked in both directions, bringing a way of life to Florida that was the *new life*. The Jacksonville once spurned by Henry Flagler had become "a town with its great hotels illuminated from top to basement, its sounds of dance music in all the great parlors, and its long porches crowded with ease-taking men and women in flannels and tennis caps and satin slippers and russet gowns, the shops full of gimcrack souvenirs the peanuts and soda water the odor of perfumery."[52]

The great Plant System never grew too great, however, to lose sight of its origins. The diary of a small-town citizen provides a glimpse of the founder's typical daily activities while traveling north on the South Florida route, April 19, 1895:

[Mr. Plant] viewed the depot at half past three while but a few of the local people were present; among others from St. Leo's College were Rev. Fr. Benedict and Dr. Corrigan, who had in readiness two carriages in which to carry Plant & party through the town to the college. For want of time Mr. Plant could not accept this offer, so after stopping at San Antonio for eleven minutes the train carried him to St. Leo station and made a stop of eight minutes there.[53]

From the *Fort Myers Press*, October 15, 1897:

A BIG DEAL

H.B. Plant Purchased the Ft. Myers Steamboat Co.'s Steamers

Messrs. H.B. Plant, Frank Q. Brown and the chief engineer and electrician of the company arrived in Fort Myers Saturday. Mayor Johnson and

---

[51] Harpers, 205-6.
[52] Ralph, "Dixie" in Ayers, 61.
[53] Horgan, "San Antonio", 2.

several of our prominent citizens were at the landing to receive him and after driving around our little city a short time ... he conversed with a number of our citizens on the future prospects of Lee County.

While here Mr. Plant consummated a deal with the Roan Bro's in which he becomes owner of the steamboat company's line of steamers and warehouses.

He expressed himself as agreeably surprised at the enterprise and thrift exhibited in our city and while he said Lee County would have no railroad soon, he would give us a steamer service that could not be surpassed. His coming means more to our county than one would think as his magic touch, wherever he has invested, has built cities and thrown whole sections of the country open to development. In the course of his remarks he said that so soon as our county raised enough produce to justify the building of a road, one would be built.

With the raising of the Plant flag on December 8, 1897, the Tampa Bay Hotel opened for its fifth season, far the most promising since the first. The Casino was offering something classy for everybody this time, a schedule of popular entertainments ranging from Shakespeare to Strauss. North of the exhibition hall, a half-mile racetrack, with grandstand, was in the final stages of construction. Working all summer and fall, groundskeepers had cleared, filled, and graded a sinkhole jungle west of the main building. Now an authentic Scots athlete, Mr. John Hamilton Gillespie, a strikingly handsome gentleman in a kilt, appeared in the region to seek his own fortune. He laid out a nine-hole golf course. In the attire of an English squire, Henry Plant sank the first putt.[54] With a few more seasons such as this one was going to be, "friend Henry" on the East Coast might start worrying.

Then at the southern end of the Plant System, on February 15, 1898, the last taps sounded for 266 sailors in Havana Harbor. The battleship *Maine* had blown up. Tampa's mayor and congressman promptly petitioned Secretary of War Russell Alger for protection against the Spanish Navy. Leading citizens and the Board of Trade demanded a military presence and the funding of coastal defense sites. From the armchair admirals in Washington, no response. Then on March 22nd, Henry Plant wrote Secretary Alger personally, calling attention to the multi-million dollar investment in Port Tampa. On March 25th, Alger sent his Chief of Engineers to begin fortifications on Egmont and Mullet Keys.

---

[54] Covington, 68.

With that, Florida, Tampa, and Henry Plant were in the still-undeclared war. The *Olivette* had already made one run for Assistant Secretary of the Navy, Theodore Roosevelt, delivering ammunition to Key West. Later Winston Churchill, an ambitious young British journalist and a recently decommissioned subaltern in Her Majesty's 4th Hussars, rode the Plant System railroads New York-Tampa and took the *Olivette* to Cuba, where he would come under fire for the first time.[55] Local papers began boosting Tampa as the obvious supply point for operations in the Caribbean. At the end of March a real-life, seagoing admiral checked into the Port Tampa Inn. On behalf of the Plant System, Henry Plant's second in command, Franklin Q. Brown, gave "Fighting Bob" Evans a tour of the harbor. The admiral passed the word to the press corps. In the event of war, make way for the Navy! Fifty thousand troops would be embarked from Port Tampa.

All that time Henry and Margaret Plant had been guests of the Flaglers in Palm Beach and Miami. When they returned aboard the *Mascotte* on April 5th, Brown was on his way to Cuba. On April 14, he brought his report straight to Washington for a meeting with President McKinley and Secretary of War Alger. One month later seven regiments of infantry were on their way to Tampa.[56]

Henry Plant was 78 years old. Why not leave everything to Brown, as he had to Wood? Brown had proved himself as capable and dedicated an executive as any retiring chief could wish for. And behind Brown—since Judge Chisholm's death in 1892—stood the astute and still youthful Robert Erwin, who had been taking charge of both PICO and the SF&W.

If the Cuba operation had been just another long-term vexing business problem, maybe Henry Plant would have said, "Leave it all to Brown and Erwin." But the Cuba operation was much worse than long-term and vexing. It had to be solved right away. And it was never less than a hellacious misery.

—o—

The old drama of the downtrodden in distress, gloating villains ripe for punishment, and the promise of battlefield glory, as whipped up by the "yellow" press, introduced the national consciousness to new and higher standards of instant gratification. Supplies and soldiers came rushing pell-mell down the Plant System into Tampa: an inconceivable, monumental glut, at once teeming and inert.

The supplies were of questionable value from first to last. A pitiful enemy would inflict only 385 of the Army's 2,446 casualties. Aside from the ravages of

---

[55] Pilpel, *Churchill,* 18-20.
[56] Covington, 68-73. Mueller, 30-35.

malaria, American soldiers ate poison from their mess kits: the unsanitary "bully beef" supplied by War Department contractors. The materiel of war itself, when it did arrive at the right place on time, was of dubious value. Though far better equipped than their foe, U.S. soldiers wore uniforms and carried weapons left over from the Civil War.[57]

For that matter, a plaintive lesser drama of the national spirit held that nothing would do better than another war to heal the wounds festering in the South since Appomattox. Just as single-shot rifles and woolen trousers for summer wear in the tropics came out of mothballs, so did Confederate generals and their equally antiquated Union counterparts. What better place to serve as a headquarters for these glorious old fossils than the Tampa Bay Hotel? At taps, one superannuated general would wrap himself in his cloak and sleep on the ground, just as he had when campaigning through Virginia. Only now he was sleeping, or attempting to, on the verandah, right above the rathskeller. All night, every night, the bar was packed with journalists and college boys in tailored uniforms. They were working selflessly to perfect what would be their lasting contribution to *Cuba Libre*.[58]

Margaret Plant certainly spent that summer between the Branford farm and the Manhattan mansion and likewise for Morton, Nellie, and little Henry. The baby would have a predominantly New England upbringing. Florida's infant mortality rate remained horrifyingly high for many years, and cut across all social classes.

Henry Plant, who had turned the hotel operations over fully to Franklin Brown, doubtless took up residency at the Inn, to be near the port. But he only slept there in bouts, infrequently, from exhaustion. It would be remarkable if he paid much attention to the frantic military preparations going on all around him. The *Olivette* and *Mascotte* were being converted to hospital ships. That was probably as close as he came to the glory side of military preparation. A few members of the resurrected high command may have known—thirty-five years before—the kind of relentless, grueling schedule of high-pressure decisions required of Mr. H.B. Plant day and night, but he had not known since chaos-tormented Augusta.

He would be 79 years old soon. Yet was there anyone else who could handle the mess on the waterfront, really? He told a popular magazine of the day: "I regard work as one the essential principles of my success—my personal supervision of every detail of my business. I believe in never leaving to others what I can do myself."[59]

---

[57] Wynne, "Spanish American War," 6-10.
[58] Harner, 27. *Success,* "The King of Florida." 5.
[59] "Report of the Commission," 17.

His experience in loading cargo went back sixty years. He knew what the government report was going to say, "very poor facilities for transferring troops and supplies arriving at Tampa via the Florida Central and Peninsular Railroad to the Plant System leading directly to Port Tampa." Well, whose idea was it that the Florida Central could handle the job? His men had done the government a big favor, locking the switch to the Plant System tracks. What had happened to cause the disaster in the rail yards and on the wharves was not his doing. In fact, it had been done to him, to the Plant System. Now only Henry Plant could set it all right, make it all shipshape, up to his standards, the way it was supposed to be. He would drive himself to have the job finished if it killed him. And, of course, it was killing him.

Privately, he had already begun to make arrangements. In January 1898, a trusted confidant of long standing, George H. Tilley of Darien, Connecticut, came down from the New York office. The two discussed the feasibility of uniting all Plant-owned properties into a Henry Bradley Plant Company, "to perpetuate the name."

He had first acknowledged what would become a growing fascination with the possibilities of perpetuity after becoming a grandfather in 1895. That year the city honored the sixty-seventh birthday of "Tampa's greatest benefactor." Some 3,000 of the more than 12,000 Plant System employees gathered on the grounds of the Tampa Bay Hotel. As Henry Plant arose to speak, he indicated a bouquet on the flag-draped platform beside him, "Those beautiful flowers are a gift from my little grandson, and I speak on his behalf a thanks for all the love and affection which you have shown me, and express the hope that in days to come, when I am no longer with you, that he may be one of yourselves and a co-worker in the enterprises which all the employees of our companies sustain by their energies and by their work."[60]

Henry Plant must have been yet more concerned with the future of those enterprises by the time he immersed himself in the desperate waterfront crisis that summer of 1898. The hectic, relentless weeks of making decisions and issuing orders must have provided some relief from his own desperate crisis, long brewing inside him. The protocol of that occasion, when he publicly committed his hopes to his infant grandson, created an awkward moment. On the platform smiling under the

---

[60] Harner, 26.

pennants and banners, sat Morton Plant, the child's distinguished-looking 43 year-old father.

—o—

Soon it was time for the family's move to the comfort and safety of the Northeast. In the vanguard, Henry and Morton Plant, with Wilson, the valet, left Tampa in Special Car 100. Arriving the next day at the Pennsylvania Railroad depot in Jersey City, they would have taken the ferry across the Hudson River, as on many previous occasions. But suddenly, suffering all the symptoms of a serious heart attack, Henry Plant collapsed. Taking the ferry was for now out of the question. Morton and Wilson spent that night and most of the next day with him, back in Special Car 100. When at last he could be transported across the river, the elegant, familiar carriage was waiting at the 23rd Street Station. Doubtless Dr. Chaisi Durant, his personal physician, rode with him to the Fifth Avenue brownstone. There—surely to a disgruntled response—the patient was ordered to avoid all forms of exertion over the next several days. sent the valet for help. A carriage was immediately available, and with the help of the driver, Plant was lifted into the carriage. The conveyance pulled away at speed and raced uptown to the office of Plant's personal physician, Dr. Chaisi Durant. Quite likely by the time the patient arrived at Dr. Durant's office, he was feeling much better and pooh-poohed attempts at further assistance. Nonetheless, Henry Plant was given a thorough examination and sternly ordered to avoid all forms of exertion over the next several days.[61]

That was in the early summer of 1898, and from then on the decision he had been in the process of making over the past three years—at least—must have assumed a new urgency. By November he had made up his mind. He was going to change his will. He would look to the future of his holdings.

—o—

Henry Plant was back in Tampa when the hotel opened for the season on December 5. Had he discussed his concerns with his family? As far as what people knew about the Plant estate, the traditional arrangements were in effect.

From *The Orange Blossom*, the newsletter of the Tampa Bay Hotel, March 26, 1998, under a handsome photograph of Morton:

---

[61] Covington, 73.

Morton Freeman Plant
Son of the President and one of the vice-presidents of the Plant System is a man of ability and affability, and will some time assume the management of the entire Plant System with credit to himself and honor to the distinguished name he bears.

In the interval arrangements for the future of the Plant System had altered drastically. On the president's return to Florida, action commenced on the plans for perpetuating his name. These were the plans that he had discussed in such closely guarded privacy with George Tilley at the beginning of the year. In January, in equally strict privacy, Henry Plant began conferring with Judge Lynde Harrison, down from New Haven, one of the original PICO officials and now his personal attorney. Though a small, frail-looking man, Harrison was known for a "forceful character." His canny advice must have been to simply change the designated name on the original PICO charter. On April 13, 1899, by decree of the Superior Court of the State of Connecticut, the Southeastern Investment Company became the Henry Bradley Plant Company.

Meanwhile, in Florida, another busy year began.[62] The Plant System acquired a line with connections to Deland, Tavares, and Mt. Dora—the Jacksonville and St. Johns River Railroad that, after the demise of the JT&KW, had inherited the slogan, the "Tropical Trunk Line." In Tampa—though the crowds were still flocking to the Flagler attractions of the East Coast—an even busier season than that of the year before was underway. And this year, too, the troops came marching down the streets. They did so proudly, but looking a little subdued, reminding him of his own attempt to walk upright through Pennsylvania Railroad depot, after his attack of vertigo. On February 23, 1899, a cheering crowd of 10,000 gathered to wish bon voyage to an occupation force headed for Cuba. The hotel orchestra gave a concert on the wharf at Port Tampa. With Margaret at his side, a tired-looking Henry Plant viewed the festivities from a balcony at the Inn.

By this time a significant amount of property had been transferred to the new company, and right to the end Henry Plant would be busy preparing deeds of conveyance. For now he was striving to put everything in order so that his namesake, his little grandson, could carry on the work of his lifetime. When the hotel—far in the red once more—closed for the 1898-99 season, he was ready to add the final codicils to his will. After that, he would be done with striving in the old way.

---

[62] Covington, 73. Turner, 64.

That spring he took his last trip to New York aboard Special Car 100. On May 24, he met with Lynde Harrison and Robert Erwin to draft the codicil, signed the next day, which would guarantee the perpetuation of his name. All that the guarantee lacked was that Henry Plant would establish his legal domicile in Connecticut. He told Harrison and Erwin that he would soon be looking at a fine home, the Hotchkiss House, in New Haven.[63]

About a month later he spent the whole of three consecutive days in the office on 23rd Street, going over the books with George Tilley. For years past it had been a familiar sight along Fifth Avenue, late in the day, to see the founder of the mighty Plant System walking home deep in thought, wearing a broad-brimmed hat and black frock coat. Reaching the house on the two previous evenings, while other members of the family were away, he had spoken with the coachman about a ride uptown to view a piece of promising residential property. This time he went silently inside and had dinner. That night Henry Plant suffered a massive heart attack. Only Dr. Durant was at his bedside when he died the next afternoon,[64] six months before the end of the American century he had helped to make, on June 23, 1899.

---

[63] Cleaveland, *Scrapbooks*, 6.
[64] Cleaveland, 6.

~ X ~

BEYOND THE PRIZE

The will became a battleground. From the moment he felt his health threatened, to have his will, the best precaution available to Henry Plant would have been to make sure that he drew his last breath in Connecticut. The extraordinary codicils added in recent years had been drafted with Connecticut's rules of probate specifically in mind.

The main extraordinary codicil had two provisions. First, everything, everything just as it was, must be held in trust for his four-year old grandson, Henry Bradley Plant II. Then, unless the heir's life should be cut short, the trust could not be dissolved until—a long way down the road—the 21st birthday of the heir's youngest child.[1] Meanwhile, Henry Plant envisioned that life for the rest of the family would go on just as before. Margaret and Morton were to be, in effect, pensioned off with handsome annuities. Though named executors, they would have only a "say" in any decision-making, against three company appointees.

—o—

The will was doomed the moment Dr. Durant pulled the sheet over Henry Plant's face in New York City—in New York State, where provisions for such extensive entailments were discouraged. A lot was at stake though, and it was not to be supposed that the will could be easily broken.

---

[1] Cleaveland, *Scrapbooks*, 6.

Finally, however, the question of the legitimacy of the will was brought before the courts in New York for adjudication.[2]

> Supreme Court, State of New York
> - Special Term -
> December 1901
>
> Margaret J. Plant, individually and as a trustee under the trusts created by the last will and testament and codicils of Henry Bradley Plant, deceased, vs. Lynde Harrison, Morton Freeman Plant, George H. Tilley and Robert G. Erwin, individually and as trustees under the last will and testament of Henry Bradley Plant, deceased and Henry Bradley Plant, an infant.

—o—

For the past year the courtroom battle to determine to fate of the "Plant Millions" had been recorded in the headlines of the time as "This Famous Case." Everything depended on the issue of domicile. The Plant house in Branford was a family home. Henry Plant's visits over the years had established it as a secondary, not a primary, residence. Everything depended on the issue of conclusive intent. When he died, was the testator a resident of the state of New York or the state of Connecticut? Both sides submitted convincing evidence, even seemingly irrefutable evidence. For instance, on the last day of Henry Plant's "conceded residence in New York," he had written:

> June 16, 1899
> Mr. Erwin H. Peaslee, Chairman,
> Finance Committee, Twenty-seventh Assembly
> District, Republican Club.
> Nos. 767 and 769 Sixth Avenue, City
>
> Dear Sir—I am in receipt of your favor of the 9th inst., which has been delayed acknowledgment because of my absence from the city. It is my expectation within a very short time to change my residence to Connecticut, my birthplace, in consequence of which I do not expect to again be able to cast my vote in New York City. I wish the party, however, every success, and especially in national affairs.
> Respectfully,
> (Signed) H.B. Plant[3]

---

[2] Cleaveland, 6.
[3] Cleaveland, 6.

This was on a Friday. The letter must have been signed before midafternoon, because at 3 o'clock Henry Plant caught the train on his journey to Branford. He was accompanied by his valet, Wilson, and by Mary Cahill, a maid. Before their departure the housekeeper had prepared a basket of food, and placed it in the care of Mary Cahill. Wilson would testify that he carried two bags for Mr. Plant. The housekeeper had packed the first with "one shirt, a pair of slippers, and stockings enough to last him two or three days." Wilson had packed the second bag himself. It contained "the instruments Mr. Plant required in consequence of his illness."

Clearly at this stage, attending to these instruments (medicines) was an important responsibility, for Henry Plant had spent almost the whole of his Branford stay in bed. He got up only to visit the cemetery. On Sunday afternoon a relative called, the wife of a second cousin. Her testimony was, "[Mr. Plant] told her that Mrs. Plant had not accompanied him, as he could only stay a short time, and that he had orders from his family physician to return on Tuesday back home. On Monday evening the pastor of Branford's Catholic Church came to call. Father Edward Martin found Henry Plant in bed. The sick man told him "that he had been ill for several days and that he had already remained too long."[4]

From the text of the decision rendered by Justice Leventrit as reported in the New Haven *Register,* "my house on Crown Street and my house with Mrs. Hoadley" refer to this arrangement. The judge then briefly explained why he could "attach but slight importance to these declarations" and to the intended purchase of the Hotchkiss House. The text resumed:

At its conclusion [the visit to the Harrison office] ... he returns to New York, goes straightway to his old house, where his coming was awaited, and in which things were moving in the same grooves as they had for thirty years past. He announces no change in his household. He resumes the routine of his life where he had left off four days previous. He tells his housekeeper the same evening that he was very glad to be "home" again; he tells his wife in the presence of the housekeeper that on the following day he proposed to go to Riverside Drive to look at a house with a view to purchase, as the house they occupied was on leased property, and he wanted one with an elevator in it; he gives instructions to his coachman to call for him the next morning and drive him there. The following morning he goes to his office on Twenty-Third Street for the same hours as for years theretofore, and while there he writes a letter to the defendant Erwin, saying that "I was rather tuckered out when I got home from New Haven." When the coachman calls he is feeling unwell and postpones the

---

[4] Cleaveland, 6.

drive to the morrow. In the course of that day, while continuing as theretofore the course of his New York life, he executed a deed of Halifax property to the Henry Bradley Plant Company, describing himself in New York as a New Haven resident. This fact, as much as any, shows the character of the would-be domicile in New Haven as purely nominal in any event as obviously acquired to for ulterior purposes. On the day he attends his office as usual. After his return to the house at the accustomed hour, the carriage came for the accustomed drive. Mr. Plant, however, was again unable to go, being taken down with the illness that, on the day following, resulted in his death.

Now, abruptly and tightly, Judge Leventrit began to draw his conclusions. With these next words, some faces in the courtroom must have paled visibly.

If Mr. Plant considered himself a resident of New Haven by virtue of the occurrences culminating on the 20th day of June in New Haven, I am quite satisfied that his intent was not bona fide. It must be obvious that Mr. Plant was acting under the guidance of his Connecticut legal advisor, who directed his steps and prompted him to the declarations he was to make. It does not require an extensive search to discover a motive. Mr. Plant's proposed testamentary disposition was invalid under the laws of the state of New York, but valid under the laws of Connecticut.

—o—

The New Haven *Union* announced the settlement of the court battle on February 15, 1902:

SETTLEMENT OF HENRY PLANT ESTATE

A meeting of the executors of the $17,000,000 estate of the late Henry Bradley Plant of Branford and New York, held in the probate of this city yesterday, produced some important and unexpected changes in the management of the vast fortune. The meeting was held before Judge Cleaveland, and was held as a hearing on the accounting of the estate.

The account shows that an inventory of the estate made in January 1900, reported the fortune to include 49,960 shares of the capital stock of the Henry Bradley Plant Company, the other 40 shares having been given to Morton Plant, his son, during the lifetime of the president of the company.

The net earnings of the company, which, of course, represents the greater part of the fortune since July 1, 1899, to February 1 this year, in addition to $300,000 which are dividends to the estate, amounting to $724,619.88.

The next step of the meeting was the resignation of two of the executors. They are Judge Lynde Harrison, of this city, and Robert Erwin, of Savannah. Their action in resigning the important positions came as a surprise. The withdrawal of the two executors means that the big estate will be withdrawn from the Connecticut courts and transferred to the New York tribunal. This will give the widow her dower right of $6,000,000. The balance will go to the tester's son, Morton Plant.

(An interesting paragraph in the account contains the statement that all of the legacies in the will have been paid except $15,000, which is not yet due under the terms of the will. This amount will go to the children of Charles and Emma Hoadley, when they have reached the age of 21.)

The New Haven *Palladium* filled in more details in its issue of February 17, 1902:

EXECUTOR GOT $161,625

The account that was submitted by Judge Lynde Harrison of the conditions of the estate of the late millionaire Henry Bradley Plant, prior to his resignation as one of the executors of the estate in April, was the subject of open debate in Probate Count. Judge Lucien Burpee of Waterbury, whose clients are the Hoadleys of Waterbury, claims that this state should have jurisdiction of the estate, claims that his questioning of Judge Harrison was merely for the purpose of familiarizing himself with the figures of the account.

During his questioning Judge Burpee asked of Judge Harrison, "What are your fees for your services as executor?"

The witness hesitated a second and then answered, "They were $161,625."

"Did the other executors receive a like sum?"

"I know only what I've heard," was the answer.

"Who told you?"

"I object," said Mr. Shipman who was representing the New York executors of the estate.

"Upon what," recurred Judge Burpee, "was that fee based?"

Judge Harrison explained that is was based upon the New York valuation of the estate. "That valuation was also used as the basis for fees in Connecticut." he added.

Judge Harrison said that the same fees, $161,625, were paid to executors Tilley and Erwin, the latter of whom resigned at the time of Judge Harrison's resignation.

(The final report ending of February 14, 1902, showed the estate to be worth as follows—Personal property on hand February 4, $16,560,214.48; value securities in Henry Bradley Plant Company to February 1, 1902, $742,619,98; cash in treasury of Henry Bradley Plant Company, $105,488.86. Total, $17,408,323.22

The value of the estate as fixed by the New York courts is now $26,000,000, and it was on this value that the fee was fixed. The increase in the value of the estate is based on the great value of the securities held by the estate.)

On July 11, 1902, the New Haven *Leader*, carried the following story:

PLANT COMPANY GOES

On the short calendar of the superior court this afternoon was the application of the Henry Bradley Plant Company for an order limiting the time for the presentation of claims. The company has gone out of existence by a vote of directors passed on March 18 of this year, and the superior court's notice has been brought to that vote of dissolution.

The company was incorporated in 1899 for the purpose of operating the various large interests of the late Henry B. Plant of Branford. It succeeded the South Eastern Investment Company.

Since he died so soon after adding the disputed codicils to his will, Henry Plant's last decisions might be regarded as ill considered as well as ill advised. From his speech of 1895, however, we know that he gave the matter lengthy reflection. But was it within the range of his planning, within the range of his thoughts, to ponder the psychological ramifications? What would be the status, in daily reality, of a small child destined to wield an immense financial authority brought up in a household by adults financially neutered on his behalf? A large part of the child's executive minority would have been dominated by the legal executors of the estate, Harrison, Erwin, and Tilley. Then, a long uneasy period of youthful awareness, a kind of interregnum, before majority and the assumption of total control. The failure of such arrangements to produce a capable, a "whole" adult human being, goes far to explain the failure of every dynasty since the beginning of history.

Henry Plant - Pioneer Empire Builder

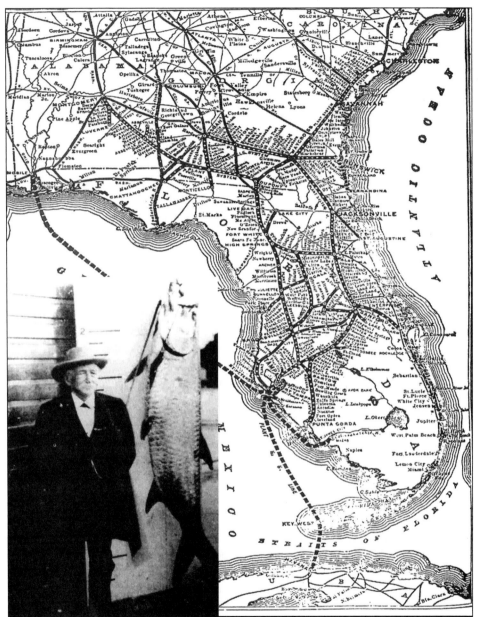

The Plant System complete, and its founder with another big fish. Henry Plant could have spent his last years visiting the many recreatioanl facilities along the sunny routes he had established. His benevolent presence would have been welcome everywhere and by everyone—especially by his employees. But though he and his friend Henry Flagler were among the prime instigatorsof fun-filled retirement, they never knew it up close.

It was a desperate solution. But what had been the problem? The rise and fall of financial dynasties in America is briefly told, from shirt-cuffs to shirttails, in three generations. The gene for successful massive acquisitiveness is only rarely, rarely inherited. Henry Plant must have realized quite soon after Morton, age sixteen, went to work with the Southern Express Company, that his son lacked his own aptitude for business. But at the time, in 1868, the observation was hardly worth more than a half-conscious review from year to year.

Finally, just the fact that Morton never struck out on his own was enough. With a generous allowance as well as a salary, he had the funds to make considerable investments. After all, for Henry Plant's kind of success, the first requirement was simply to exercise the combination of a searching, bright eye and an ever-active mental acuity, to notice somewhere out there a good thing. Then, "get a-holt" and make the most of it—develop your opportunity. True, the final requirement was vision, but that could come later. And who was a better example of the "later" principle than himself? In between, of course, there had been many promising indications. The father must have been well pleased to observe that the young man had a good head for figures, that his judgment was sound, and that he was industrious, sober, and absolutely honorable and reliable in all his dealings.

If the boss's son did not readily assume command, that could be just because he was the boss's son. Certainly, in whatever positions of command he did eventually assume, Morton earned the dignified respect of colleagues and subordinates. And that polite respect was enough for him. In family company after company, Morton Freeman Plant had been appointed to the office of vice-president. Never would he seek to rise any higher.

It only struck the father when he was near the end of his life that his son's lack of initiative disqualified him as an heir to his legacy. For he was passing on not just "a vast fortune." Had that been all, Morton would have been an ideal heir. Rather, Henry Plant must have been starkly aware for some time that he had achieved his wildest dreams. His concerns had paid wages to many thousands of employees in 14 states. His railroads ran on close to 2,000 miles of track, His ships navigated the high seas of the world. He had created and was the master of an empire. He was required to think grandly, in terms of dynasty.

Yet precisely because of this, the grandeur of dynasty, he must keep his thinking secret. His wife, for all her appreciation of the Plant System's vast wealth, had never committed herself to its legacy under the Plant family name. From the beginning, her enthusiasm for her role as his son's stepmother had diminished. Now, was she more than distantly aware of his grandson's future?

Whatever discussions he may have had with his associates in business, it was in solitude, then, that Henry Plant resolved on a desperate measure. By the second codicil to his will he sought to cast the control of his empire as far as he could into the future. But in making this extraordinary attempt, he restricted the locality of its application.

On the eve of having his way after death, the man who had done so much to conquer geography would have his last wishes thwarted by mere distance. The man, who had done so much to make travel easy and available, took one trip too many. The man who had bought so many places, failed to buy the last place.

The ultimate result would reduce to insignificance the share of the legacy eventually inherited by Henry Bradley Plant II. Though there would be, still, a fortune left.

For reasons of legal strategy, Margaret brought suit against the executors, including Morton, who was recovering at the time from a near-fatal attack of typhoid fever. Actually the two of them were acting in concert to break the will. That done, they proceeded with all haste to disentangle their interests, and their relationship.

Very little was heard about Margaret thereafter. From her donation in 1902 of costly decor imported from France to the Church of the Immaculate Conception, we know of her continuing attachment to Branford's Catholic community. For a while she and Morton wrangled over the ownership of the Tampa Bay Hotel. But antagonists rarely contend for very long over a drain to their mutual assets. By default, Morton took over. Still, Margaret was disappointed. She had made plans years before to make the entire property over to the local Jesuit order.[5] After a brief, valiant attempt to turn things around, Morton betook himself to a better bet across the bay, the Belleview.

From then on he became a "sportsman"—one of the world's premier yachtsmen—and a gentleman farmer. Typically, Morton was at sea with Nellie aboard their championship schooner, the *Ingomar*, when his father died. In one European season the *Ingomar* won 21 of 25 races and was the envy of King Edward and Kaiser Wilhelm. These two monarchs owned the world's largest steam yachts. In 1907 Morton commissioned the third largest, the *Iolanda*, which cost $1,000 a day to operate. When he and Nellie spent the summer of 1908 cruising the Mediterranean and entertaining royalty, Morton was proclaimed "Commodore Plant."

---

[5] Mueller, *Steamships*, 48.

A few years later he commissioned what was to be the nonpareil racing vessel of the time, the super-sleek *Elena*. Then, in the middle of a triumphant 1913 season, a fever epidemic swept the eastern seaboard. Nellie died. Morton sold his fabulously expensive pleasure craft and never again sailed in competition.[6]

With the immediate proceeds of breaking the will, he and Nellie had acquired some land, by the shore in Groton, Connecticut. She had attended the Sorbonne, studying architecture, and in 1902 they built a "summer retreat," 18,900 square feet in the heroic baronial style. Complete at a cost of $3,000,000, Branford House—with its profusion of "ornate gardens—embellished with rose-colored marble and reflecting pools," surpassed even the Tampa Bay Hotel in its effects "of overpowering ornamentation."[7] Nearby, Morton established the 330 acre Branford Farms, in every detail a model operation, and bred prize-winning cattle and poultry. The 72-acre estate of the Branford House yielded a profusion of flowers, fruit, and vegetables, distributed through the countryside. And when landscaping exposed a run-down resort hotel, marring their vista, the Plants bought the property and demolished the old structure—then summoned a leading architect to build a new hotel, under the same terms given John Wood. The next season eleven-year-old Henry Plant II raised the Plant System flag over the suitably heroic Griswold Hotel, which became "the most fashionable hotel on the Connecticut coast."[8] To insure the orientation of newly arriving guests, Morton would replace the old Groton town hall by the depot at his own expense—in the baronial style, of course.[9]

Though always behind the scenes, he was revered, too, as just a plain good sport. He bought the local baseball team in New London, renamed them "The Planters," and made them minor league champions. Later he became part owner of the Philadelphia Phillies.[10] It was in advancing the game of golf, however, that Morton made his permanent contribution to sports, if from far behind the scenes. After losing interest in the problems of the Tampa Bay Hotel, Morton made the Belleview in Clearwater the family's winter retreat. At the Griswold Hotel he had put in a splendid golf course. Those traditional vistas of gleaming and shadowy emerald, however, had never been duplicated in Florida. The gritty soil, the blis-

---

[6] *Branford Review,* 7, "Morton F. Plant."
[7] Heckman, "Rare Photographs." *Groton's Historic Houses*
[8] Kimball, "Prominent Citizen."
[9] "Groton Historic Houses."
[10] "Morton F. Plant."

tering sun, the often-rainless weather made a Florida golf course an unlovely affair of dusty fairways and putting greens of hard-packed sand.

For two years at his Belleview Hotel, Morton Plant took up the challenge of building traditional golf courses in Florida. He spared no expense in developing the technology that would water the acres of the special grasses he was attempting to grow. After experimenting with many soil types, he finally brought down trainloads of topsoil from Indiana. It worked. The water held, the grass grew and stayed green. In 1910 he commissioned the outstanding golf course architect of the time, Donald J. Ross, to design two championship courses outside the hotel. Legions of approving golfers have played them ever since.[11]

The year the golf courses opened, Henry Bradley Plant II was going on sixteen, a plump, somewhat owlish-looking young man. Unlike his paternal progenitors, he had grown up knowing only great wealth. His mother and father went quietly about a full social life, but were never less than devoted parents. Once, in a bicycle accident at the Belleview, young Henry badly injured his right leg. Morton sent Special Car 100 to Chicago for a specialist, and kept the doctor at the hotel for a month.[12] After Nellie's death, life changed dramatically in the Plant household. Within the year (1913) Morton Plant began a courtship and embarked on a marriage worthy of tabloid coverage. In Waterford, Connecticut, Sara Mae "Masie" Cadwell, the town's school teacher, had married a member of the local gentry, Seldon Manwaring. They were the doting parents of a son, Phillip, an exceptionally goodlooking, active young lad. Mr. Manwaring was the proprietor of a popular local establishment that would later become a resort for city folks, the Oswegatchie House. Here, Masie was adding a few artistic touches to the sign out front when Morton—visiting Waterford to inspect the trolley line he owned—came sauntering along. The two met. Shortly thereafter Seldon Manwaring found himself maneuvered into a compromising predicament with a young woman in a New York hotel room, enabling Masie to sue for a divorce. Shortly after that, Masie gave Morton her hand, receiving from him the splendid mansion he had built in 1904 on the northeast corner of Fifth Avenue and 52nd Street.[13]

The consequences of such generosity, however, eventually excised the Plant nameplate. Popular legend has it that one day a jeweler, newly come over from Paris, showed Masie a string of perfectly matched Oriental pearls, which was a steal at $1,200,000. When her new husband failed to appreciate the opportunity,

---

[11] Board and Colcord, *Belleview,* 20.
[12] Board and Colcord, 15.
[13] Bachman, *Waterford, 12-13.* Dance, *Scrapbook,* 83. Gray, "Millionare's Row," 7.

she went back to the jeweler, whose name was Henri Cartier. He was willing to bargain. Smoothly the two arranged to swap the wedding gift for the pearls.[14] The less colorful but likely much truer, version stipulates a straightforward real estate transaction.[15] In any case, the present address of Cartier & Company boasts a corner entrance at 2 East 52nd Street.

The next year Morton died in the influenza epidemic that swept Europe and America at the end of the First World War. Mrs. Masie Caldwell Manwaring Plant inherited the great part of his fortune, said to be in the neighborhood of $50,000,000. At the time of their marriage Morton had formally adopted her wild thirteen year-old son, Phillip. Terrifically handsome and athletic now, Phillip Manwaring Plant would go on to be—for the rest of his short life—the exemplary Hemingway-Fitzgerald hero. After three glamorous marriages, he died on expedition in 1941.[16] The heir designated by the founder to carry on the Plant empire was twenty-three at the time of his father's death. Except for a short life span, he resembled his younger stepbrother not at all. In 1917 Henry Bradley Plant II married Amy Warren of Connecticut. He led a quiet life, fathered two daughters, enjoyed sailing, and died in obscurity.[17]

The daughters, Amy Capron Plant and Mary Ellen Plant, spinsters both, lived to a great old age.[18]

After the decree of the New York Supreme Court at the end of 1902, the Plant empire began breaking apart like a mighty iceberg. As years went by people would no longer remember that a single man had established and ruled the powerful transportation systems so much a part of their daily lives—the Atlantic Coast Line Railroad, the Peninsular & Occidental Steamship Line, the Railway Express Agency.

The Southern Express would hold on the longest, the way Henry Plant had created it. The newly formed Interstate Commerce Commission subpoenaed the company records shortly after the founder's death. It was discovered that the 1861 charter authorized the issue of 50,000 shares of stock. The initial distribution of 588 shares can only be approximated. The ICC report concluded, "None of the

---

[14] Board and Colcord, 29.
[15] Gray, 7. Phinizy, "Millionare," 27.
[16] Board and Colcord, 35
[17] Board and Colcord, 36
[18] Board and Colcord, 30

original twenty-four stockholders are now living, and there is no existing record to show how much was realized from its distribution."[19] A record does indicate, however, that at his death Henry Plant owned 38,000 shares. The company treasury then held millions in undivided profits, and had unfailingly paid eight percent in dividends from the beginning.[20]

The loyal, and astute Michael J. O'Brien, Plant's business associate since 1863, left his name on the map of Florida—modestly. When the Plant System completed the line through Lafayette County from Live Oak to Rowland's Bluff, the citizens of the ingloriously titled mid-way village of Dab's Hole decided to claim O'Brien as their namesake. When he arrived for the ceremony, however, Mr. O'Brien had need of all his Irish charm. The sign on the new depot that day proclaimed, "O'Brine." Rowland's Bluff, the larger village to the south, subsequently honored Henry Plant and became New Branford, then Branford. From Plant's demise, Michael O'Brien served as president of the Southern Express Company until his own death in 1909.[21] In 1918 Congress, acting on ICC recommendations, united all interstate delivery services under government supervision as the Railway Express Agency.

Henry Plant's first love in the world of transportation, his steamship interests, passed into friendly hands. That Caribbean cruise of 1893 must have smitten Henry Flagler, who began expanding the Florida East Coast Steamship Company. While the will was on its way to court, he struck up a deal to incorporate the much larger Plant maritime interests with his own. Between 1900-02 the Peninsular & Occidental Steamship Company was formed. Morton Plant served for a while as vice-president. Before very long, naturally, Flagler ran everything.[22] For a while it appeared that Morton would take over the chain of eleven luxury hotels. But he soon narrowed his interest to the Belleview, which became more and more successful.[23] Passing in the 1920s into the Biltmore organization, and in the 1990s into international ownership, the Belleview Resort Hotel is today among the world's largest inhabited wooden structures, and still a success.[24]

Even such a masterful hotelier as Franklin Q. Brown, who assumed overall control of the chain, could do little for the Tampa Bay Hotel. In 1905 it became city

---

[19] Harlow, *Old Way Bills,* 324
[20] Harlow, 325.
[21] Mueller, 47.
[22] Mueller, 71-120.
[23] Board and Colcord, 19-25.
[24] Board and Colcord, 34-123.

property for less than one percent of its cost to build and went into mothballs for decades.[25] Today, gorgeously restored, the Tampa Bay Hotel has become the campus of the University of Tampa. The once-residential north wing houses a walk-through time machine, the Henry B. Plant Museum.

None of the other luxury hotels survive. But in Sanford the quaint structures of the Pico Building and the Pico Hotel still stand, maintained in mint condition.

Henry Plant's truly namesake achievement, the keystone of the entire financial structure, the Plant System—his railroad, his railroads—went quickly. In his first act as executor, Robert Erwin negotiated a sale to the Atlantic Coast Line,[26] and almost immediately afterwards in 1902 was appointed corporate attorney and president.[27]

The Tampa *Morning Tribune* signaled the end of Henry Plant's dream on July 1, 1902:

GOODBYE PLANT SYSTEM

Yesterday was the last day of the existence of the Plant System of Railroads. Today there isn't a Plant System train, a Plant System depot, a Plant System rail or a Plant System employee anywhere in the world.

The absorption of the Plant System—a system that has been closely connected with the up-building of the South and particularly the State of Florida—by the Atlantic Coast Line, went into full effect last night at mid-night. In the *Tribune* this morning, the familiar heading of the advertisements and schedules of the Plant System disappears. Gradually, the old name will vanish over the entire system, and the Plant System of Railways will be but a memory.

The man who more than any other put Henry Plant's railroads on the map, Henry Haines, never built or ran railroads again after he left Florida. He promoted American railroad interests in Europe for a while, and then returned to become commissioner of the Southern States Freight Association, and vice-president of the Atlantic and Danville Railroad. In 1905 and 1907 Boston University invited Haines—who never attended college—to deliver a series of lectures on railroad management. His six volumes on the subject, published over the next ten years, were widely translated. For the rest of his life he served as an engineering consult-

---

[25] Mueller, 39.
[26] Dozier, Atlantic Coast Line , 145-7
[27] Mueller, 6.

ant to foreign governments. Henry Haines died in Lennox, Massachusetts in 1926, at the age of 82, and was buried in Savannah.[28]

Henry Sanford did more than any one else to bring Henry Plant to Florida. Strong of spirit, but in frail health all his life, he died in 1891. None of his extravagant plans ever amounted to much, except for the small city named after him, which slowly prospered.[29] James Ingraham, Henry Sanford's youthful assistant whose enthusiasm "sold" the idea of building a railroad to Tampa, remained a vital spirit in the Plant System so long as there was something to build. Then he went to work for Henry Flagler, supervising the extension to Key West. When Flagler took an interest in taking up where Hamilton Disston had left off, draining the Everglades, James Ingraham surveyed the project.[30]

Henry Flagler was 80 years old when he came to Key West in 1910 to celebrate the completion of the Florida East Coast Railway, the "Eighth Wonder of the World." Still, his 914 miles of track could hardly match Plant's 2,235. Taking charge to the last, Henry Flagler lived until 1913. His Key West extension became the roadbed for the highway to the Keys when a hurricane blew away the rails in 1935.[31]

That vital human asset Henry Plant had acquired with the purchase of the Florida Southern Railroad in 1885, Franklin Q. Brown, saw to the liquidation of the last elements of the Plant empire. Afterwards Brown settled in Dobbs Ferry, New York, where he lived until 1955, active in business and civic affairs to the last.[32] Immediately after Robert Erwin accepted his appointment with the corporation that succeeded the Plant System, his health began to decline. The alert and courteous young lawyer who came to counsel Henry Plant on building a railroad to Florida in 1879, and who had stayed to give shrewd advice from then on, was a railroad president for only two years. He resigned from the Atlantic Coast Line in 1905 and died a few months later.[33] Lynde Harrison's death followed the next year. The birdlike little man of "forceful character" left a sizable estate, the large part of it represented by his executor's fee of $161,625. Probate went swiftly, though the eldest son had been entirely cut off. At the bottom of the assets of the Harrison estate, listed in diminishing order:

---

[28] Johnson, "Plant's Lieutenants," 290-91
[29] Fry, Sanford, 164-75
[30] Tebeau, *History of Florida*, 239.
[31] Chandler, *Henry Flagler*, 267-8.
[32] Johnson, 385-7.
[33] Johnson, 380.

Plant Investment Company ... 17 shares ... $100.00[34]

The most widely beheld symbol of the Plant System's power, efficiency, and opulence, however, continued to run for many years and still survives, intact. Following the breakup of the System, Special Car 100 passed through many adventures, and is currently on permanent display at the Illinois Railway Museum in Union, Illinois.[35]

—o—

Of course trains are running on the tracks of the Plant System to this day. But the way they ran on March 1, 1901, would have given Henry Plant the most satisfying thrill of his life. And maybe the old railroad king was around somewhere, for this would be a train race with a miracle finish.[36] For every railroad line, a U.S. Post Office contract was the big-money ticket. In bidding for the Jacksonville-West Indies route, a tie resulted between the brand-new Seaboard Airline Railroad and the Plant System, operating in the last full year of its existence under that venerable name. It was agreed to settle on the basis of the best time in a race run, on their separate tracks, from Savannah to Jacksonville.

The Seaboard ran a straight-ahead coastline route. The Plant System's triangular inland route was longer by 32 miles. To stay competitive, the old-timers from Tampa had contracted with the Rhode Island Locomotive Works for big ten-wheelers of the same model that was going to make Casey Jones a legend. With each contender hauling four equally-loaded freight cars, the race began in the early morning hours of March 1, 1901. South from Savannah the rival tracks ran parallel down a 12-mile stretch, and immediately the more powerful Plant System engine established a seemingly insurmountable lead. But its firebox began overheating. Abruptly, feebly, the mighty vehicle labored to a halt, wreathed ignominiously in its own smoke. Moments later the Seaboard engine went by, the crew waving and jeering. Their victory clinched so soon, so easily, they began making celebratory stops at each station down the line.

When cooled off, the ACL engine limped into Fleming, eight miles away. Just then the northbound local came in, pulled by the other and practically brand-new, high-stepping Casey Jones ten-wheeler, "The Rhode Island Lady," Engine 111. Desperately—and doubtless amid near-mutinous passenger consternation—the

---

[34] Cleaveland, 8.
[35] Kramer, Clark and Weart, "Private Car."
[36] Burnett, "Great Train Race." Hurst, *Magic Wilderness,* Pettengill, *Florida Railroads,* 95-6.

newly arrived cars were put onto a siding. The locomotives were switched. The engineer of "The Rhode Island Lady" and his fireman—Albert Lodge and Charlie Johnson, respectively—now took over.

If Henry Plant had chosen a driver for the race, he would have chosen tiny Albert Lodge, who had exactly his own imperturbable demeanor and steady gaze. For the sake of the historical record, luck would further have it that two veteran railroad men, S.S. McClellen and James "Uncle Jimmy" Ambrose, were deadheading a ride and came aboard. The two were still admiring the cab's state-of-the-art equipment when the depot at Jesup flashed by. McClellen shouted, "This train is going awfully fast." His voice, a bellow really, sounded small in the screaming thunder of the cab. At the 69th milepost he and Uncle Jimmy punched their stopwatches. At the 74th post they looked at each other, gaping. The current land speed record of 112.5 mph had been recently set, supposedly for many years to come, by the New York Central's famous Engine 999. Down the straightaway from Jesup, Albert Lodge had been flying along at 120 mph.

Instants later, outside Waycross, McClellen and Ambrose clapped their ears shut against the shrieking of the wheels. McClellen later wrote, "I shall never forget the things that passed through my mind as the train reached the top of the hill just a little south of Screven and started down [toward] the Santilla River. There is a little curve just after passing over the river, and I wondered whether the train was going to take the curve at its speed or take to the woods." Then they were highballing toward the dangerous convex curve at Race Pond. From McClellen's narrative, "Albert Lodge closed up the throttle three notches. I prepared to heave a sigh of relief. But then he immediately pulled it out five notches. We hit the curve. Uncle Jimmy grabbed me and I grabbed the hot iron pipes on the boiler head, which now felt rather cool."

Engine 111 finally slowed down for the signals at the Jacksonville yards, and coasted over to the far side of the depot. Quite a while later the rival train arrived, heavily bedecked in victory flags. The staff at each small town depot, alerted by telegraph, had been turning out to hail their heroes. Stopping now right at the Jacksonville station, the Seaboard men took their precious time disembarking, taking into account what must be the initially sophisticated restraint of the big city. Their glory would be crowned soon enough by a raucous surprise-party welcome at a breakfast fit for the gods, such as they now were, in the restaurant. But when they came sauntering into the big room, they found it crowded but strangely quiet. At last their majestic conductor asked, "Has that broken down Plant engine been heard from yet?" The tumult of laughter went on until the Seaboard men singled out the smiling crew from Engine 111, and became part of it too. Then, in one of the last gestures of the Plant System's tradition of generous hospitality, the real celebration began.

—o—

In the twilight of the Gilded Age, in his last years, celebrations were the most visible part of Henry Plant's life. Hitherto, his style of meeting the public had been a buggy ride to the crossroads store. Such grand events as the 1895 Atlanta Cotton Exposition were something new. But how could he stay away? "Georgia, the South, and Atlanta owe more to Henry B. Plant than to any other man," said mayor Porter King.[37] When acknowledging progress in the 1890s, Henry Plant was a main attraction.

Called on to speak, he dwelt on his gratitude for the people who had joined him in making the progress possible. Almost eighty years old, he spoke eagerly, at length, and in perfect humility on one theme, the loyalty of those who worked for him, the employees of the Plant System. And this loyalty had been established on the basis of mutual respect; the Plant System had never been idled for even one hour by a strike.[38] Even when his passion for dynasty became overmastering, he never lost sight of that, the rewards of association. Forging ahead when the slightest progress meant sacrifice and risk, *together*, they had created an empire.

And from highest to lowest they had worked together in an atmosphere of total respect. From his obituary that summer in the *New York Times*, "Mr. Plant never treated a subordinate unfairly or harshly, and no subordinate of his was ever heard to speak an unkind word about him. Mr. Plant did as much as any one man toward bringing the North and the South together after the Civil War."[39]

An earlier encomium sums up the specific aspect of his legacy that has left the widest, the most significant, and the most lasting application. Of all the lavish praise heaped on him from the time he became the widely celebrated Mr. H.B. Plant, nothing could have pleased him better than this one sentence from the *Atlanta Constitution* on the occasion of his 77th birthday, "More than any man living he represents the great industrial revolution which has come over the Southern States and which marks the success of free over slave labor."[40] It came down to that, the secret of all his riches, under the best terms available, making each day's work a fully rewarding individual accomplishment.

Henry Plant brought the promise of that possibility with him when he came to the South, when he came to Florida. It took courage, cunning, and relentless effort to keep it alive, the promise of working hard and working free. In the end, the empire gone, the promise would live on, always a little closer to fulfillment.

---

[37] Mueller, 39.
[38] Nolan, 115.
[39] *New York Times,* June 27, 1899.
[40] *Atlantic Constitution* in Harner, *Promoters,* 26.

WORKS CITED
- Books -

Agnew, J.L. and Lee, S.D. *Historical Record of Savannah*. Savannah: Still and Company, 1869.

Akin, Edward N. *Flagler: Rockefeller Partner & Florida Baron*. Kent: Kent State University Press, 1988.

Arsenault, Ray. *St. Petersburg and the Florida Dream*. Gainesville: University of Florida Press, 1986.

Atkins, Caius Glen & Fagley, Fredrick L. *American Congregationalism*. Boston: Pilgrim Press, 1942.

Ayers, Edward, L. *The Promise of the New South*. New York: Oxford University Press, 1992.

"Benjamin F. Newcomer," *Baltimore and Its People*. Various Contributors. Volume II. New York: Lewis Publishing Company, 1912.

Beebe, Lucius. *Mansions on Rails: The Folklore of the Private Railway Car*. Berkeley: Howell-North, 1959.

Black, Robert C. *Railroads of the Confederacy*. Chapel Hill: University of North Carolina Press, 1950.

Board, Prudy Taylor and Colcord, Ester B. *The Belleview: A Century of Hospitality*. Virginia Beach: Donning, 1996.

Branden, Susan. *Architects of Leisure*. Gainesville: University of Florida Press, 2002.

Brown, Canter. *Florida's Peace River Frontier*. Orlando: University of Central Florida Press, 1991.

Bruton, Quinilla and Bailey, David E., *Plant City: Origins and History*. Winston-Salem: Hunter Publications, 1984.

Butterfield, Roger. *The American Past*. New York: Simon and Schuster, 1947.

Cashin, Edward J. *The Story of Augusta*. Augusta: Richmond County Board of Education, 1950.

Chandler, David Leon. *Henry Flagler*. New York: Macmillan, 1986.

Conrad, Joseph. *The Nigger of the Narcissus and Other Stories*. New York: Dutton, 1978.

Coleman, Kenneth, ed. *Dictionary of Georgia Biography*. Athens: University of Georgia Press, 1983.

----. *A History of Georgia*. Athens: University of Georgia Press, 1997.

Corey, Elizabeth. Introduction by Bell I. Wiley. *Confederate City*. Columbia: University of South Carolina Press, 1986.

Covington, James. *Plant's Palace*. Louisville: Harmony House, 1991.

Crane, Stephen. "Maggie, a Girl of the Streets." Stephen Crane: *Stories and Tales*. New York: Vintage Books, 1955.

Craven, Avery. *The Coming of the Civil War*. Chicago: University of Chicago, 1974.

Davis, William C. *A Government of Our Own*. New York: The Free Press, 1994.

----. *Jefferson Davis: The Man and His Hour*. New York: Harper-Collins, 1991.

Dayton, Fred Erving. *Steamboat Days*. New York: Fredrick A. Stokes Company, 1925.
Derr, Mark. *Some Kind of Paradise*. New York: Morrow, 1989.
Derrick, Samuel M. *A Centennial History of South Carolina Railroads*. Spartanburg: Reprint Press, 1975.
Dillard, Annie. *The Living*. New York: Harper Collins, 1992.
Doggett, John. *The New York City Directory for 1842 and 1843*. New York: Doggett, 1842.
Dozier, Howard D. *The Story of the Atlantic Coast Line Railroad Company*. New Haven: Yale University Press, 1920.
Dutcher, Salem. *Memorial History of Augusta, Georgia: From the Close of the Eighteenth Century to the Present*. Spartanburg: Reprint Press, 1980.
Ellis, Edward Robb. *The Epic of New York City*. New York: Kodansha America, 1997.
Federal Writers Project. Connecticut: *A Guide to Its Roads, Lore, and People*. Cambridge: Riverside, 1938.
Fleming, Barry. *Autobiography of a City in Arms*. Augusta: Richmond County Historical Society, 1976.
Foner, Eric. *Reconstruction: America's Unfinished Revolution*. New York: Harper & Row, 1988.
Fry, Joseph A. *Henry S. Sanford: Business and Diplomacy in Nineteenth-Century America*. Reno: University of Nevada Press, 1982.
Gannon, Michael. *The New History of Florida*. Gainesville: University Press of Florida, 1996.
Gillett, Timothy P. *The Past and Present in the Secular and Religious History of the Congregational Church and Society of Branford*. New Haven: Morehouse and Taylor, 1858. New Haven: New Haven Colony Historical Society.
Glisson, J.T. *The Creek*. Gainesville: University Press of Florida, 1998.
Grismer, Karl. *Tampa*. St. Petersburg, 1950.
Gordon, Sarah H. *Passage to Union*. Irvin R. Dee: Chicago, 1996.
Hanna. Alfred J. and Katherine A. *Lake Okeechobee*. Dunwoodie, Georgia: Burke, 1973.
Hanson, Robert. *Safety-Courtesy-Service: History of the Georgia Railroad*. Johnson City: Overmountain Press, 1996.
Harlow, Alvin F. *Old Way Bills: The Romance of the Express Companies*. New York: Arno Press, 1976.
Harner, Charles E. *Florida's Promoters*. Tampa: Trend House, 1973.
Harpers Magazine. *The South*. Editors. New York: Gallery Books, 1990.
Herr, Kincaid. *The Louisville & Nashville Railroad, 1850-1963*. Louisville: L&N Public Relations Department, 1964.
Hoffman, Glenn. *Building a Great Railroad: A History of the Atlantic Coast Line Railroad*. Richmond: CSX Corporation, 1998.
Hofstader, Richard. *American Political Tradition*. New York: Vintage, 1961.
Homberger, Eric. *The Historical Atlas of New York City*. New York: Henry Holt, 1994.
Horgan, James. *Pioneer College: The Centennial History of Saint Leo College, Saint Leo Abbey, and Holy Name Priory*. Saint Leo: Saint Leo College Press, 1991.
Hurst, Robert L. *Magic Wilderness*. Waycross: Wilderness Publications, 1982.

James, Marquis. *The Raven: A Biography of Sam Houston.* Austin: University of Texas Press, 1988.

Jensen, Oliver. *American Heritage History of Railroads in America.* New York: Random House, 1975.

Jones, J.B. *A Rebel War Clerk's Diary of the Confederate States Capitol.* Howard Swigget, ed. New York: Sagamore Press, 1958.

Johnson, Angus James. *Virginia Railroads in the Civil War.* Chapel Hill: University of North Carolina Press, 1961.

Johnson, Paul. *A History of the American People.* New York: HarperCollins, 1997.

Karlen, Arlo. *Men and Microbes.* New York: Putnam, 1995.

Kirkland, Edward Chase. *Men, Cities, and Transportation.* Cambridge: Harvard University Press, 1948.

Klein, Maury. *History of the Louisville & Nashville Railroad.* New York: Macmillan, 1972.:

Kolchin, Peter. *American Slavery, 1819-77.* New York: Hill and Wang, 1993.

Landau, Elaine. *Tuberculosis.* New York: Venture Books, 1993.

Larkin, Jack. *The Reshaping of Everyday Life: 1790-1840.* New York: Harper and Row, 1988.

Lyman, Susan Elizabeth. *The Story of New York.* New York: Crown, 1975.

Mancini, Martin. *One Dies ...Get Another - Convict Leasing in the American South, 1866-1928.* Columbia: University of South Carolina Press, 1995.

Mann, Robert. *Rails 'neath the Palms.* Burbank: Darwin, 1983.

Martin, S. Walter. "Henry Bradley Plant." *Georgians in Profile,* Horace Montgomery, Ed. Athens: University of Georgia Press, 1958.

----. "Morton Freeman Plant." Robert L. Frey, ed. *Encyclopedia of American Business History and Biography.* New York: Facts on File, 1988.

McPherson, James M. *Battle Cry of Freedom: the Civil War Era.* New York: Oxford University Press, 1988.

McWhiney, Grady. *Cracker Culture: Celtic Ways in the Old South.* Birmingham: University of Alabama Press, 1988.

Mitchell, Lonzo B. *The Right Way: Central of Georgia Railway Company.* Savannah: 1963.

Mormino, Gary R. and Pizzo, Anthony P. *Tampa: The Treasure City.* Tulsa: Continental Heritage Press, 1983

Mueller, Ed. *Steamships of the Two Henrys.* DeLeon Springs, Florida: Painter Printing, 1996.

Murdock, R. Ken. *Outline History of Central Florida Railroads.* Winter Garden: Central Florida Chapter, National Railway Historical Society, 1999.

Nevins, Allen. *Ordeal of a Nation: A House Dividing, 1852 - 1857.* New York: Scribners, 1947.

Newby, I.A. *The South: A History.* USA: Holt, Rinehart, and Winston, 1978.

Nolan, David. *Fifty Feet in Paradise.* New York: Harcourt Brace Jovanovich, 1984.

Osterweis, Rollin G. *Three Centuries of New Haven, 1638-1938.* New Haven: Yale University Press, 1964

Pettengill, George W. *The Story of the Florida Railroads*. Jacksonville: The Southeast Chapter of the Railway and Locomotive Historical Society, 1998.

Phillips, Ulrich Bonnell. *A History of Transportation in the Eastern Cotton Belt to 1860*. New York: Columbia University Press, 1908.

Pilpel, Robert H. *Churchill in America*. New York: Harcourt Brace Jovanovich, 1976.

Patrick, Rembert W. and Morris, Allen. *Florida under Five Flags*. Gainesville: University of Florida Press, 1967.

Powell, John C. *The American Siberia, or Fourteen Years Experience in a Southern Convict Camp*. Gainesville: University of Florida Press, 1976.

Ralph, Julian. *Dixie, or, Southern Scenes and Sketches*. New York: Harper and Brothers, 1896.

Rivers, Larry E. *Slavery in Florida*. Gainesville: University of Florida Press: 2000.

Rogers, William W. *Thomas County, 1865-1900*. Tallahassee: Florida State University Press, 1973.

Rowland, Ray and Callahan, Helen. *Yesterday's Augusta*. Miami: Seeman, 1976.

Ryan, Frank. *The Forgotten Plague: How the Battle against Tuberculosis Was Won and Lost*. Boston: Little, Brown & Company, 1993.

Schwartz, Alvin. *When I Grew Up Long Ago*. New York: J.B. Lippincott, 1978.

Seig, Edward Chan. *Eden on the Marsh: An Intimate History of Savannah*. Los Angeles: Monitor Press, 1982.

Shofner, Jerrell H. *Nor Is It Over Yet: Florida in the Era of Reconstruction, 1863-77*. Gainesville: University of Florida Press, 1963.

Shore, Laurence. *Southern Capitalists: The Ideological Leadership of an Elite, 1832-85*. Chapel Hill: University of North Carolina Press, 1986.

Simonds, Rupert J. *A History of the First Church and Society of Branford*, Connecticut, *1644-1919*. New Haven: Tuttle, Morehouse & Taylor, 1928.

Smiley, Nixon. *Yesterday's Florida*. Miami: Seeman, 1974.

Smith, Jean Edward. *John Marshall: Definer of a Nation*. New York: Henry Holt, 1996.

Smith, Patrick D. *A Land Remembered*. Sarasota: Pineapple Press, 1998.

Smyth, G. Hutchinson. *The Life of Henry Bradley Plant*. New York: Putnam, 1898.

Stott, Richard B. *Workers in the Metropolis*. Ithaca: Cornell University Press, 1990.

Stover, John F. *American Railroads*. Chicago: University of Chicago Press, 1997.

Taylor, George Rogers and Neu, Irene D. *The American Railroad Network, 1861 - 1890*. Cambridge: Harvard University Press, 1956.

Taylor, Robert A. *Rebel Storehouse: Florida in the Confederate Economy*. Tuscaloosa: University of Alabama Press, 1995.

Tebeau, Charles W. *A History of Florida*. Coral Gables: University of Miami Press, 1971.

Tosches, Nick. *Where Dead Voices Gather*. London: Jonathan Cape, 2002.

Towbridge, John T. *The Desolate South*. New York: Duell, Sloan, & Pearce, 1922.

Turner, Gregg. *Railroads of Southwest Florida*. Charleston: Arcadia, 1999.

----. *A Short History of Florida Railroads*. Charleston: Arcadia, 2003.

Waring, Joseph Fredrick. *Cerveau's Savannah*. Savannah: The Georgia Historical Society, 1973.

Warner, Joe. *The Singing River*. Bradenton: Manatee County Historical Society, 1992.

Williamson, Edward C. *Florida Politics in the Gilded Age, 1877-1893*. Gainesville: University of Florida, 1976.
Woodward, C. Vann. *Origins of the New South*. Baton Rouge: Louisiana State University Press, 1951.
Wynne, Lewis and Taylor, Robert. *Florida in the Civil War*. Charleston: Arcadia, 2001.

- Articles and Documents -

Bachman, Robert L. *An Illustrated History of the Town of Waterford*. Waterford: Waterford Bicentennial Committee, 2000.
Barbour, George M. *Florida for Tourists, Invalids, and Settlers*. Facsimile Reproduction of the 1882 Edition. University of Florida Press: Gainesville, 1964.
Bramson, Seth. "A Tale of Three Henrys." *Journal of Decorative and Propaganda Arts*, 1998, 23.
Branford Budget. June 30, 1899
"Branford." New Haven: New Haven Colony Historical Society. Monograph.
Brown, Canter. "Tampa and the Coming of the Railroad, 1853-1884." *Sunland Tribune*, November 1991, Vol. XVII.
Brown, C.K. "The Southern Railway Security Company." *The North Carolina Historical Review*, April 1929, Vol. VI, No. 2.
Browning, Alex. "Alex Browning and the Building of the Tampa Bay Hotel: Reminiscences." James Covington, ed. *Tampa Bay History*, Vol. 4, No. 2, Fall/Winter, 1982.
Brunswick *Advertiser and Appeal*. March 9, 1888.
Burnett, Gene. "How the Great Train Race Proved Plant's Power." *The Flatwheel*, February, 1997. Winter Garden: Central Florida Chapter, National Railway Historical Society.
Carr, John C. Ed. "Old Branford." Branford: Historical Research Committee, 1946.
Cauthen, Charles Edward. "South Carolina Goes to War, 1860-65." *James Sprunt Studies in History and Political Science*, Vol. 32, 1950.
Cleaveland, L.W. *Scrapbooks of Judge L.W. Cleaveland*. New Haven: New Haven Colony Historical Society.
Commercial and Financial Chronicle, June 12, 1880.
Corliss, Carlton J. "Building the Overseas Railway to Key West." *Tequesta*, Number XIII, 1953.
Covington, James. "The Tampa Bay Hotel." *Tequesta*, Number XXVI, 1966.
Dance, Arnold Guyot. *Scrapbooks*. Vol. 84 "The Old Timer." New Haven: New Haven Colony Historical Society.
Fort Myers Press, October 15, 1897. Bradenton: Manatee County Historical Society.
Franks, Norman H. "Drug Supply in the Confederacy." *Georgia Historical Quarterly*, December, 1953, Vol. XXXVII.
Gray, Christopher. "The Jeweler That Conquered a Millionaire's Row." *New York Times*. Real Estate. January 28, 2001.
Gibson, Pamela. "Sport Hunting in Old Miakka." *Sarasota Herald-Tribune*. September 13, 2000.

"Great Southern Railway: a Trunk Line between the North and the Tropics to within Ninety Miles of Havana." New York: Hickok, 1878. Athens: Central Library, University of Georgia.
Groton's Historic Houses and Sites. "Branford House." Groton: Electric Boat Division of General Dynamics, 1977.
Hegel, Richard. "New Haven Views Jefferson's Embargo." *Journal of the* New *Haven Historical Society*. Spring, 2000, Vol. 46.
Horgan, James. "The San Antonio Railroad Depot." Typescript. Saint Leo: Saint Leo College, History Department, 1992.
Ingraham, James E. "Sketch of the Life of Mr. Henry B. Plant." *Sunland Tribune*. February, 1985, Vol 7.
"John Lovall." New Haven: New Haven Colony Historical Society. Monograph.
Johnson, Dudley S. "The Florida Railroad after the Civil War." *Florida Historical Quarterly*. January, 1969, Vol. XLVII.
----. "Henry Bradley Plant and Florida." *Florida Historical Quarterly*. October, 1966, Vol. XLV.
----. "Plant's Lieutenants." *Florida Historical Quarterly*. April, 1970, Vol. XLIX.
----. "The Southern Express Company: A Georgia Corporation." *Georgia Historical Quarterly*. April, 1972, Vol. LVLL.
Jones, John Richard. "Tampa - The Early Days." Typescript. Bradenton: author's collection.
Kennedy, George A. "Running a Locomotive in 1856: The Log of H.S. Haines." *Railroad History*, Spring, 1991, Number 165.
Kentsch, Joe. "Hamilton Disston and the Development of Florida." Typescript. Address for Central Florida Community College. February 8, 1997.
Glover, F.H. "Henry Plant - Genius of the West Coast." *Sunland Tribune*, February 1925, Vol. I.
Harrison, Lynde. "James Blackstone and His Family." New Haven: New Haven Historical Society. Monograph.
Jacksonville City Directory, 1887. Jacksonville: Jacksonville Historical Society.
Kimball, Carol W. "Morton F. Plant." *Tidings*. New London, July, 1989.
_____. "Groton's Most Prominent Citizen." *Groton Standard*. June 5, 1982.
Kramer, Roger; Clark, George; Weart, Walter. "Private Car 'Ely' Has Its 104th Anniversary!" *Rail & Wire*. November 1993, Issue 142.
Lord, Angela. "Diary." New Haven: New Haven Colony Historical Society.
Louisville City Directory, 1859. Louisville: Filson Club.
McLaws, Layfette. "Henry Plant." Gainesville: George A. Smathers Library, University of Florida. Typescript.
"Morton F. Plant Started Career at 16." *The Day*. New London, February 17, 1965.
Neff, Mary and Edith. *Scrapbooks*. Cincinnati: Cincinnati Historical Society. Documents.
New Haven *Directory, 1845*; New Haven *Directory, 1862*. New Haven: New Haven Colony Historical Society.
New York *Times*, June 27, 1899. New York: New York Public Library.
"Notes, 1849-50," entry of March 1, 1849. Francis Collins Papers.

The Orderboard. Newsletter. Tampa: Tampa Bay Chapter of the National Railway Historical Society, September, 1999.

Pettengill, George W. *The Story of Florida Railroads*. Railway and Locomotive Historical Society, Bulletin No. 86, July, 1952.

Pfeifauf, Nick. "History of Local Railroads." *Sanford Herald*, September 8, 1996.

Phinizy, Catherine. "Big-Hearted Millionaire." *Connecticut College Magazine*, Spring, 2000.

"Report of the Commission Appointed by the President to Investigate the Conduct of the War Department in the War with Spain." Washington: Government Printing Office, 1899.

Ross, D. Reid and Wiester, C.W. "The Relationship between Urban Growth and Transportation Developments in the Cincinnati-North Kentucky Area." *Bulletin of the Historical and Philosophical Society of Ohio*, April, 1963, Vol. 21, 2.

Savannah *Morning News*: October 11; November 5; December 4; December 8, 1879. Savannah: Thunderbolt Library.

Singleton, Royce Gordon. "Stages, Steamers, and Stations in the Ante-Bellum South." *Florida Historical Quarterly*. October, 1966. Vol. XLBV.

_____. "Northern Interests in Southern Railroads, 1865-1900." *Georgia Historical Quarterly*. September, 1955, Vol. XXXIX.

_____. "The Pennsylvania Railroad's Southern Empire." *Pennsylvania Magazine*. Vol. XXX1, 1957.

Sparrow, Laurie Lee. "ACL Hospital Comes Down After 66 Years of Service." Waycross *Journal Herald*. Centennial Edition. April, 1974.

"Town and City Directory, 1830." *Connecticut Herald*, January 5, 1830. New Haven: New Haven Colony Historical Society.

Vince, Thomas L. "John Brown of Hudson & Harpers Ferry (1800-59)." Hudson, Ohio: Hudson Library and Historical Society. Monograph

Winter, Michael. "Hell in Harness Screams into Town." *Tampa Tribune Centennial*, September 25, 1994.

Wynne, Lewis N. "The Spanish American War Was the U.S.'s First World War." *Florida Historical Horizons*. September, 1998. Issue 1, Number 1.

(Per Secondary Sources)

Cincinnati *Enquirer*, November 27, 1881. Neff, Scrapbooks.

Daily Augusta Chronicle & Sentinel. July 11, August 2, 1861. Johnson, "The Southern Express Company."

Columbus *Sun*. Johnson quoting Augusta *Chronicle & Sentinel*. October 13, 1861.

Macon *Index*. Johnson, quoting Augusta *Chronicle & Sentinel*. March 16, 1861.

New Haven *Leader*, July 11, 1902. Cleaveland. Scrapbooks of Judge L.W. Cleaveland.

New Haven *Palladium*, February 17, 1902. Cleaveland.

New Haven *Register*, January 16, 1900. Cleaveland.

New Haven *Union*, February 15, 1902. Cleaveland.

New York *Times*, 1890s. Smyth, The Life of Henry Bradley Plant.

Orange Blossom, March 26, 1898. Gainesville: George A. Smathers Library, University

Kelly Reynolds

of Florida. Newsletter.
Tampa *Morning Tribune*, July 1, 1902. Tampa: Hillsborough Public Library.
Thomasville *Times*, August 30, 1884. Poughkeepsie, NY: Annon Adams Collection.
Weekly Montgomery Confederation. August 2, 1861. Johnson.

INDEX

A.

Adams, Alvin. Significant refs. *in passim:* 42, 50, 77; beginnings, his "discovery" and development of express business; 40-1, 55-6, competition vs US Post Office; 39, 65-6; hires and promotes HBP, 50-2; sends HBP to develop Southern District, 56 possible attendance at Louisville meeting, 81; retirement, pro-active, 78, 100

Adams Express Co. (originally Adams Company, Adams and Company). Significant refs. *in passim:* 55, 56, 65, 100, 102, 176; dominates East Coast express business, 50-1; and national express business, 55-6, 68, 69; as threatened by Confederacy, 75, 79, 80; as HBP's gateway to fortune, 50-2, 62, 67-8, 70, 75, 78; BP acquires Southern District, 80-3; becomes Southern Express; 85-6; Gold Rush, as crucial to, 62, 68-9; role in siege of Atlanta, 96; mystery of HBP's ongoing remuneration, 85, 110

Aiken, William. 76, 77

Alabama Midland Railroad. Ref. Plant System, railroads, 164, 177

Albany, Georgia. 179

Albany, New York. 111

Alger, Russell. 181

Alsa (steamship). Ref. Plant, Henry(2), the South, arrival, 98

Amazeen, Captain Jon J. 163

Amazon Basin (West Indies and Caribbean). Ref. as Confederate slave empire, 91; potential riches of, see Plant, Henry (1) (2), grand strategy, 49-50, 139

Ambrose, James. 203

Amelia Island, Florida. Ref. Tampa-Sanford connection, 142

American Congo Exploration Company. Ref. Sanford, Henry, business ventures, Africa, 111

American Eagle (steamboat). Ref. New Haven, Steamboat Wars, 38

Ancient Arabic Order of Nobles. Ref. Plant, Henry (2), decor, Middle Eastern, and Pico Hotel, construction of, 163

Anderson, Captain (auctioneer). 129-30

Anderson, Jerry T. 165

Anita (steamboat). Ref. Plant System, People's Line, 163

Anna Maria Island, Florida. Ref. Plant System, tourism, 175

Apalachicola, Florida. 22, 74, 128, 137

Apopka, Florida. Ref. Florida Midland Railroad, 179

Arcadia, Florida. Ref. Florida Southern Railroad, 164

Athens, Georgia. 58, 61; as site of ante bellum industry, 68

Atlanta, Georgia. 68, 70, 72, 81, 106, 125; ref. Spooner, travels with HBP, 67; ref. Adams Express, siege of, 96; also Southern Express, post bellum headquarters 109; and Plant, Henry (3), valediction, 205

Atlantic Coast Line Company. Ref. Plant, Henry (2), shrewdness of, 133-4

Atlantic Coast Line Railroad. 126; ref. Plant, Henry (2), shrewdness of, 133-4, 135; ref.

Plant System, becomes ACL, 200; and fate of, 198, 201

Atlantic & Danville Railroad. Ref. Haines, later accomplishments, 200

Atlantic & Gulf Railroad (formerly Savannah, Albany & Gulf; later Savannah, Florida & Western). 60, 112; ref. Haines, early career and meets HBP, 128; ref. Savannah, site of auction, 129- 130; becomes SF&W, 132

Atlantic and Gulf Canal and Lake Okeechobee Land Company. Ref. Disston, Kissimmee Valley, 115

Augusta, Georgia. 58, 65, 72, 80, 85, 91, 102, 109; headquarters, Adams Express, 63; arrival, Henry and Ellen Plant, 79, 161; residency, Henry and Ellen Plant, 88-9, 98, 101; industrial base, 79-80, 86, 96; railroad "fever", 80-6; HBP's "Yankee"difficulties, 91-2; Civil War period, 92-3, 95-6; as Confederate stronghold, 104, 118, 119, 130-1; and demise, 31-2, 137, 138; post bellum, 103-5, 107, 146; residence HBP, widower, 100, 123; headquarters, Southern Express, 120

Augusta Canal. 56, 57

Augusta, National Bank of. Founded by HBP, 106; appointments: of Dinsmore, as president, 106, and Bullock to board, 122; unique power of, 107-8

Augusta & Savannah Railroad. 84

B.

Babcock, I.W. Ref. testimony, Einstein vs Adams, 110

Bainbridge, Georgia. Ref. Atlantic & Gulf, 60, 128, 129; Savannah, Florida & Western, 179

Baldwin, James. 51, 86

Baldwin, D.H. 86

Banks, Nathaniel. 76

Bar Harbor, Maine. Ref. Plant System, maritime interests, steamships, 174

Barr's Tram Railway. Ref. Plant System, railroads, 177

Bartow, Florida. 155; ref. South Florida Railroad, 138; Florida Southern Railroad, 64

Beach, John. 144

Beauregard, General Pierre. 95, 96

Beecher & Company. Ref. Plant, Henry (1), early business career, 50

Bellamy, John (Bellamy Road. 2, 8, 13

Belle (steamboat). Ref. New Haven, Steamboat Wars, 38

Belleview, Florida. Ref. Belleview Hotel, 172

Belleview Hotel (Belaire, Florida). 9; ref. Plant System, hotels, 172-3;. Plant, Morton, hotel interests, 195, 196-7; fate of, 199

Benedict, Rev. Father. 180

Berger, Mr. and Mrs. G.W. 171

Bermuda, West Indies. Ref. Plant, Henry (3), historical events, Civil War, 98

Best Friend (locomotive). 67; short and happy life of, 58

Birney, James. 49

Black Belt. 119-20, 121, 128, 155

Black Codes. Ref. Plant, Henry (2), historical events, Reconstruction, 120

Black Tuesday. Ref. Plant, Henry (2), historical events, 124

Blackstone, James (father-in-law). 49
Blackstone, Lorenzo (brother-in-law). 49; ref. Plant, Henry (2), friendships, 127
Bleeding Kansas. Ref. Plant, Henry (2), historical events, Civil War, 77
Bloxham, William. 116, 132, 137, 155
Boston, Massachusetts. 98, 113; ref. Adams, Alvin, beginnings, 41; ref. Plant System, maritime interests, Plant Line,164; ref. Plant System, maritime operations, 174
Boston University. Ref. Haines, later accomplishments, 200
Bradenton, Florida. 159; as possibility for HBP's West Coast terminal, 143, 144; site of record-setting hunt, 171
Branford Academy. Ref. Plant, Henry (1), education, formal, 26
Branford, Connecticut. 23, 24, 27, 28, 29, 43, 183; topography, 17, 19, 20-21, 22; early history, 17-8, 19, 21; daily life, 17-8, 19, 26-7, 29-30, 23; typhus epidemic, (and Plant household), 25-6; as seaport, 17, 19, 21, 30; funeral of Henry George Plant, infant, 50; as childhood of Morton Plant, 55, 71; HBP weds Margaret Loughman, 99; residency, HBP, legal issue of, 188, 189, 190, 192,; see final internment, Ellen Plant, 74, 174; see Margaret Plant, Catholicism, 195; see also Branford, Florida, 199
Branford, Florida. (formerly O'Brien, formerly New Branford). Ref. Branford, Connecticut, 199
Branford Farms (Groton, Connecticut). Ref. Plant, Nellie, architectural interests, 196; Plant, Morton, gentleman farmer, 196
Branford, First Church and Society of. Ref. Plant, Henry (1), moral influences, 21
Branford House. Ref. Plant, Nellie, architectural accomplishments, 196
Breakers Hotel (Palm Beach). Ref. Flagler, hotel interests, 171
Brock, Captain C.H. 163
Brooke, Colonel George Mercer (quoted). 6
Brooks, Preston. 77
Brooksville, Florida. Ref. Florida Southern Railroad, 138
Brown, Franklin Q. 138, 199; ref. Adams Express, siege of Atlanta, heroism, 96; during Spanish-American War, 181-3; later accomplishments, 201
Brown, John. 78
Brown, Joseph. 92, 93
Brown, Tom. 7
Brunswick, Georgia. 54, 179; ref. HBP's benevolence, 125; and Wood, John, 166
Brunswick & Western Railroad. 166; ref. Thomasville, 167; ref. Plant System, 167
Bullock, Major Rufus. 122, 124 ; directorships, courtesy HBP, 106, 177-8
Bunker Hill (steamboat). Ref. New Haven, Steamboat Wars, 39
Burpee, Lucian. 191
Butler, Andrew Pickens. 77

C.

Cahill, Mary.188; as witness during dispute over HBP's will, 189
Calhoun (steamboat). Ref. Plant, Henry (2), first Florida trip, 54
Calhoun, John C. (quoted). 64
Calhoun, Patrick. 178

Call, Wilkenson. 132
Callahan, Georgia. Ref. Waycross Short Line, 135
Cameron, J.D. 126
Caribbean (region). Ref. Plant, Henry (1) (2), grand strategy, 49-50, 139
Carnegie, Andrew. 20
Carrere, John. 161
Carter's Mill (near Lakeland, Florida). Ref. Tampa, Tampa-Sanford connection, Golden Spike," 157
Cartier, Henri. 197-8
Cass, George W. 126
Cato Bell (steamboat). Ref. Plant System, maritime interests; Cedar Key, 137
Cedar Key, Florida. 69, 119, 150; HBP's connections to, residency, legal issue of 137; as transportation hub, 142; see also Plant, Henry (2), equanimity, loss of, 144
Central of Georgia Railroad. 61, 62, 84, 178; ref. Spooner, partnership with HBP, 67
Central Rail Road & Canal Company of Georgia. 59
Central Rail Road and Banking Company of Georgia. 60; ref. Savannah, Gulf & Western (per Atlantic & Gulf), 129
Charleston, South Carolina. Ref. Plant, Henry (2), the South, first visit, 67; as crucial to New Haven economy, 46; and to pioneer USA railroad, 57-8; and proposal for Confederate slave empire, 91; HBP's post bellum return, 102; ref. Southern Express, post bellum headquarters 109
"Charlestonites." Ref. Plant, Henry (2), initial contacts, the South, 30
Charleston & Savannah Railroad (formerly Savannah & Charleston). Ref. Plant System, railroads, 129, 133
Chattahoochee & East Pass Railway. Ref. Savannah, Florida & Western, 137
Chilton, William Parrish. 86, 88
Chipley, Colonel William. 148
Chisholm, Judge Walter S. 129, 131, 134
Chubb, Florida (later Lake Alfred). Ref. South Florida Railroad, 138
Churchill, Winston. 181
City Hotel. As Civil War hospital, 95
City Hotel (Augusta); also Second General Hospital (Augusta). Ref. Augusta, Civil War period, 95
Citizens Line. Ref. New Haven, Steamboat Wars, 38-9, 42-3
Clay, Henry. 49, 76
Clearwater, Florida. Ref. Belleview, 9, 172
Cleaveland, I.W. 190
Clemens, Samuel. 17, 29
Cleopatra (steamboat). Ref.New Haven, Steamboat Wars, 42-3
Cleveland, Grover, 165
Cleveland, Ohio. Ref. Flagler, early career, 160
Climax, Georgia. Ref. Savannah, Florida & Western, 137
Clinton, DeWitt, 11
Cobb, Thomas (quoted). 60

Columbus, Georgia. As site of ante bellum industry, 68; ref. Plant, Henry (2), the South, approval of HBP from Vigilance Committee, 89

Confederate Express Company. 94-5

Confederate Post Office. 94-5

Congregationalism. Ref. Plant, Henry (1), religious commitment, 20-1

Conrad, Joseph (quoted). 37

Convict Lease System. 148; during Tampa-Sanford connection, 153-5

Cooke, Jay. 124

Corrigan, Felix. 180

Cotter, W.T. 163, 167

Crane, Stephen (quoted). 47

Crocker, Charles F. 165

D.

Dana, Richard. 36

Davis, Jefferson. 70, 72, 75, 79, 80, 88, 90, 104; possible interview with HBP, 89

DeBary, Count Frederick. 161

Deland, Florida. Ref. Jacksonville & St. Johns River Railroad, 185

Dickens, Charles (quoted). 33

Dickison, Captain J.J. 119

Dinsmore, William. 41, 52, 55; succeeds Alvin Adams, 77, 80-1; directorships, courtesy HBP, 106, 108; ref. Plant, Henry (1), friendships, 78; ref. testimony, Einstein vs Adams, 110

Disston, Hamilton. 113, 173, 201; plans for Kissimmee Valley empire, 114-6; and Vose injunction reprieve, 133, 137

Disston Land Company. Ref. Tampa-Sanford connection, 144

Disston Purchase. Ref. Sanford, Kissimmee Valley empire, 138

Dorsey, Dennis. Ref. Plant, Henry (2), slavery, 63-4

Dunellon, Florida. Ref. "West Coast Route," 177

DuPont, Georgia. Ref. Live Oak, Tampa & Charlotte Harbor Railroad, 137; ref. Savannah, Florida & Western, 177

Durant, Dr. Chaisi. 184, 186, 187

E.

East Florida Railway Company (Georgia). Ref. Plant System, railroads, 132, 134

Edison, Thomas ("the wizard"). 169

Egmont Key, Florida. Ref. Plant System, tourism, 175

Eiffel Tower. Ref. Plant, Henry (3) (quoted), historical events, Paris Exposition, 168

Einstein vs Adams (Einstein Brothers). Ref. testimony, Babcock, Dinsmore, Hoey, Sanford, Edward and Henry, 109-10

El Paso, Texas. Ref. Texas Express, 69

The Ely. Ref. Special Car 100, fate of 202

"End of Line" (later Plant City). 151

Erie Canal. Ref. Plant, Henry (1), historical influences, 11, 22, 45
Erwin, Robert. 134, 164; in dispute over HBP's will 188, 191, 192; ref. Plant System, becomes Atlantic Coast Line, 200; later accomplishments, 201
Eustis, Reverend W.T. (quoted). Ref. Gillett, eulogy as pert. HBP's vision and character, 27
Evans, Admiral Robert. 181

F.

Farmington Canal (Hartford-New Haven Canal). 59; Ref .Plant, Henry (1), transportation, early influences, 22-3
Fernandina, Florida. Ref. Tampa-Sanford connection, 142
Fernandina, Tampa & Key West Railroad. 142
Fiche, Anton. 170
First Church and Society of Branford. Ref. Plant, Henry (1), moral influences, 21.
Fitzgerald, Captain J.W. 163
Flagler, Henry Morrison. 20, 122, 126; early career, 160, and Rockefeller's quote re Flagler as Standard Oil "villain," 124; first Florida visit, 117-8; second visit, 160; friendship with HBP, 8, 176; cruisewith HBP and Margaret, 176; as financer: railroad interests: Florida East Coast Railway, 8, 171; Key West extension, 201; hotel interests: Ponce de Leon, 118, 160-1, 170, Royal Poinciana, 171, Breakers, 171; maritime interests: Florida East Coast Steamship Company 199; Peninsular & Occidental Steamship Line, 199; quoted in praise of developments, 118; later accomplishments, 201
Fleming, Georgia. Ref. Plant, Henry (3), folklore legacy," Great Train Race," 202
Florida Central and Peninsular Railroad. Ref,. Yullee, anti-Tampa villain, 155; ref. "West Coast Route," 177; ref. Plant, Henry (3), Spanish-American War, participation, 183
Florida East Coast Railway. Ref. Flagler, railroad interests, 8, 171; Key West extension, 201
Florida East Coast Steamship Company. Ref: Flagler, shipping interests, 199
Florida Midland Railroad. 179
Florida Railroad. Ref. Tampa-Sanford, 142; see also Florida Transit & Peninsular
Florida Southern Railroad. 138, 201; ref. Plant System, railroads, 164
Florida Transit Railroad. Ref. Tampa-Sanford connection, 142; see also Florida Transit & Peninsular
Florida Transit & Peninsular Railroad (formerly Florida Railroad; Florida Transit). Ref. Tampa-Sanford connection, 143
Folks, Dr. (railroad owner). 132
Fort Brooke, Florida (later Tampa). 6
Fort Myers, Florida. 159, 164, 180; ref. Plant System, hotels, 172
Fort Myers Steamboat Company. Ref. Plant System, maritime interests, 180
Fort Sumter, South Carolina. Ref. Plant, Henry (2), historic events, 85
Fort White, Florida. Ref. Florida Southern Railroad, 138
Frederick DeBary (steamboat). Ref. Plant System, People's Line, 161
Fulton, Robert. 32

G.

Gainesvilles, Florida. 137, 179; ref. Florida Southern, 138;. "West Coast Route," 177
Gaither, Alfred. 81, 84, 100
Galt House (Louisville, Kentucky). Ref. Louisville, HBP acquires Southern District, Adams Express, 80
Geo. M. Bird (steamboat). Ref. Plant System, People's Line, 163
Georgia Central Railroad. 81, 85, 86, 119
Georgia Railroad. 61
Gillespie, John Hamilton. 181
Gillett, Timothy F. 23-5, 50; ref. Plant, Henry (1), moral influences, 21; quoted on education, 24-5; eulogy, pert. to HBP's character and vision, 25
Gold Rush. Ref. Adams Express, as crucial to, 62, 68-9
Gordon, General John B. 122; negotiations with HBP during Tampa-Sanford connection, 155-6
Gordon, William Washington. 59-60
Grand Masonic Lodge of New York. Ref. Plant Henry (2), decor, Middle Eastern, and Pico Hotel, construction of, 163
"Grand Skidaddle." 95
Grant, General Ulysses S. 95, 96, 132, 165
Greeley, Horace. 64
Green Cove Springs, Florida. Ref. Tampa Bay Hotel, construction, 166
Griswold Hotel (Groton, Connecticut). Ref. Plant, Nellie, architectural accomplishments, 196
Groton, Connecticut. Ref. Plant, Nellie, architectural accomplishments, 196; and Plant, Morton, gentleman farmer, 196

H.

Hackley, Richard. 4-6
Haines, Colonel Henry Stephen. 13, 131, 173, 176; early career and meets HBP, 128; builds Jackson-Waycross Short Line, 133, 134; builds Tampa-Sanford connection, 146-9; friendship with HBP, 128; later accomplishments, 200-01
Halifax (steamship). Ref. Plant System, Plant Line, 174; ref. Flagler, cruise with HBP and Margaret, 176
Halifax, Nova Scotia. Ref. Plant, Henry (2), historical events, Civil War, 98; ref. Plant System, maritime interests,
  Plant Line, 164; ref. Plant, Henry (3), last will, dispute, 190
Hamburg, South Carolina. Ref. South Carolina Canal and Railroad Company, 58; ref. Central of Georgia, 61, 62
Hansa (steamship). Ref. Plant, Henry (2), the South, arrival, 98
Harlow, Alvin F. (quoted). 77, 85, 108, 110, 111
Hartford, Connecticut. 17; ref. Plant, Henry (1), historical events, Steamboat Wars, 32, 34; ref. Adams Express, 41, 43
Harrison, Lynde. Ref. Plant, Henry (3), last will, planning, 185; in dispute over HBP's

will, 188, 189, 191, 192; later accomplishments, 201
Hastings, Thomas. 160
Havana, Cuba. 143, 146, 155; ref. Plant System, maritime interests, Plant Line, 164; ref. Plant System, tourism, 173, 179
Hayden, "Doc." 166
Hayden, Thomas. 170*H.B. Plant* (steamboat) 8; ref. Plant System, People's Line, 161-2, 161-2, 163; ref. Savannah, residence, maritime, 134; during Tampa-Sanford connection, 145-6, 151-2
H. B. Plant Hotel (Tampa, Florida). Ref. Tampa Bay Hotel, decision, 165
Henry B. Plant Museum (Tampa). Ref. Tampa Bay Hotel, fate of, 200
High Springs, Florida. Ref. Plant System, hospitals and "West Coast Route," 177
Henry Bradley Plant Company (formerly the Southeastern Investment Company). In dispute over HBP's will, 183; in disposition of HBP estate: shares, 190; monies, 191; grand total, 192
Hoadley, Betsey Bradley Plant. See Plant, Betsey Bradley.
Hoadley, C. E. (step-nephew). 173, 191
Hoadley, Emma (wife of Charles Hoadley). 189, 191
Hoadley, Henry P. 27, 127
Hoadley, James (step-brother). 27
Hoadley, Mrs. (sister-in-law).
Hoadley, Philomen (step-father). 27; 55; death of, 96
Hoadley (as family of Philomen). 36, 43, 55, 71, 99, 191
Hoary, Eias. 76
Hoey, Joe. 56, 100; ref. testimony, Einstein vs Adams, 110
Hoffman, Glen (quoted). 133
Homosassa, Florida. Ref. Plant, Henry (2), historical events, Phosphate Rush, 178
Horry, Elias. 76
Hotchkiss House (New Haven). Ref. New Haven, residency, dispute over HBP's will, 186, 189
Houston, Sam. 79-80; (quoted) 80
Hudson (steamboat). Ref. New Haven, Steamboat Wars, 36
Hudson, Ohio. Ref. Plant, Henry (2), historic events, slavery, 78

I

Ingraham, James. 13, 144, 160; meets HBP, helps negotiate contract for Tampa-Sanford connection (and quoted), 145, 146-7; helps negotiate Tampa Bay Hotel contract, 165; friendship with HBP, 145-6; later accomplishments, 201
Inman, John C. 178
Inn at Tampa Bay (Tampa). Ref. Plant System, hotels; as residence during Spanish-American War, 183; last days, HBP, 186
Interstate Commerce Commission. Ref. Southern Express, 199

J.

Jackson, Andrew. 3, 6, 49

Jacksonville, Florida. 4-6, 8, 119, 163; ref. Plant, Henry (2), first Florida visit, 53-4, 141; ref. Flagler, first Florida visit, 117-8; as site of Tampa-Sanford deal, 145, 147; as crucial to Tampa-Sanford connection, 149, 151; Waycross-Jacksonville Short Line, 132, 134-5; under Flagler, 118; and after HBP, 179; see also Plant, Henry (3), folklore legacy," Great Train Race," 202-4

Jacksonville & St. Johns River Railroad. Ref. Plant System; 185

Jacksonville Street Railway. Ref. Plant System, railroads, 132

Jacksonville, Tampa & Key West Railroad. 185; Ref. Plant System, 148; during Tampa-Sanford connection, 147-8, 150, 155; see also. Land Grants, 176

James, Fred. 167

Jefferson, Thomas. 21-2

Jenkins, Thomas K. 133

Jersey City, New Jersey (Pennsylvania Railroad depot). Ref. Plant, Henry (3), critically ill, 184-5

Jesup, Morris K. 128, 133, 131

Johnson, E.A. 49, 50, 51, 52

Johnson, Andrew. 120

Johnson, Paul (quoted). 72

Johnson, General John K. 119

Jones, C.C. (quoted). 85

Jones, S.H. 69, 88

Jones, Starr S. 69

Judson Hotel (Manhattan). 47-8, 52, 71-2

K.

Kendrick, William. 149

Key West, Florida. 9, 116, 132, 146, 201; ref. Plant System, maritime interests, steamships, 164, 173, 179

Kimball, Hannibal I. 121-2

King, J.H. 170

King, Porter (quoted). 205

King Philips War. Ref. Brandon, early history, 18

Kinsley, A.B. 56

Kississimmee (steamboat). Ref. Plant System, People's Line, 175

Kissimmee, Florida. 133, 145, 151, 172; ref. Tampa, Tampa-Sanford connection, celebration, 156

Kissimmee Valley. 111; ref. Disston and Sanford, Henry, dreamed-of empire, 114-6

Kosciusko (steamboat). Ref. Vanderbilt; and New Haven, Steamboat Wars, 36-7

L.

Grande Duchesse. Ref. Plant System, Plant Line, 10, 175; see also Plant, Henry (3), dubious investments, 10, 175

Land Grants. Ref. Plant System, 176-7
Lake Alfred, Florida (formerly Chubb). Ref. South Florida Railroad, 138
Lake City, Florida. Ref. Florida Southern Railroad, 138
Lakeland, Florida. During Tampa-Sanford connection, see Carter's Mill.
Lanier, Sidney (quoted). 141
Law, General A.B. 130
Lee, General Robert E. 86, 93, 95
Leesburg, Florida. Site of banquet praising (quote) HBP, Tampa-Sanford connection, 155
Lennox, Massachusetts. Ref. Haines, later accomplishments, 201
Leventrit (Justice of Supreme Court, State of New York). 189, 190
Levi, Morton. 168
Lincoln, Abraham, 65, 74, 76, 79, 104, 120
Live Oak, Florida. Ref . Atlantic & Gulf, 60; ref. SF & W, 129, 132, 137, 199
Live Oak & Rowlands Bluff Railroad. Ref. Savannah, Florida & Western, 137
Live Oak, Tampa & Charlotte Harbor Railroad. 137
Livingston, Johnston. 56
Livingston, Robert. 32
Lodge, Albert. 203
London, UK. 101; ref. Plant, Henry (1), ancestry, 17; ref. Sanford, Henry, Kississimmee Valley empire, 137; Plant, Henry (3), decor, taste in, 168
Long Wharf (New Haven). Ref. Plant, Henry (1), transportation, influences, 23, 30, 36, 47
Lott, Dr. (railroad owner). 132
Louisville, Kentucky. Ref. Adams Express, HBP acquires Southern District, 81-2
Louisville & Nashville Railroad. Ref. Alabama Midland, 177
Lowville Academy (Branford). Ref. Plant, Henry, education (1), formal, 27

M.

Macon, Georgia. Pert. first Georgia railroad, 59, 60; as site of ante bellum industry, 68
Manhattan (See also New York Harbor and New York, NY). 3, 183; arrival, HBP as Vanderbilt employee: 43-5, 47, 48, 51;HBP as Adams employee, 52, 57; post bellum] return, 103; Plant System headquarters, 127
Manwaring, Seldon. 197
Marco Island, Florida. Ref. Sanford, Henry (2), Kississimmee Valley Empire, 138
Margaret (steamboat). Ref. Plant System, People's Line, 8, 159, 175
Marion (steamboat). Ref. Plant, Henry (2), first Florida trip, 54
Martin, Father Edward. 189
Martinsburg, New York. 29; ref. Plant, Henry (1), transportation, early influences, Upper New York State, 28
Mascotte (steamship). Ref. Plant System, Plant Line, 173-4; in cigar-running operation, 175; during Spanish-American War, 183
McClellen, S.S. 203
McDaniel, James. 88
McKinley, William. 181
McMahon John. 129

Memphis, Tennessee. 61, 70; ref. Plant, Morton, practical education, and as headquarters, Southern Express, 109

Mercier, Captain G.J. 163

Meriden, Connecticut. 43

Miami, Florida. Ref. Flagler, developments, 118; ref. Plant, Henry (3), friendships, 118

Middlesex, UK. Ref. Plant, Henry (1), ancestry, 17

Mikisukee. 8

Mitchell, Henry L. Ref. PICO, top officials and founding of Plant City, 151

Mitchell House (Thomasville, Georgia). As site of ante bellum industry, 68; ref. Wood, previous inspirations, 167

Mizzen Top Hotel (Duchess County. New York). Ref. Wood, previous inspirations, 167

Mobile, Alabama. 63, 69, 72 {missing passage}, 150; ref. Haines, early career, 128; ref. Plant System, Plant Line, 164

Mohawks. Ref. Branford, early history, 18; ref. Plant, Henry (1), transportation, early influences, Upper New York State, 28

Mohegans. Ref. Branford, early history, 17-8

Molineux, Major General Edward L. 104, 107; and quoted, 104

Montgomery, Alabama. Significant refs *in passim*: 72, 176; ref. Spooner, travels with HBP, 67; ref. Southern Express, post bellum headquarters 109; ref. Davis, interview with HBP, 89; ref. Plant System, Alabama Midland, 164, 177; ref. Plant System, Montgomery Belt Line Railway, 164

Montgomery Belt Line Railway. Ref. Plant System, 164

Morgan, J.P. 20, 178

Dora, Florida. Ref. Jacksonville & St. Johns River Railroad, 185

N.

Narragansetts. Ref. Branford, early history, 18

Nashville & Cattanoga Railroad. 81

Newcomer, Benjamin F. Ref. Atlantic Coast Line, 126; Plant, Henry (2), dubious investments, 126-7, 178; and friendship with HBP, 127

New Haven, Connecticut. 17, 18, 20, 22, 50, 52, 98, 122; influence on HBP: commercial activities, 35; Inventive Spirit, 39-40, 46; vacation spot for Southerners, 44; waterfront and Long Wharf, 23, 30, 36, 47; Steamboat Wars, 38-9, 42-3; during Civil War, effect of memories on HBP, 92; post bellum return, HBP, 99; HBP's residency, 43; residency as factor in dispute over HBP's will, 187-90; and Hotchkiss House; see also Plant, Morton, childhood.

New Haven Colony. 18, 20

Haven Colony. 13, 25, 28

New Haven County Medical Society. 29

New Haven-Hartford Canal. See Farmington Canal.

New Haven & Hartford Railroad. 50; ref. New Haven, Steamboat Wars, 38

New Haven Steamboat Company (Vanderbilt Line). Ref, Plant, Henry (1), aboard *New York*, 37, 38-9; 60-1; see Vanderbilt, steamboat empire, 34-5, 36, 38-9; and New Haven, Steamboat Wars, 38-9, 42-3

New London Planters. 196; see Plant, Morton, baseball team owner.
New Manchester, Georgia. As site of ante bellum industry, 67
New Orleans, Louisiana.148; ref. Southern Express, 46, 61, 69; ref. Plant, Morton, childhood, 70 (Madi Gras); and proposal for Confederate slave empire, 91
New York, New York (See Manhattan and New York Harbor). Significant refs. *in passim*: 98, 113, 135, 167; arrival, HBP as Vanderbilt employee, 37-8, 43-5, 66-69; arrival, HBP as Adams employee, 50-2; arrival, HBP, post-bellum, 101-2; HBP's 1873 legal address, 126; during Tampa-Sanford connection, 144, 145; ref. Plant System, Tampa-New York route, 176; headquarters, PICO, 127, 163, 185, 189; and ref. Tilley, last will, planning for, 183, 185; residency, HBP and family, 62), 116, 183; last days, 184-5, 185-6; in dispute over will, legal issue of, 188-90; see Flagler, first Florida visit, 160; and hotels, 161; see also Plant, Morton, fate of Fifth Ave. mansion, 197 New York City Custom House. Ref. Adams Express, HBP's gateway to fortune, 51
New York Central Engine 999. Ref. Plant, Henry (3), folklore legacy," Great Train Race," 202-4
New York Harbor (See also Manhattan and New York, New York). 11, 23, 43; site of *United States* explosion, 32
New York, State Supreme Court of. Ref. Einstein vs Adams, 110; ref. Plant, Henry (3), breaking of. 188, 199
New York (steamboat). Ref. Plant, Henry(1), education, practical, 37; and quoted on value of, 39
Northeast Railroad Company. Ref. Plant, Henry (2), shrewdness of, 133
Norwich, Connecticut. . Ref. Adams Express, 41

O.

O'Brien, Florida (formerly Dabs Hole, later Branford). 199
O'Brien, Michael J. 96, 109, 134, 199
Ocala, Florida. Ref. Florida Southern, 143; ref. Plant System, hotels, 172
Oglethorpe Hotel (Brunswick, Georgia). Ref. Wood, previous inspirations, 166
Olivette (steamship). Ref Plant System, Plant Line, 173-4; record setting run, 173; in cigar-running operation, 173-4; during Spanish-American War, 181, 183
Orange Belt Railroad (later Sanford & St. Petersburg). Ref. Plant System, Belleview, 172
Orange House Hotel (Tampa). Ref. Tampa, Tampa-Sanford, celebration, 141, 156
Orlando, Florida. Ref. Sanford, Henry, Kississimmee Valley Empire, 114
Osceola. 18

P.

Pacific Ocean. As goal of projected Southern transcontinental railroad. 70
Palatka, Florida (East Palatka). 2, 118, 155; ref. Sanford, Henry, first Florida visit, 117; ref. Florida Southern, 132
Palm Beach, Florida. Ref. Flagler, developments, 118; ref. Flagler, hotels, 171; ref. Fla-

gler, friendship with HBP, 181

Paris, France. Ref. Plant, Henry (2), Confederate passport, problems of, 101; and Plant, Henry (3), historical events, Eiffel Tower (quoted), 168

Parslow, Alfred. 148

Pavilion Hotel (New Haven). Ref. Plant, Henry (1), transportation, early influences, 30

Peaslee, Erwin H. 188

Peninsular & Occidental Steamship Line. Ref: Flagler, shipping interests, 199?

Pensacola, Florida. 3, 6, 12, 22, 128, 150; ref. Haines, Tampa-Sanford connection, 148

Pensacola & Atlantic Railroad. 137

People's Line. Ref. Plant System maritime interests, 161

Pequots. Ref. Branford, early history, 17-8

Pettingill, George W. (qouted). 135

Philadelphia, Pennsylvania. Significant refs. *in passim:* 66, 124; ref. Philadelphia Mint, 51; ref. Sanford, Kississimmee Valley empire, 112, 132, 137; ref. Disston, Kississimmee Valley empire, 114; ref. *Mascotte*, 173

Philadelphia Mint. Ref. Adams Express, HBP's gateway to fortune, 51

Philadelphia Phillies. 196; see Plant, Morton, baseball team owner.

Phillips, Wendell. 64-5; (quoted) 65; (quoted) 78

Phosphate Rush. Ref. Plant, Henry (3), historical events, Phophate Rush, 177-8

PICO (Plant Investment Company). 173; founded, 139; during Tampa-Sanford connection, 147, 148, 156; top officials and founding of Plant City, 151; ref. Tampa, contracts for Tampa-Sanford connection, 150; ref. Tampa Bay Hotel, HBP solo decision, 165; Paris Exposition, 168

"PICO Block" Sanford, Florida. Ref. Pico Hotel, construction, 163

Pico Hotel (Sanford, Florida). Design and construction of, 163-4; post-HBP fate, 200

Pierpont, James. 106

Piney Woods Hotel (Thomasville, Georgia). Ref. Wood, previous inspirations, 167

Plant, Amy Capron (great-granddaughter). 198

Plant, Amy Warren (granddaughter). 198

Plant, Anderson (father). 23, 26, 27

Plant, Betsey Bradley (mother). 14, 36, 39, 40-2, 53, 62, 77, 146; weds Philomen Hoadley, 27; devotion to HBP, 26, 35; devotion to Morton Plant, 13, 77; death of, 163

Plant City, Florida (formerly "End of Line"). Ref. PICO, top officials and founding of, 151

Plant,Eliza Ann (sister). 35

Plant, Ellen Elizabeth Blackstone (first wife). 141; courtship and marriage to HBP, 48-9; birth and death of infant, George Henry Plant, 50; birth of Morton Freeman Plant, 71; and tuberculosis, 53-4, 55, 72; therapeutic visit to Florida, 53-4, 117, 141; helpmate to HBP, 56; residency in South, see Augusta, residency; during final illness in Planters Hotel, 72-4; illness; death of, 74; final internment, 74, 174

Plant, George Henry (son). 50

Plant, Henry Bradley (1). Early years (1819-1835): BACKGROUND: Ancestry, 17; activities, childhood, 29-30; devotion to family, 9-10,27; illnesses and accidents, 25-6, 29; education, formal, Branford Academy, 26;Lowville Academy, Lovall Academy, 30, 35;

Lacasterian system, 30; education, practical, with Washington Webb, 49-50, 99-100, 138; aboard *New York*, 37, 38-9, 42, 48; 60-1; quoted on value of, 39; see also New Haven, Steamboat Wars; also Adams Express, HBP's gateway to fortune, 51; transportation, early influences: Upper New York State, 3, 28; Farmington Canal, 22-3; New Haven waterfront, Long Wharf, 23, 30, 36, 47; Pavilion Hotel, 30; political interests, Whig Party, 49, 76, 120, 132; HISTORIC EVENTS, Embargo Act (aftermath), 30-1; Erie Canal, 11, 22, 45; Steamboat Wars, 38-9, 42-3; PERSONAL EVENTS: New Haven area typhus epidemic, 24-6; religious commitment, 20-1, 26, 27; Moral Influences, village church, 21, 27, 28; Gillett, Timothy, 26-7; family life, see Plant, Betsey; John; Sarah; Personal Relations: weds Ellen Blackstone, 48-9; bereavement at death of George Henry Plant, 50; fatherhood, birth of Morton Freeman Plant, 71; early business career: Washington Webb Company, 49; Plant & Webb, 49- 50; Beecher & Company (becomes Adams Express, 50); see Adams Express, HBP's gateway to fortune; envisions grand strategy, 49-50; and vision, 27; further see: Branford, Connecticut, daily life, epidemic, village green, seaport; New Haven, commerce, waterfront; New York,, arrival, HBP as youth; grand strategy, 49-50

Plant, Henry Bradley (2). Middle years (1836-82): CHARACTERISTICS AND CONSEQUENCES: geniality and equanimity, 35, 67, 111, 137, 143 145-6; loss of, curse on Cedar Key, 144; shrewdness: 61-2, 67, 81-2, 97-8, 100-7, 108, 110, 116, 131, 133-4, 135, 147-8, see also Einstein vs Adams; dubious investments of, see Southern Railroad Security Company, 126, 127; Richmond and West Point Terminal Company, 178; successful grand strategy, Amazon Basin, 139; geniality, 43-4, 180, 181; New England heritage, "grit," 82, 97; probity, 68; benevolence, 125; personal relations: devotion to Ellen Blackstone Plant, 56, 3-4, 80, 142; friendships: see Blackstone (Lorenzo), Dinsmore, Flagler, Haines, Ingraham, Newcomer, Sanford, Henry and Edward; HISTORICAL EVENTS, Impacting on HBP: Panic of 1837, 60; protective tariffs, 64; Free Soil, 76; slavery, 62, 63-4, 65, 71, 77, 78; Bleeding Kansas, 77; Sumner assault, 77; Fort Sumter attack, 85; Black Tuesday, 124; PERSONAL EVENTS: the South; first visit, 67; as Adams official, 67-9; see also Augusta, arrival, Henry and Ellen Plant and residency, Henry and Ellen Plant; pre-Civil War, antagonism toward HBP, 86-88, approval of HBP, 89, 94; initial contact, 43, social system, 68, 97; historic events, participation of HBP; Civil War: during formation of Confederacy, 84; during hostilities, 89, 90-3, 94; HBP's Confederate citizenship, advantages of 80, 82, 99; and problems of 92, 97-8 , 101-2; see also New Haven, effect of memories, 92; Reconstruction, 119-21, 123; European trip, 99-101; European decor taste in, 100; and Middle Eastern decor, 163; HBP's post bellum return: see New Haven, New York, Charleston, Savannah, Augusta; formulates grand strategy, 139;

Plant, Henry Bradley (3). Later Years (1883-99): CHARACTERISTICS AND CONSEQUENCES: geniality and equanimity, 176, 180, 181; shrewdness: 164, 167, 173-4, 175-6, 177-80, 183-4, 185; dubious investments, *La Grande Duchesse,* 10, 175; Tampa Bay Hotel, 10, 165; and golf, 170, 181; decor taste in, 169-70, 171-2; religious commitment and benevolence, 164, 174-5; HISTORIC EVENTS, Participation of HBP: yellow fever epidemic of 1888, 164; Paris Exposition, 168; standard gauge conversion, 176; freeze of 1895, 177; Phosphate Rush, 177-8; Spanish-American War, 19-20, 181, 182-5; Paris

Exposition and Eiffel Tower, quoted on impermanence of, 168; hard work, quoted on value of, 183; folklore legacy," Great Train Race," 202-4; PERSONAL EVENTS: critically ill, NYC, 184-5; death of, 186; Final Will and Testament: planning for, 15, 175, 183-4; breaking of, 187-91; see Branford, residency, legal issue of; New Haven residency, legal issue of, and quoted, 266 ; and New York, residency, legal issue of; Post Mortem: valediction, 184, eulogy, Atlanta, 205

Plant, Henry II (grandson). 8, 183; birth, 175; designated HBP's heir, 14, and publicly, 184; as beneficiary of HBP's disputed will, 188, 195; 186, 187, 195; residence at Belleview, 196; accident at Belleview, 197; marries Amy Warren; death of, 198

Plant, John (grandfather). 17-8, 27

Plan183; possible estrangement from Plant family, 175; ardent Catholicism of, 175, 195; decor, taste in, 151, 159, 163, 166, 165, 168, 169-70; affection for canines, 170; christening of *Mascotte* (quoted), 173; ref. Flagler, cruise, 176; during Spanish-American War, 181, 183; during HBP's last days, 186; legal maneuvers vs HBP will, 187, 188, 195; ends relationship with Plant family, 195; in disposition of HBP estate, 190; departure of, 195

Plant, Mary Ellen (great-granddaughter). 198

Plant, Morton Freeman (son). 50, 116 166; birth, 71; childhood and youth, 14, 55, 62, 70, 100, 102, 109, 116, 134; and 2nd home, New Haven & Branford, 71; formal education, Russell School, 109; practical, Memphis, Southern Express, 109; as parent, 8, 183, 196, 197; activities, gentleman farmer, 196; golfer, 170, 197; baseball team owner, 196; yachtsman, 195-6; marriages: 1st, Nellie Capron, 165; 2nd and its repercussions, see Cadwell, Sarah; filial responsibilities, challenge and difficulties of, 184, 192; as heir to Plant empire, HBP's likely assessment of, 194; with HBP at health crisis; 184-54; in dispute over HBP's will, 187, 188, 190; conflict with Margaret, 195; executive capacities: hotel interests, Belleview, 195, l96-7, 199; Tampa Bay Hotel, 196, 197; steamship line, with Henry Flagler, 199; legal maneuvers vs HBP's will, 187, 188; in disposition of HBP estate: shares, 190; monies, 191; death of, 198

Plant, Nellie Capron (Morton Plant's first wife). 165, 175; architectural interests, 195

Plant, Phillip Manwaring (Morton Plant's adopted son). 197, 198

Plant, Sarah (grandmother). Devotion to HBP, 26, 35; moral influence of, 29, 41, 55; plans for HBP's education, 10, 27, 30, 35; and career, Yale Divinity School, 34

Plant, Sara Mae ("Masie") Cadwell Manwaring (Morton Plant's 2nd wife). 196-7; ref. Plant, Morton, fate of Fifth Avenue mansion, 197

Plant System. 8, 13, 15, 25, 30, 138, 165 inception, 60; major upgrading, Pullman Palace Cars, 139; during Tampa-Sanford connection: strategy, 142, 146; officials and founding of Plant City, 151; southern extension, see Florida Southern Railroad, 164; agriculture, vital relationship, 177; major maritime acquisitions, 174; HOTELS (noted as to opening and/or inclusion): commercial hotel, Pico Hotel (Sanford), 163-4; luxury and resort hotels: Belleview Hotel, 172-3 Port Charlotte Hotel, 164; Ft. Myers Hotel, 172; Ocala Inn, 172; Punta Gorda Hotel, 164, 172; 172; Tampa Bay Hotel, 169-70; Tropical House (Kississimmee); Seminole Inn (Winter Park), 165; RAILROADS (noted as to ground breaking and/or inclusion): Alabama Midland Railroad, 164, 177; Barr's Tram Railway. Ref. Plant System, railroads, 177; Brunswick & Western Railroad, 167; Charleston & Savannah Railroad (formerly Savannah & Charleston), 129; East Florida Railway Company, 132; Florida Southern Railroad, 138; Jacksonville & St. Johns River Railroad, 185; Jacksonville, Tampa & Key West Railroad, 148; Jacksonville Street Railway, 132; Live Oak, Tampa & Charlotte Harbor Railroad, 137; Montgomery Belt Line Railway, 164; Sanford & St. Petersburg Railroad, 172; Savannah, Florida & Western Railroad, 130; Silver Springs, Ocala & Gulf Railroad, Florida Railroad, 138; South Florida Railroad (Tampa-Sanford connection) 148; Waycross-Jacksonville Short Line, 134-5; also land grants and total mileage, 176. Famous rolling stock, ACL # 40, "fast mail,"135; Special Car 100. 3, 14, 159, 173, 184, 186, 197; fate of, 202; Plant System Engine 111, "The Rhode Island Lady", 201-3. See also: Tampa-Sanford connection, strategic importance, 142, 146, 148; hospitals, 163, 177; Tampa-New York route, 176; and ref. Plant, Henry (2), historic events, standard gauge, 179; MARITIME INTERESTS: operations, Boston, 174; Tampa, Port Tampa facility, 164, 178. Steamboats: *Cato Bell,* 137; People's Line inland and coastal waters of Florida and Georgia: *Anita,* 163; *Frederick DeBary,* 163; *Geo. M. Bird,* 163; *H.B. Plant,* 131, 145, 159, 161-2, 163; *Kississimmee,* 175; *Margaret,* 8, 159, 175-6; *Rosa,* 163; Plant Line (Tampa-Key West-Havana, Tampa-Mobile, Boston-Halifax): steamships: *La Grande Duchesse,* 10, 175; *Mascotte,* 173-4, 175, 181; *Tarpon,* 175; Fort Myers Steamboat Company; Tourism: Anna Maria-Egmont cruises, 175; Boston-Bar Harbor-Halifax run, 174; Tampa-Key West-Havana run, 164, 173, 179

Planters Hotel (Augusta). Ref. Plant, Ellen, final illness, 72-4

Polk, James K. 49

Ponce de Leon Hotel. Ref. Flagler, hotel interests, 117, 161, 170

Port Charlotte, Florida. 114, 143; ref. Plant System, hotels, 164; and Savannah, Florida & Western, 138

Port Tampa. Port Tampa Project, 164; phosphate shipping, 177-8; and, Plant, Henry (3), Spanish-American War, 181, 182-5

Pullman, George. 165

Pullman Palace Car Company. Ref. Plant System, major upgrading, 139

Punta Gorda, Florida. Ref. Disston, plans for Kissimmee Valley empire, 114; and Plant System, hotels, 164, 172

Punta Rassa, Florida. Ref. Disston, plans for Kissimmee Valley empire, 114

Q.

R.

Raines, Colonel George Washington. 93

Railway Express Agency. 111; ref. Southern Express, 198, 199

Raney, George P. 137

Reed, Governor. 143

Regan, John. 104

Rhode Island Locomotive Works. Ref. Plant, Henry (3), folklore legacy," Great Train Race," 202

Richmond, Virginia. 93; ref. Southern Express, post bellum headquarters, 109

Richmond County, Georgia. See Augusta.

Richmond & Danville Railroad. Ref. Plant, Henry (2), shrewdness of, 133

Richmond and West Point Terminal Company. Ref. Plant, Henry (2), dubious investments, 178

Rockefeller, John D. 8, 20, quoted re Flagler as Standard Oil "villain," {in parentheses}, 126

Rome, Italy. Ref. Plant, Henry (2), European travel, 101

Roosevelt, James. 126

Roosevelt, Theodore. 13, 181

Rosa (steamboat). Ref. People's Line, 163

Ross, Donald J. 172

Rowlands Bluff, Florida. Ref. Live Oak & Rowlands Bluff Railroad, 137

Royal Poinciana Hotel (West Palm Beach). Ref. Flagler, hotel interests, 171

Russell School (New Haven). Ref. Plant, Morton Freeman, formal education, 109

S.

St. Augustine, Florida. 12, 53; ref. Flagler, hotel interests, 118, 161, 165

St. Leo, Florida (St. Leo's College). Ref. Plant, Henry (2), geniality and equanimity, 180

San Antonio, Florida. Ref. Plant, Henry (3), geniality and equanimity, 180

St. Petersburg, Florida. Ref. Plant System, hotels, Belleview, 172

Sanford, Edward S. 56, 81; testimony, Einstein vs Adams, and friendship with HBP, 110

Sanford, General Henry Shelton. 144, 172; as ambassador to Belgium, meeting with HBP, 100; business ventures, HBP, 78, 131; at Louisville, 81; at Einstein trial, 110; Tampa-Sanford connection; 145, 147-8; Kississimmee Valley empire and Disston, 113-6, 132-3, 136; business ventures, personal; in Africa, 111; in Louisiana, 111, in South Carolina, 111; in Florida, 112, 132;first Florida visit, 112, 117, 118; friendship with HBP, 56, 78, 1 11, 131, 142, 144; death of, 201

Sanford, Florida. Ref. Sanford, Henry, Kississimmee Valley Empire, 113, 132-3, 135-7; during Tampa-Sanford connection, 144, 145, 147, 151, 155; ref. Plant System, hospitals, 163; ref. Pico Hotel, 163-4, 200; as PICO headquarters, 164

Sanford & St. Petersburg Railroad (formerly Orange Belt). Ref. Plant System, railroads, 172

Savannah, Georgia. 46, 54, 56, 57, 60, 109, 131; HBP's post bellum return, 102-3; ref. Southern Express, post bellum headquarters 109; site of auction for HBP's first railroad, 129-30; as residence, maritime, 134; ref. Haines, later ccomplishments, 201; and Plant, Henry (3), folklore legacy, "Great Train Race," 202-4

Savannah, Albany & Gulf Railroad (later Atlantic & Gulf). 128

Savannah & Charleston Railroad (later Charleston & Savannah. 129

Savannah, Florida & Western Railroad (formerly Atlantic & Gulf). 130-31, 137; ref. Plant System, 130

Schleman, Arthur. Ref. Bradenton, record-setting hunt, 171

Scott, Tom. 123-4, 126

Screven, Georgia. 203; ref. Plant, Henry (3), ref. folklore legacy, "Great Train Race," 203

Screven, John C. (quoted). 112

Seaboard Airline Railroad. Ref. Plant, Henry (3), folklore legacy," Great Train Race," 202

Sebring, Edward. 86

Seig, Edward Chan (quoted). 103
Seminole Inn (Winter Park, Florida). Ref. hotels, Plant System, 165
Seminoles. 53
Sessacus. 18
Shaw, Captain W.A. 163
Sherman, General William Tecumseh (and March to the Sea). 94-5 , 96, 102-3, 125-6
Shipman, Mr. (attorney). 191
Shoemaker, S.M. 56, 133
Silver Springs, Ocala & Gulf Railroad. Ref. Plant System, 178; ref. Plant, Henry (3), historical events, Phosphate Rush, 178
Small, A.B. 96, 108, 109,125
Smith, Buckingham (quoted). 115
Smith, Milton H. 179
Smyth, G. Hutchinson. 63 (quoted), 174
Snead Island, Florida. Ref. Tampa-Sanford connection, 144
South Carolina Canal & Railroad Company. 57, 61, 67, 76
South Florida Railroad. 145, 151; Lake Alfred-Bartow connection, 138; ref. (David Yulee) Tampa, Tampa-Sanford connection, 143; ref. Plant System, railroads, 147-8; ref. Tampa, Port Tampa Project, 164
Southeastern Investment Company (later the Henry Bradley Plant Company). In dispute over HBP's will 185, 190; disposition of shares, 192
Southern Express Co. 85, 96, 98, 106, 124, 174; ref. Adams Company, HBP acquires Southern District, 60-1; becomes SEC; continuing relationship, 102, 108, 110; pseudo-Southern Express, 86; good name attacked, 86-8; good name of, vindicated, 88-9; Confederate asset, 90-1; post bellum headquarters established per HBP, 109; post bellum solvency and HBP's bounty, mystery of, 154; post bellum power of, 182-3; good Works of, 125; good Works of, 125; good works of, 125; rates of (questionable), 134; final reckoning, HBP, 198-9; see also, Plant, Morton, education, practical 109
Southern Railway Security Company. Ref. Plant, Henry (2), dubious investments, 126,127
Southern States Freight Association. Ref. Haines, later accomplishments, 200
Spanish-American War. Ref. Plant, Henry (3), historical events 19-20, 181, 182-5
Splendid (steamboat). Ref. New Haven, Steamboat Wars, 36, 39
Spooner, Clapp. 56, 78-9, 94-5; sales partner and travels with HBP, 67
Steamboat Wars. Ref. New Haven and Plant, Henry (3), historical events, 38-9, 42-3
Stephens, Alexander. 79, 89, 104
Stephens, Thaddeus. 120; and quoted, 120
Stone, Captain Bartlett S. 39-40, 71-2; and quoted, 71-2
Sumner, Charles. 77
Sutherland, Duke of. 165
Swann, Samuel. 137

T.

Tallahassee, Florida. 120, 132, 134
Tampa, Florida. Significant refs. *in passim*: 69, 119, 179; Tampa-Sanford connection: pre-

HBP tribulations, 142-3; ref. Plant System, strategic importance, 142, 146, 148; ref. Ingraham, contract for Tampa-Sanford connection, 145, 146-7; City Council contracts with PICO, 150; during construction, 148, 150; first locomotive, 152-3; celebration, 141, 156; Tampa-New York route, 176; ref. Plant System, Tampa-Havana run, 164, 173, 179; see also Port Tampa, Tampa Bay Hotel.

Tampa Bay Hotel. 10; begun per HBP solo decision, 165; ref. Ingraham, TBH contract, 165; construction, 166, 168-9; design, 166-9; grand opening, 169-70; facilities and activities,169-70, 180-1; see also Bradenton, record-setting hunt, 171; horticulture, 170 and Spanish-American War, 13, 182; and ref. Plant, Nellie, architectural interests, 196; see Plant, Morton, hotel interests; and Plant, Margaret and Plant, Henry (2) (3), decor, taste in; post-HBP fate 195, 196, 199-200

Tarpon (steamship). Ref. Plant System, Plant Line, 175
Tavares, Florida. Ref. Jacksonville & St. Johns River Railroad, 185
Telegraph (steamboat). Ref. New Haven, Steamboat Wars, 38, 43-3
Tennessee Coal, Iron, and Railroad Company. 178
Texas Express Company. 69, 108. 125, 175
Texas & Pacific Railroad Company. 132
Thackery, William Makepeace (quoted). 57
Thompson, John Edgar. 61
Thomasville, Georgia. 166; ref. Wood, previous inspirations, Mitchell House and Piney Woods Hotel, 167
Tilley, George H. Ref. Plant, Henry (3), last will, planning for, 183-4, 185; as active in dispute over HBP's will, 188, 192
Trinity College (Hartford). 135
Twain, Mark. See Clemens, Samuel.

U.

Union, Illinois (Illinois Railroad Museum). Ref. Special Car 100, fate of, 202
United States (steamboat). 36; ref. New Haven, Steamboat Wars; explosion of, 32
U.S. Post Office. 41, 66

V.

Vanderbilt, Cornelius ("Commodore"). 48; builds steamboat empire, 34-5, 36; ref. New Haven, Steamboat Wars, 38-9, 45-3
Vanderbilt Line. See New Haven Steamboat Company.
Vicksburg, Mississippi. 72; ref. Southern Express, post bellum headquarters per HBP, 109
Vose, Francis. 113. 116
Vose Injunction. 113, 115, 132, 137

W.

Wade, Ben. 76; quoted 76
Waleka (steamboat). Ref. Plant, Henry (2), first Florida trip, 54
Walters,W.T. 133

Warner, Warburton. 144
Washington, DC. As "rightfully" Southern city, 77
Washington Webb Company. Ref. Plant, Henry (1), early business career, 49
Waterford, Connecticut. ref. Plant, Sara Mae "Masie, 197
Waycross, Georgia. Ref. Waycross-Jacksonville Short Line 132; ref. Plant, Henry (2), "Great Train Race," 202
Waycross-Jacksonville Short Line Railroad. 8, 143, 163; ref. Plant System, railroads, 134; ref. Tampa, Tampa-Sanford connection, strategy, 143; ref . see Haines, builds, 133, 134; and builds Tampa-Sanford connection, 146-9; also Haines, later accomplishments, 200; see also Plant, Henry (3), folklore legacy," Great Train Race," 202-4
Webb, Washington. Ref. Plant, Henry (1), practical education, 49-50, 99-100, 138; see also Washington Webb Company.
Webb & Plant Company. Ref. Plant, Henry (1), early business career, 49
Webster, Daniel. 49, 76
"West Coast Route." 177
West Indies. Ref. Plant, Henry (1) (2), grand strategy, 49-50, 139
West Palm Beach, Florida. 161; ref. Flagler, hotels, 171
West Point Foundry. Ref *Best Friend*, short and happy life of, 58
Western & Atlantic Railway. 58, 61, 81
Western Reserve Territory. Ref. Plant, Henry (2), historical events, slavery, 78
Whig Party. Ref. Plant, Henry (2), political interests.
Whitman, Walt (quoted). 45
Whitney, Eli. 46, 56
Wilmington, Delaware. 46, 98; ref. Plant System, maritime interests, *H.B. Plant*, 131
Wilmington & Weldon Railroad. 98; ref. Plant, Henry (2), shrewdness of, 133
Winston Lumber Company. Ref. Phosphate Rush, 178
Winter Park, Florida. Ref. Plant System, hotels, 165
Wood, John A. Ref. Tampa Bay Hotel, construction of, 167-9; design of: previous inspirations, Brunswick, Oglethorpe Hotel, 166; Duchess County, Mizzen Top, 167; Thomasville: Mitchell House, Piney Woods Hotel, 167; design flaws, 171
Worcester, Massachusetts. Ref. Adams, Alvin, beginnings, 41

X

Y.

Yale College (later University). 10; ref. Plant, Sarah, HBP's education, 27, 30, 35
Yale Divinity School. Ref. Plant, Sarah, HBP's career, 34
Ybor, Vincinte Martinez. 173-4
Yullee, David Levy. 113, 124; as anti-Tampa "villain," 142-3, 151; negotiations with HBP, 143-34; failure of negotiations, see Plant, Henry)2), curse on Cedar Key, 144

Z.

Come see our store at 435 Brevard Avenue, Cocoa Florida 32922, phone (321) 690-0099. Or visit us on line at www.florida-historical-soc.org and click on The Print Shoppe